Signposts in Fostering
Policy, practice and
research issues

Acknowledgements

We would like to thank the authors of all the papers contained in this collection for their kind permission to reproduce them. Although every effort has been made to trace each of the authors, we have not been able to do so in every instance and have selected each paper on the assumption that the author would have willingly given permission if we had been able to approach them.

We are also very grateful to Malcolm Hill (Commissioning Editor of *Adoption & Fostering*) for selecting and introducing the papers in this anthology and to Miranda Davies (Production Editor of *Adoption & Fostering*) for her help with the preparation of this book.

Shaila Shah
Head of Communications

Note about the Editor

Malcolm Hill is Director of the Centre for the Child and Society, University of Glasgow, and has authored several studies and journal articles. He was the Commissioning Editor of *Adoption & Fostering* until late 1998 and will be back on board as Commissioning Editor from September 1999.

Signposts in Fostering

Policy, practice and
research issues

Edited by Malcolm Hill

British
Agencies
for **A**doption
and **F**ostering

Published by
British Agencies for Adoption & Fostering
(BAAF)
Skyline House
200 Union Street
London SE1 0LX

© BAAF 1999

Charity registration 275689

British Library Cataloguing in Publication Data
A catalogue record for this book is available
from the British Library

ISBN 1 873868 72 3

Designed by Andrew Haig & Associates
Cover photographs (posed by models):
John Birdsall Photography
Cover illustration by Andrew Haig
Typeset by Avon Dataset Ltd, Bidford on Avon
Printed by Russell Press Ltd. (TU),
Nottingham

Contents

Preface

What we know today as "The Journal" began life as "The Bulletin" of the Standing Conference of Societies Registered for Adoption. The first edition was published in October 1951 and was available for member societies only – membership was then open to all registered adoption societies on payment of an annual affiliation fee of £2 and 2 shillings! It was edited by its founder, Margaret Kornitzer, who was also the Press Officer of the Standing Conference; Tony Rampton was Honorary Secretary and Treasurer. It was all of 14 pages long and typed with only a few errors, clearly at a time when Tippex was not invented.

This first edition introduced readers to the purpose of the Bulletin. It promised that it would tell members 'what the Standing Conference is doing as an organisation, with your money, to further the cause of adoption, whether by approach to official bodies or otherwise. It will contain general items of news, advance notices of meetings, information on special points that have presented difficulties to member societies, and anything else likely to be interesting . . .

. . . In large measure we must depend on you to make this Bulletin your own, both by reading it and commenting on its contents, and by contributing to it yourselves when you have something worth saying. From time to time we hope also to print short articles by experts. Let us know what you would like to see in these pages . . ." (p 2)

That edition included short "newsy" items on family allowances, the filing of adoption applications, the difficulties of defining domicile and residence, adoption by US citizens stationed in

Britain, and the concerns of member agencies about the numbers of mothers of illegitimate children who were driven to adoption not because they wanted to give up their children but because they could not find accommodation. The book reviews section kicked off with Dr Bowlby's *Maternal Care and Mental Health*, a study that has since been cited frequently in the pages of the journal.

By January 1953 the Bulletin had acquired a name – *Child Adoption*. Two years later *Child Adoption* took on a different garb – it was professionally printed with the titles of the articles appearing on the front cover. In keeping with this change of status, it stopped describing itself as a "Bulletin" and became the more scholarly "Journal". It carried on like this until 1970 with a gradual increase in the number of pages.

By 1970, *Child Adoption* was published by the Association of British Adoption Agencies. A sizeable 52 pages long, the journal cost five shillings. It was in 1976 that it rechristened itself and became *Adoption & Fostering*, the journal of the Association of British Adoption and Fostering Agencies (ABAFA) – a further change of status bringing it into line with journals published by professional and learned societies. Now 72 pages long, it also had a new Editor, Sarah Curtis, following the retirement of its founder Editor, Margaret Kornitzer, after 25 years in post.

The journal was to go through still more changes. ABAFA changed its name and became British Agencies for Adoption & Fostering (BAAF) and the first edition of *Adoption & Fostering* published by BAAF in 1980 had further improved its presentation. In 1987, a brand identity in the shape of BAAF's logo was introduced on the cover. A single copy then cost £3.00

and the first revamped edition contained an article on *Fostering Outcomes: interpreting breakdown rates* by Jane Rowe.

In 1997, to coincide with *Adoption & Fostering's* 21st birthday, the Journal was relaunched yet again, now 80 pages and with a spine to hold it together (to the delight of Felicity Collier, Director of BAAF, who had agitated for a spine ever since she joined us) and an impressive peer review panel in place assuring quality standards of papers submitted to the journal for publication. The first relaunched issue, published on the eve of the 1997 General Election, attracted statements from the key health spokespeople of the Liberal Democrat, Conservative and Labour parties who commented on the Draft Adoption Bill – a coup for the journal. Alongside the well established tradition of practice-based and accessibly written academic articles, this provided testament to the confirmed status of *Adoption & Fostering* as *the* authoritative journal on adoption and fostering matters in the UK.

Leigh Chambers and Shaila Shah
BAAF
1999

Introduction
Fostering in the UK

Malcolm Hill

Foster care is at the same time a very ordinary activity and an extraordinary undertaking. Looking after children is something that the great majority of adults do at some period in their lives, relying largely on common sense and their own experience. Taking in someone else's child can be seen as an act of good neighbourliness and an extension of everyday parenting. Yet fostering poses significant challenges. A child from a different background may not readily adjust to a new family. The foster family's routines, expectations and activities have to adjust not only to the presence of an initially strange child, but also to contacts with that child's wider family and friends. When foster carers have children of their own, as many do, they have to learn to share their lives, home and possessions with an "outsider". Individual and family privacy gives way to personal exposure, through professional assessment and monitoring, as well as the critical gaze of the foster child and her or his original family.

It is commonly recognised that in general the fostering task has become increasingly complex and in many respects more difficult over the last few decades. In the past foster care often involved either straightforward physical care of a child on a temporary basis or else long-term substitute parenting. It was not unusual for the foster carers (then known as foster parents) to bring up the child virtually as a full member of their own family on a quasi-adoptive basis (Rowe *et al*, 1984). According to Triseliotis *et al* (1995b) 'formal fostering until the end of the Second World War was largely long-term in nature with little or no contact between children and their birth parents' (p 7). This traditional fostering role was not always easy, but nowadays considerably more is expected of foster carers for three main sets of reasons.

Firstly, it is now much more rare for a child to be fostered unless there are very serious family or personal difficulties, often both. Developments in prevention and family support have raised the threshold for children to become looked after away from home, while local authority policies and practices have led to higher proportions of children being adopted from foster care than formerly, including many of the more settled individuals (DoH, 1991; Fox Harding, 1991). Negative attitudes about residential care, especially for pre-teen children, have meant that many who would formerly have been placed in children's homes are now fostered. A high proportion of looked after children are now recognised to have significant problems related to experiences of abuse, including sexual abuse. Some are themselves physically or sexually aggressive.

Secondly, practice and legislation have in many ways increased the demands made of foster carers. Obligations to encourage contacts with birth families have been strengthened. More frequent and formalised involvement is required in planning, decision-making and reviews. Greater emphasis is placed on children's participatory rights and more attention is given to children's cultural heritage and identity (Borland, 1998). Discriminatory attitudes with respect to "race" and disability are no longer acceptable.

Thirdly, fostering today is located within a child care scene which has a less certain sense of direction. The 1980s witnessed a dominating framework of permanency planning, which stressed focused planning and action to return children swiftly to their families or else to secure them a permanent alternative, preferably through adoption in order to achieve a sense of permanent belonging (Fox Harding, 1991; Smith, 1995). Another source of clear direction was the development of closely prescribed procedures for responding to child abuse and an emphasis on legal controls on parents when abuse was demonstrated. The 1990s saw increased questioning and even rejection of certain trends promoted by permanency planning, such as the ready use of the law to cut off parental contact and to move children to adoption against parental wishes. The Children Act 1989 stressed partnership with parents rather than opposition; family support rather than compulsory separation (Packman and Jordan, 1991; Aldgate *et al*, 1994). Both practice and research developments favoured a more co-operative approach to child protection (Thoburn *et al*, 1995; DoH, 1995). It was accepted that for some children the permanency principles did still apply, but for many – particularly adolescents – it was not relevant. Therefore alternative and more complex guiding principles were required, taking account of continuity, resilience, multiple identities and network support, as well as permanent belonging (McFadden and Downs, 1995; Gilligan, 1997).

To some degree, the greater challenges to foster carers have been matched by better recognition and remuneration, though many still regard these developments as inadequate. For more than 20 years now the notion of fostering as a professional role has been promoted, but the extent to which this has been put into practice remains patchy. The perception that fostering is and should be an unpaid voluntary activity remains strong in some quarters, including a minority of foster carers themselves (Rhodes, 1993: Triseliotis *et al*, 1998).

This present volume aims to give insights into some of the main developments in foster care in the UK during the 1990s. It provides a selection of articles from BAAF's journal, *Adoption & Fostering*, as a companion publication to one covering adoption (Hill and Shaw, 1998). In both texts, space considerations have meant that interesting papers about fostering or adoption outside the UK have not been included. Inevitably the range of topics on which articles were submitted and accepted by the journal also affects the coverage. Important insights are given about the organisation of services and new developments in recruitment and training. The nature of contacts between foster and birth families has become a vital consideration in practice and several papers address this. Previously neglected issues have received considerable attention, such as the perspectives of foster carers' birth children and placement endings.

On the other hand there are noteworthy gaps, most of which mirror the wider literature. For example, little has been written about longer-term or permanent fostering, which received so much consideration in the 1980s. Broad assessments or critiques of the principles, theories and policies underpinning fostering practice are hard to find anywhere. Little material has been reproduced in the journal that incorporated children's perspectives. Fortunately a growing body of such material is available elsewhere (e.g. McAuley, 1996; Hill, 1997; Thomas, 1998). The experiences of black children are largely absent, though work by Barn *et al* (1997) and Ince (1998) provide useful correctives to this. We know very little about the current state of private fostering.

The articles have been grouped thematically and each section is preceded by a short introduction to discuss the context and summarise key points from the chapters that follow. References to these are indicated in bold (e.g. **Cleaver, 1997**) to distinguish them from references to others' books and articles whose details are placed at the end of the book.

Before embarking on the first section, it is helpful to review briefly key aspects of fostering in the UK.

Fostering today

The legal basis for fostering in the 1990s was established by the Children Act 1989 in England and Wales, the Children (Scotland) Act 1995 and the Children (Northern Ireland) Order 1995 (Hill and Aldgate, 1996). These statutes introduced new principles and terminology. The child's welfare was reinforced as the primary consideration in decision-making. Emphasis was placed on the idea of partnership between local authorities and families in need of services. Whenever it is consistent with children's welfare, social workers and other professionals should seek to work co-operatively with parents and children to support families and sustain family relationships. In keeping with this spirit, the new terms "accommodation" and "looked after" were introduced to refer to circumstances when children are placed away from home, formerly known as "in care". It is recognised, of course, that in some instances parents' wishes and children's views may need to be overridden in the child's best interests, usually subject to a court order or, in Scotland, a children's hearing requirement.

Although this book concentrates on fostering, with its distinctive characteristics and issues, it is important to remember that foster placements usually constitute only part of a sequence of experiences in children's lives, and sometimes just a brief episode. Many fostered children spend most of their upbringing with their birth families. A number experience several moves away from and back home. Moreover it is fairly common for children in foster care to have come from or move onto a

5

residential home (Rowe *et al*, 1989; Bullock, 1990). The various sequences that children may undergo are often referred to as "care careers" (Little *et al*, 1995). By taking a care career perspective, professionals and carers are helped not only to ensure that current practice and children's own understandings are rooted in knowledge of the past, but to make decisions on a long-term basis in the light of future options and implications.

Fostering is the principal form of care provided for children who live away from home under local authority auspices. The numbers of children in care or looked after away from home have decreased substantially since the 1970s, but virtually all this decline has been in the residential sector. The numbers of children fostered have remained fairly constant, which means that foster children make up a higher proportion of children looked after than 20 years ago. In England and Wales on 31 March 1997, just over 33,000 children were placed in foster care, compared with approximately 10,000 who were in a residential home or school (DoH, 1999). In Scotland a higher proportion of children are in residential establishments, but foster children are still in the majority (Scottish Office, 1998). In Northern Ireland, by contrast, the numbers of children fostered have doubled in the last 25 years. Several factors explain this difference, including a strong consensus about the positive value of foster care, its cheapness and the rare use of adoption as a route out of care (McColgan, 1991; Kelly and Coulter, 1997).

Roughly one in six of the foster children in England and Wales are living with relatives. Fostering is a very significant service for teenagers as well as younger children. Over half of foster children are aged ten or more, although nearly two-thirds were aged under ten when they first arrived. Nevertheless the age profile is very different from that of residential care, where well over 90 per cent of residents are adolescents (DoH, 1999). African-Caribbean and mixed parentage children are over-represented (Rowe *et al*, 1989). Socio-economic disadvantage, external referral processes (e.g. by police and schools) and social workers' negativity about prevention all appear to contribute to this, though there is also evidence of some very good practice with black families (Rhodes, 1992; Barn, 1993; Barn *et al*, 1997).

Most foster families have been recruited and are supported by local authorities. Some voluntary agencies and increasingly certain private agencies run foster care services, usually of a specialist nature, although legal responsibilities for the children placed are held by the local authority. It appears that a few thousand children are privately fostered. For many years, this activity has involved mainly children of West African parents placed with white carers (Atkinson and Horner, 1990).

Diverse terms are used by different agencies to describe the kinds of foster care on offer. These classifications tend to encompass two dimensions: expected length of stay and specialisation by type of child or task. Typically distinctions are made between respite, emergency, short-term, intermediate and long-term or permanent fostering (Triseliotis *et al*, 1995b). Some carers or schemes specialise with teenagers, children with disabilities or children with challenging behaviour. Certain projects have an even more specific focus, for instance, remand placements, as alternatives to custody or for homeless young people (Graham *et al*, 1992; Field, 1992).

Foster care may have a variety of functions (Rowe *et al*, 1989; Berridge, 1996; Sellick and Thoburn, 1996). These include:
• emergency provision of a "roof over head";
• temporary care;

7

- respite;
- assessment;
- remand/alternative to custody;
- preparation for adoption or long-term placement;
- treatment;
- long-term or permanent care;
- bridge to independence.

The same placement may serve several functions for the same child or sibling group, either at the same time or in succession.

Holman (1976) observed that foster carers could be seen as having different orientations to the task. Some saw themselves as looking after the child with minimal involvement or interference from birth family or social workers. He described this as an exclusive model. In contrast others had an inclusive approach, seeking to share care and decision-making with parents and professionals. Nowadays the practice emphasis is very much on inclusiveness (partnership), but there is evidence that certain foster carers find this approach difficult (Kufeldt *et al*, 1996; Triseliotis *et al*, 1998). Although inclusiveness refers to engagement with birth families, its rationale is based on the needs of the fostered child for continuity, contact and understanding of the past (Kufeldt, 1994).

The outcomes of foster care placements have been a matter for investigation and debate for over 40 years. For much of this period, placements were simply divided into those that lasted and those that broke down. This disregarded the fact that a continuing placement might be an unhappy one and that children could gain many benefits from a placement that ended prematurely. Nevertheless, worrying evidence was produced of breakdown rates of up to 50 per cent for longer-term placements. More recent research suggests 30 per cent as a more typical rate for placements meant to last two years or more (Triseliotis, 1989; Triseliotis *et al*, 1995b). Success rates for short-term placements seem to be much better, taking into account perceived benefits and whether needs were met, as well as actual length compared with expected duration (Rowe *et al*, 1989). Not surprisingly, the risk of a poor outcome is higher for older children and those with significant emotional or behavioural difficulties. Broadly speaking, the success of foster placements, however judged, seems to be no better but also no worse than residential placements (Sellick and Thoburn, 1996; Berridge, 1996). The present picture seems somewhat improved compared with the past, despite the increased challenges, and this may represent a tribute to current foster carers as well as recruitment practices and support. Nevertheless, the proportion of unsuccessful placements remains significant. Moreover, the specialisation of placements by duration or type means that many children are exposed to planned as well as unplanned changes of placement As a result, emotional, social and educational adjustments need to be made by children already adversely affected by family disruption and separation. There is no room for complacency.

The nature, quality and outcomes of foster placements depend on the kinds of families who put themselves forward and are accepted, following a thorough assessment process. Also important are the preparation and support received as carers carry out their vital and demanding roles. Both practice wisdom and research suggest that the organisation of services, the approach to recruitment and the ongoing relationship between carers and fostering agencies have a significant impact on the service provided and the experiences of children (Berridge, 1996). Therefore we begin this anthology with these elements of the fostering service. They are not always seen as the most exciting aspects of fostering, but structures, policies and formal arrangements provide the vital framework for the more personal and interpersonal matters dealt with in later chapters.

Section I
The organisation of fostering services

Organisational aspects of fostering services have not received a great deal of attention in writing and research, perhaps because they lack the human interest of foster care processes and relationships. Yet children, foster carers and birth families are only too aware of how their experiences are affected by the attitudes and behaviour of councils, departments and agencies, mediated through contacts with social workers, managers, receptionists, administrators, finance officers and so on. Structures, policies and procedures impinge on foster families through seemingly mundane matters, like the timing of payments or the authorisation of school trips which can be speedy and straightforward or frustratingly slow and awkward. The nature of the agency also affects more general aspects of the fostering service such as the levels of recruitment, foster carer morale and hence choice of placements or the degree to which key decisions are experienced as participatory by the various parties concerned.

In Northern Ireland statutory responsibility for foster care lies with Health and Social Services Boards and Trusts, as part of the NHS (Kelly and Pinkerton, 1996; Kelly and Coulter, 1997). Elsewhere in the UK local government has the prime responsibility for looked after children. Local authority social services were subject to a number of important changes in the 1990s. Central government encouraged the development of purchaser/provider arrangements and competitive tendering, so that some authorities significantly increased the commissioning of child welfare services from the voluntary and private sectors. In Northern Ireland service delivery was similarly transferred to Health and Social Services Trusts as the providers in relation to the purchaser role of the Boards. According to Waterhouse (1997) just under half of English authorities had introduced a purchaser/ provider split in children's services, with fostering located in the provider arm. It is not easy to quantify the effects of different arrangements, but Richards (1998/9) presented evidence that authorities with purchaser/provider splits had poorer numbers of foster placements at a higher price, compared with those operating on more traditional functional lines.

The most significant development in many areas has been local government reorganisation, which was carried out piecemeal in England and comprehensively in Wales and Scotland (Black, 1995; Herts, 1997). In most places this resulted in unitary authorities smaller than those previously responsible for social work services. While some people have welcomed increased local autonomy, critics have pointed to financial problems, lost economies of scale and disruptions to established service patterns and policies (Craig and Manthorpe, 1998). Smaller authorities may be less able to deploy specialist staff with the skills and experience to support innovatory or demanding work (see **Gilchrist and Hoggan, 1996** in Section II). Many authorities took the opportunity to introduce new departmental structures. In some cases this has meant that councillors and even senior staff responsible for fostering had little specialist knowledge in this area, at least in the short term (Herts, 1997; Triseliotis *et al*, 1999).

Shortly before the creation of unitary authorities in Wales, the Welsh Office Social Services Inspectorate commissioned a review of services (**Pithouse and Parry, 1997**). This revealed a considerable variety of structures. For instance, responsibility for fostering was sometimes located in local child and family teams, but elsewhere was geographically and operationally separate. Links to adoption and child protection services were diverse.

Similarly the three authorities which took part in the study by Barn *et al* (1997) each had a different structure. A survey of all English authorities showed that nearly all distinguished between fieldworkers, responsible for children and their families, and family placement workers, concentrating on the fostering service. Sometimes both worked in the same teams, but more commonly they were separate and often authorities had a centralised family placement or fostering team (Waterhouse, 1997). Fostering is far more often integrated with adoption services than with residential care.

In Wales, despite the diversity of organisational structures, policy documents were broadly similar, with a strong emphasis on close co-operation between foster carers and parents. Monitoring and performance review mechanisms were not well developed, so it was difficult to assess the effectiveness of policies in practice. Similar conclusions were reached in a Scottish study of fostering services (Triseliotis *et al*, 1999). A survey by Singh and Patel (1998) revealed that only about half of Scottish local authorities had specific policies relating to the needs of black and minority ethnic children and a similar proportion had ethnic monitoring systems.

In some Welsh counties but not others, experienced carers were involved in recruitment and preparation of new carers. The development of carer groups was patchy. At the time of the All Wales Review, respite services were poorly integrated with other forms of foster care (see also Section III).

The Welsh research confirmed the findings of other surveys that patterns of payment are highly variable between and even within authorities (Bebbington and Miles, 1990; Lowe, 1990; NFCA, 1998; Triseliotis *et al*, 1998). This resulted in unfairness, "poaching" and resentment. The remuneration issue highlights a longstanding ambiguity in the status of foster carers. Are they good-hearted volunteers, who require only compensation for any costs incurred, or professionals carrying out a skilled task meriting a proper salary (Rhodes, 1993)? Or perhaps they are somewhere in between. Present payment patterns include each of these positions. Moreover, the calculation of costs is not straightforward and the criteria and arrangements for making enhanced allowances are highly variable.

One reason for the diversity of payment levels and systems has been the development of specialist schemes. The model for these was the Kent Family Placement Project set up in the 1970s. This showed that foster care could hold and help teenagers with major behaviour difficulties (Yelloly, 1979; Hazel, 1981). The early model was based on the use of contracts, targets and time limits. Schemes for young people proliferated in the 1980s and in addition certain projects were set up to place children with disabilities (Shaw and Hipgrave, 1983).

For some time, specialist schemes were seen to be in the vanguard of progress. They remain common, but increasingly doubts have been voiced about the divisive consequences of categorising placements into specialist and mainstream, especially as it seems that few placements can any longer be regarded as straightforward. **Pithouse and Parry (1997)** found that some specialist schemes for troubled young people were seen as insulated from other kinds of fostering. Also restrictive admission criteria could result in very challenging children being placed with "ordinary" foster families who lacked the same levels of support and remuneration. In 1992 a national survey of fostering agencies was undertaken, using a similar questionnaire to one developed in North America so that international comparisons could be made (**Hill** *et al*, **1993**). Responses were received from three-quarters of UK agencies. About one-third of these had a special scheme. A number of others indicated an intention to introduce a scheme, whereas a few had already dismantled separate projects. This illustrated the divergence in attitude about specialisation, which emerged and intensified during the 1990s. A later survey by NFCA (1998) again revealed that half of the fostering agencies operated specialist schemes, which most regarded as very effective, yet significant numbers of others had disbanded separate schemes because of their inflexibility, unfairness in offering higher rewards or budgetary considerations.

The British-North American comparative study found that nearly three-quarters of the children in specialist foster homes were aged 12 or over. The majority of British schemes paid a fixed amount (retainer) with additions when a child was actually present, though some only paid for days when a child was placed. In contrast to North America, payment levels usually changed with the age of the child but were not affected by the experience or skills of the carers. The latter arrangement has subsequently been introduced in a few areas. Compared with North American programmes, few British schemes had an explicit and specific treatment model, though some were influenced by systems thinking or behavioural/social learning approaches.

More recently, many statutory and voluntary agencies have developed another kind of scheme focused on leaving care. Interestingly, although children and young people are no longer referred to as being "in care", it is still common to refer to them afterwards as having left "care" or receiving "after care". The notion of through care has also become current, representing the idea of children and young people's placement being part of a sequence in their lives, in which preparation for leaving needs to play an important part right the way through. As with specialist fostering schemes, dedicated projects were initially seen as the main response to the needs of young people leaving care, but some now believe it is better to have a more integrated model.

Surprising as it may seem, until the 1980s little formal attention was given to children once they left care, whether to return home or when they reached an upper age limit. Several studies, notably that by Stein and Carey (1986), helped to place the issue of leaving care firmly on the policy, practice and research agendas. They showed that many young people left care far sooner than the majority of their peers left their family homes. Many care leavers experienced poverty, isolation and housing difficulties. Two important consequences arose from the increased awareness of such problems. First, the preparatory and after-care duties of local authorities were strengthened in new legislation. Second, a range of policies and projects have been developed to assist young people. Partly because more teenagers are placed in residential care and also as a result of untested assumptions about the support available for young people in foster care, most attention has been given to supporting young people formerly in residential establishments. The needs of young people leaving foster care have been relatively neglected.

In his article, **Wade (1997)** draws out the particular experiences of fostered young people from a larger four-year study of leaving care services (Biehal *et al*, 1995). He stresses that leaving care should be seen as an extended process not a single event. It also represents a number of transitions, as regards family and household relationships, education and work, sources of income. Thus, young people in foster care, like all young people, may require assistance with respect to different aspects of their lives at different points in time. Young people tend to leave foster care at an older age than their peers do in residential units, but sadly a significant minority leave following a crisis or breakdown. As others have found (Triseliotis *et al*, 1995a; Stein, 1997), poor educational attainments, unemployment, homelessness and insecurity remain common risks for those who leave care early. However, according to Wade, those who do well at school, college or work are most likely to have had stable backgrounds in foster care. Case studies by Ince (1998) indicate that black care leavers make the transition more easily if they retain contacts with their extended families and have been helped to develop a positive identity rooted in their heritage.

Wade concluded that leaving care programmes were successful in many respects. They particularly helped with housing. However, early planning and involvement were usually crucial and here young people in foster care were at a disadvantage. Relationships between leaving care projects and foster carers were often distant and sometimes tense, in part due to the origins and orientation of the projects. Evidently work is needed to mesh throughcare and aftercare programmes more effectively with the needs of foster children and the resources of foster carers. As Marsh (1998/9) has illustrated, it is also important to give careful attention to the support available within young people's informal networks, including the extended family.

1 Local authority fostering in Wales:
the All Wales Review

Andrew Pithouse and Odette Parry

Andrew Pithouse is Director of Social Work Studies in the School of Social Sciences, University of Cardiff, where he chairs the Social Welfare Systems Research Group. His current inter-disciplinary team research focuses on a welfare economic study of community-based family support services in Wales. He is also about to embark upon an evaluation of training in challenging behaviour in foster care. The study will be conducted in South Wales in partnership with statutory providers, users, Barnardo's and BAAF (Wales).

Odette Parry is a Senior Research Fellow at the Research Unit in Health and Behavioural Change, University of Edinburgh. A sociologist, she has held senior researcher posts in universities in Wales, the West Indies and Scotland, and has published widely in education, health and welfare services. She is currently engaged in health education studies at Edinburgh University.

This paper was published in Adoption & Fostering, 21:2, 1997.

The Review

Prior to the introduction of unitary authorities throughout Wales in April 1996, the Welsh Office Social Services Inspectorate commissioned the Children Act Research Group at the University of Wales, Cardiff, to undertake a brief review of fostering provided by the (then eight) County Council social services departments in Wales. The main objectives of the Review were to explore the child care strategy in each local authority, locate and examine the place of fostering within these and examine the mechanisms for policy development in foster services. It was not part of the brief to investigate the relative cost and outcomes of the different schemes or their financial frameworks. Nor did the brief include reference to the activities of the independent sector. The Review was completed and disseminated throughout Wales in late 1994. It was based upon a survey of policy and procedural documents, fostering statistics generated by authorities and taped interviews with senior staff about fostering protocol and practices. One day was spent in each authority for the purpose of data collection, during which time lengthy qualitative interviews were undertaken and policy and procedural material was collected and discussed with providers. All the interviews were guided by an interview checklist and were audio-taped and transcribed. These data were supplemented with statistical information which authorities provided about their fostering services pre and post the 1989 Children Act. This paper focuses on the qualitative data concerning policy and practice. (For a full account of the findings and the methods used, see Pithouse *et al*, 1994.)

Fostering policy: aims and objectives
It was not surprising, given the different demography, local authority structures and traditions within Wales, that fostering services for children and young people varied among counties. These variations also reflected organisational characteristics. For example, responsibility for fostering might be located within area based child and family teams, or, as was more commonly the case, set up as part of family support services and functionally separate from child care teams. Differences in the physical location of fostering operational management were also prominent (central versus local). Despite these variations, however, fostering services in Wales demonstrated strong consistency in their policies. All authorities drew upon the Children Act 1989 and cast fostering as part of an integrated strategy to protect and support children in need and promote their rights to a secure and caring family life. These general aims were typically supplemented by a range of service objectives broadly related to the Act. For example, policy documents promoted fostering as a service to help keep children in their own homes; to maintain contact where feasible during a placement; to seek agreements and make decisions in partnership with foster carers, children and parents; to acknowledge the importance of cultural, linguistic and religious backgrounds of children and generally to support and promote the needs of young people no longer looked after.

In reflecting the intentions of the Children Act 1989, policy aims and objectives in Welsh local authorities generally illustrated the canons of good practice, including those documented in fostering research. For example, partnership is an important principle embodied in the Children Act 1989 (and the Children [Northern Ireland] Order 1995 and the Children [Scotland] Act 1995).

Research findings suggest that partnership, in respect of both parental contact during placement and the relationships made between social workers and foster carers, is a crucial underpinning of both quality and continuity of placement (Millham *et al*, 1986; Cliffe and Berridge, 1991; Berridge, 1996). However, while the Welsh counties had well-developed strategic policies on child and family services in general and on fostering in particular, we found limited documentation allied to this on the aims of fostering in relation to either discrete performance measures or broad targets to achieve.

In brief, it was difficult to assess practice in relation to the expressed intentions of policy. Only two of the counties (West Glamorgan and Gwynedd) had attempted to monitor overall levels of performance and to set targets in relation to their policy aims and service objectives. Other authorities, while recognising the need for such audit systems, were not in a position to carry this out in any comprehensive fashion at the time of the review. Likewise, we found that while authorities unanimously stressed the importance of involvement of carers and users in policy formulation and were committed to this, few had identified the groups, the mechanisms and the timetable through which this would be realised.

There appeared to be unifying and standardising influences at the level of procedures in respect of family placements. All authorities said their procedures were informed by sections 22 and 23 of the 1989 Act, the Foster Placement (Children) Regulations of 1991 and guidance (Volume 3, *Family Placements*) from the Children Act. All authorities had constructed administrative routines and formats in respect of these regulations and some, like Gwynedd, had combined legal requirements, departmental policy and administrative procedures within a single format. Similarly, the county of Dyfed provided clear procedures accompanied by detailed guidance on legal requirements and departmental policy. Other authorities, such as Mid Glamorgan, had basic formats and guidance in place but were in the process of introducing new procedures to promote better standards around planning and reviews. In all counties, formats such as placement agreements, end of placement reviews, children reviews and annual carer reviews provided guidance regarding the purpose of the task at hand, the statutory timescales involved and where responsibilities lay.

Policy and procedural consistency, however, does not guarantee its application and very few authorities had management information systems in place to ensure that practice conformed to the formal aims and standards espoused by councils. Accountability, service achievement and quality are in significant part promoted through information collection and monitoring. Effective systems were absent in most authorities. Although most authorities held electronically retrievable material on, for example, child movement, legal status, key worker, family members, child plan and reviews, none accumulated this routinely in relation to fostering provision and its objectives. Furthermore, none could do this without hefty time costs of additional manual aggregation and analysis.

Fostering arrangements

Fostering staff across Wales worked within varied operational structures which defined fostering provision. For instance, some social services departments had resource teams of fostering staff connected to a range of family services (such as day care, family aides and domiciliary support) but separated from child care social work teams whose members had direct case management responsibilities. Other departments had fostering staff whose brief included adoption and who could be found in family resource or child care teams. However, at the time of the Review all departments were moving towards more pronounced delineation of roles whereby fostering staff supported foster carers, and child care workers took responsibility for children placed. In brief, a prominent feature of mainstream fostering in most authorities was the creation of resource teams closely linked with child care teams which provided assessment and case management. Both fostering support workers and child care workers were usually located in the same setting and, in any case, routinely collaborated over planning and reviews. Links to other family services, through resource teams, were thought to be effective as were the links between resource teams and child protection services. It was widely stated that fostering staff were well acquainted with child protection procedures and several authorities mentioned both the training and considerable experience of their fostering personnel in this regard.

Links to residential care, a much reduced resource in most authorities, were typically made through centrally controlled access. Similarly, obtaining placements in specialist fostering projects, such as remand or special needs, were typically made through a single gatekeeping point in most counties (e.g. Gwent, South Glamorgan and West Glamorgan). Links between fostering services and after care provision were generally well established and featured in planning and procedures over most of Wales, although the after-care service itself was undeveloped in some areas. Arrangements to provide Independent Visitors were also well established and in most authorities appointments had been made or identified.

Designations of placement types in mainstream and specialist provision were not uniform across Wales. Some authorities described their mainstream fostering as comprising all or some of the following: emergency, short-term, respite, long-term or permanent. Others simply divided fostering into either transitional or long-term, incorporating other categories within these two. One authority (Mid Glamorgan) defined its fostering placements largely by reference to a payment scale based upon the child's needs at the time of placement. This variation in terminology made it difficult to make comparisons across fostering services, and in those departments which did not maintain more precise classifications the appraisal of trends and adjustment strategies were thought by respondents to be rudimentary at best.

Although the reviews of foster carers and of children and young people in placements were informed by both statute and departmental policy, it was evident that these requirements were not always uniformly met. Respondents frequently stated that social workers were diverted from routine tasks around placement reviews by the pressing demands of child protection work. Many respondents felt that their annual reviews were unlikely to be up to date due to staffing changes, organisational change and crisis work on foster placements occupied by challenging children and young people. The problem of review non-completion was particularly marked in regard to respite care services for children and young people with learning difficulties. The issue of children being administratively located within statutory adult disability provision, yet receiving their respite care from national child care voluntary agencies, was a familiar feature across the Welsh counties. It was evident from respondents' accounts that fostering regulations did not mesh easily with the practical arrangements around respite admissions and that this appeared to create problems of accountability over who should complete child care plans and reviews in relation to the "short breaks" which respite offered. Some of these difficulties had arisen in Dyfed and South Glamorgan and were, at the time of the Review, the subject of further discussion by parties to those service level agreements.

Specialist fostering: troublesome schemes for troubled youngsters?
All respondents believed that fostering should provide a range of placement opportunities and foster carer skills in order to ensure a continuum of provision. This point was clearly evidenced in Mid Glamorgan's policy and was apparent in most policy statements made by the eight counties. All departments were working towards this, but faced the organisational conundrum of wishing to offer flexibility and ease of access to services and at the same time also provide specialist foster schemes closely targeted at specific needs. It was the view of several respondents that specialist schemes sometimes become highly insulated and inaccessible through overly restrictive admission requirements. As a result, anomalies were thought to arise elsewhere in the fostering system which was then expected to absorb those cases that did not precisely match the entry conditions of special projects. Evidence of this was most often cited in respect of "difficult adolescents" who were thought to be inappropriate for mainstream placements yet failed to meet all the criteria necessary for inclusion in specialist schemes aimed at troubled youngsters. Such issues are well documented in fostering research which suggests that matching children with particular attributes and needs with specific families can be problematic (Berridge and Cleaver, 1987; Berridge, 1996), especially teenagers with a history of disruptive behaviour (Triseliotis *et al*, 1995a). As elsewhere in the UK (see Berridge and Cleaver, 1987; Aldgate and Hawley, 1988), it was

noted by respondents that emotionally deprived and difficult children can impose heavy burdens on carers and their families who may not always receive adequate support from specialist foster services. Ethnicity has also created challenges for fostering agencies seeking appropriate placements (Rowe *et al*, 1989; Ahmad, 1990; Banks, 1995). Similar difficulties, particularly in Mid and South East Wales, were identified by respondents who recognised the importance of placing children in an environment that would facilitate appropriate development and identity, but have not always been able to recruit ethnically matched carers for specialist or mainstream fostering.

The Review also noted that while specialist schemes do, quite properly, seek to control access to a service and to match needs to provision, they can inadvertently encourage duplication of resources (such as training, recruitment, panels, administration). For example, in South Glamorgan, which had an impressive array of mainstream and specialist fostering services, there were three panels that served different schemes in three different service divisions (child, adult and juvenile justice).

Foster carers
Fostering research suggests that the level and quality of support offered to carers varies significantly. While it is generally acknowledged that more training is now available to carers (Berridge, 1996), there is evidence that this is not a uniform feature of all foster services (see Triseliotis *et al*, 1995b). Within Wales the picture was similarly uneven but all authorities provided some level of training on recruitment, induction and continuing education in both specialist and mainstream schemes. Within recruitment campaigns and subsequent training programmes key topics typically included child protection, partnership working, family contact, challenging behaviour, Children Act 1989 principles on culture and background, corporal punishment and emotional needs. In West Glamorgan, certification was available via a college further education course.

By contrast, carers were not routinely involved in fostering processes and decision-making in all authorities. For instance, while panels operated in all but one authority not all the counties had carer representation on their panels and the majority of panels did not invite prospective carers to attend when considering applications. Few counties systematically involved carers in the recruitment of new families despite the evident benefits of doing this (see Berridge, 1996), particularly in respect of seeking carers from minority ethnic communities (Mountney, 1991; Caesar *et al*, 1994) where relatively little initiative by statutory providers had been taken at the time of the Review. Fostering studies have often found that carers have been given insufficient information by child care social workers and have frequently been left out of care planning and reviews (Berridge, 1996). Whether this is intentional or due to faulty communication, it nonetheless supports the case for separate social work back-up specifically for carers whose information, emotional and material requirements may be eclipsed by an understandable emphasis by social workers upon the needs of the child or young person (see Aldgate, 1989; DoH/SSI, 1996).

The need to develop strong and supportive links between carers and fostering staff was acknowledged by all respondents and has long been advocated in fostering literature (Berridge and Cleaver, 1987). Most respondents pointed to what they considered to be open and accessible contact between workers and carers, notwithstanding staff shortage and a demand-led approach to placement crises rather than providing a more rounded service to all carers. Here, the development of carer self-help groups was seen as an imperative and most interviewees described recent attempts by staff to promote such ventures. Most authorities supported these groups by servicing meetings and finding rooms, speakers and trainers. All counties provided carers with membership of the National Foster Care Association (NFCA) but few had NFCA carer groups established in local areas. Every county viewed it as essential that carers be involved in service development and several had carers on various working or planning groups. Apart from these service development fora, all counties obtained feedback from foster staff who routinely attended local groups.

Remuneration
Remuneration remains a confused and confusing aspect of foster care which is linked to a long-running debate over the very purpose of fostering. Payment variations in Wales reflected different departmental

(and individual manager) policy as to whether carers were employees, volunteers or "professionals". Thus, carers might be paid uniform allowances only, fees, retaining fees, special discretionary payments or a mixture of these depending upon the scheme and the authority. Variation in payment has been well noted elsewhere (Bebbington and Miles, 1990) and a survey of teenager fostering (Lowe, 1990) found two-thirds of local authorities paying below NFCA recommended rates. In Wales, the value of allowances varied considerably across counties and none paid the NFCA recommended level. All departments acknowledged a need to enhance payments and some recognised a need to harmonise these in order to reduce anomalies and unfairness. For example, it was regularly observed that some mainstream foster carers had a child or young person who was as challenging as those in higher paid specialist care schemes but they received far less income. A few authorities were examining the case for a standard income structure. Gwynedd, for example, had recently abandoned specialist based higher payments to provide a uniform and universal payment system.

The possibility that invidious distinctions between groups of carers (within and between counties) could arise as a consequence of differential payments was noted by several respondents, as was the experience of unhelpful "poaching" of carers by different schemes and counties offering different rewards. Another unfortunate consequence of piecemeal and unsystematic payment systems, as noted by several respondents, was that they had given rise to miscalculation and delays. This is not unique to Wales and research elsewhere has suggested that such events are likely to lead carers to question the esteem in which they are held by the agency (see Berridge, 1996). The low status attributed by some social service departments to carers is evident within fostering literature, as is a concern that some departments appear to concentrate more on the recruitment of carers and less on their retention and dropout (Berridge and Cleaver, 1987). Among respondents from all Welsh counties it was fully accepted that carers should be seen as partners, there to provide authentic purposeful supplementary care and not there as a substitute family. The case for a more professionalised fostering service whose distinctive contribution is more widely acknowledged (see Lowe, 1990) was endorsed by most respondents. All believed that adequate funding was central to this but, given their experience of budgetary constraints in local government, unlikely in the immediate future.

Parents

The research literature suggests that, for most children, maintaining contact with parents in a structured context is conducive to their social and emotional development and helps promote placement continuity (Millham *et al*, 1986; Berridge, 1996). In the past, parents have not always been encouraged to sustain contact, nor have they always been invited to make a full contribution to care plans (Berridge, 1996). Similarly, there is some evidence that statutory reviews are sometimes held without parents (Sinclair, 1984). The reasons for this may have more to do with social workers' wishes to protect placements rather than any reluctance on the part of carers to work with parents (Berridge and Cleaver, 1987). The ethos of the Children Act, promoting the reunion of families, was strongly reflected in respondent accounts and in formal policy aims seeking to reduce the length of time children remained in care. This was reinforced by carer training which encouraged parental and family contact. Contact was seen by some respondents as problematic for a minority of carers because of unrealistic arrangements imposed by courts, but they thought this had not resulted in a noticeable loss of recruits or existing carers. All respondents felt that carers had responded well to the issue of contact and all had received training in this regard.

A number of authorities reported that the objective of reuniting a fostered child with her or his family of origin could sometimes be displaced by other compelling placement related demands. A frequent observation was that reasonably settled long-term placements received less attention than they should from over-stretched staff due to the exigencies of short-term or emergency placements and crisis work. In Wales (and elsewhere in the UK; see Rickford, 1996) there is evidence that limited attention seems to have been paid to the needs and support of parents. The capacity of parents to sustain contact may be influenced by several factors. For example, visiting children at a placement or in some supervised setting is likely to call forth particular social skills and require some emotional control, but there are few sources of preparation in this regard. Children, too, may become deeply upset during and after visits, which may deter some parents from visiting as often as they might wish.

Despite the possibility that visiting may be stressful for parents it is evident that positive relationships between them and their children can be accomplished (see Millham *et al*, 1986; Caesar *et al*, 1994). Key factors influencing visiting have been summarised as social worker encouragement, foster family attitudes, family circumstances and parents' perception of their role in the child's life (Triseliotis, 1989). However, the interests of the child are paramount and these will inform arrangements. We were often reminded by respondents that in some cases the notion of reunification is not in the best interests of the child and that planning for permanency elsewhere will be the only option. Maintaining contact under such circumstances can be a highly sensitive matter that will place heavy demands on the emotions and skills of carers. In this respect, close liaison was deemed essential between all parties. Several respondents stated that the clear location of case management responsibility for the child with a child care social worker, and not with foster care services, was essential in clarifying to parents and significant others that carers and allied support staff were service providers and not the arbiters of major decisions in the lives of children and their families.

Monitoring and evaluation

Monitoring, as in the measurement of overall service activity, was undeveloped in most departments. Few authorities had formulated their strategic policy and related service objectives in the context of specific targets, timescales and performance criteria. At the time of the Review they all relied upon central computer systems that, while containing client profiles and service characteristics, did not generate the sophisticated level of data needed to appraise foster service operations. As noted earlier, a wide range of data was routinely collected on these systems but this information could not be easily abstracted to monitor county-wide practice or inform strategic planning.

During the Review, all departments were in the process of developing their management information systems and designing new software with the assistance of outside agencies or their own county planning programming staff. Some respondents spoke of delays in revising their software because of the priority placed by their authority on developing new programmes for community care plans. New data gathering systems were to be introduced by most authorities in 1995/6, but it is unlikely that these can promote comparable monitoring across Wales with any degree of depth and reliability, given their varied software design and purpose. Evaluation as a measurement of service quality and outcome was also undeveloped in most counties and occurred largely in the context of routine discussion in case management and review meetings. The need to broaden this approach to include groups of carers, children and parents was well recognised by all departments and there were a number of examples where initiatives were being planned to introduce quality action groups or standard setting groups that would involve carers.

In the course of the Review there was evidence that the pressing need for comprehensive service appraisal systems was coming to the top of departmental agendas. Some counties (e.g. West and South Glamorgan) had made considerable headway in setting up monitoring systems, but like other counties they acknowledged that information systems to appraise fostering services in respect of overall quality and outcomes were yet to be introduced. In short, notions of quality assurance in fostering as an effective element of organisational practice and culture were in the early stages of development in most counties. Given the pace of policy and practice changes that flowed from the implementation of the Children Act, it is not altogether surprising that monitoring and evaluation lagged behind these shifts during the early 1990s. Also, most interviewees remarked that the introduction of the NHS and Community Care Act (1990) exacted a high price in management time and administrative resources that might otherwise have gone into the development of information systems in child care.

Conclusion
The diversity of fostering services in Wales reflects, inevitably, the impact of organisational, demographic and funding characteristics of local authority social services departments in the very different urban, rural and valley communities of Wales. What these foster service providers had in common, and continue to share with other providers in

the UK, are the following changes and challenges noted by most respondents. First, all interviewees acknowledged that the notion of "traditional fostering" (see Cooper, 1978), where carers accept the child as part of the family and where there is little emphasis or requirement to undertake training, was now an aspect of the past. In its place, the notion of foster carer as skilled and worthy partner was widely invoked as the preferred image. The notion of "image" is not altogether inappropriate here in that the "skilled and worthy partner" might be more apparent than real in some contexts. For example, the many different fostering projects in Wales, with their varied range of allowances and payments, reflected a differential status for some foster carers, with those in the more specialist schemes likely to enjoy the social kudos and material benefits of being seen by agencies as more "professional". Gwynedd introduced its uniform rate of allowance to recognise that all their foster carers typically dealt with complex and demanding situations, with many carers, particularly in less populated areas, previously having simultaneous involvement with different specialist schemes (e.g. children with a disability, challenging behaviour, troubled adolescents), as well as being a resource for mainstream placements.

Notwithstanding the diversity of fostering schemes and operational structures, all respondents recognised the importance of "partnership" between carers and fostering staff and the need for greater involvement of carers in decision-making. This more open model (a feature of child care more generally; see Packman, 1993), which has evolved through the rise in consumer power and participatory mechanisms in welfare, has also helped empower foster carers (Butler and Owens, 1993). Furthermore, this challenge to professional dominance has been accompanied by the strictures of the Children Act 1989 over the primacy of the family of origin and parental responsibility. These requirements of the Act call forth a more inclusive style of fostering, allowing greater openness and contact between foster carer, child and her or his family. These twin principles – carer partnership and primacy of family of origin – were frequently cast by respondents as the defining features of contemporary fostering, albeit in a sometimes tense relationship. Indeed, several respondents saw the careful management of these sometimes competing interests as one of the key skills in fostering practice.

Generally it was taken for granted by respondents that, *a priori*, fostering was a "good thing", somehow sanctified by the undoubted altruism of the carers and the "obvious" benefits assumed to flow from being in a "good family". The idea that fostering might be harmful for some children, not simply due to the problems of poor matching but due to abusing carers (Fox Harding, 1997), was rarely raised. Instead, the logistical imperative for most providers was to secure a regular supply of two-parent families rather than any pressing concern for whether fostering was in some sense "effective" or that funding might be better spent on preventive measures within those communities from which fostered children frequently came to notice. Like other providers in the UK (Rickford, 1996), most respondents assumed the benefits of a two-parent heterosexual foster household. While they recognised that such families did not reflect the full pattern of households in the wider population, they cited few attempts to recruit family and carer types that might more faithfully reflect the sorts of home settings in which children grow up today. While all counties placed children with their extended family (albeit usually short term) only a few were planning to promote actively this reservoir of potential carers by developing specialist systems to train and register them quickly in order to sustain such placements for the medium or long term.

In most respects the Welsh Review found fostering to be in a steady state of activity. No dramatic departures were planned that would, for example, reduce fostering levels in order to divert investment to other areas of child and family services. Nor were significant increases in funding for fostering services on the horizon, to deliver what many respondents described as the "continuum of fostering provision" they deemed necessary to tackle diverse child and adolescent needs. Most respondents articulated the essential nature of this "continuum" as (i) providing those fostered with well-matched families who could call upon a range of developmental/ support programmes to help the child whose family of origin would also be assisted towards reunification where appropriate, and (ii) providing foster carers with adequate financial back-up, good training for the whole foster family, respite and therapeutic support when needed. This "ideal type" of provision, while firmly lodged within the professional imagination of respondents, had not been dulled by the real-world constraints of funding and organisational upheavals in Welsh local government in the 1990s. In this regard the Review, while essentially a snapshot of fostering policy and operational structures in the principality, also revealed the determination of hard-pressed staff who were still committed to achieving sometime in the future the sort of service they believed would deliver the highest standards in foster care.

Note

Since this study was completed there have been some significant changes in local authority fostering in Wales. Local government reorganisation has led to the re-configuration of SSD fostering within 22 local unitary authorities that replaced the eight county councils participating in the All Wales Review. Anecdotal evidence suggests that there is now some competition between several of these new authorities (particularly those that were once part of the same county council) in attracting foster carers and that this has led in some instances to a more responsive and supportive provider regime in order to retain carers. The proximity of several of these small authorities opens up the prospect of more "market mobility" for foster carers than hitherto and it seems clear that some carers are understandably taking a keen interest in what's "on offer" in other nearby councils. Of some concern is the view that several of the new unitary authorities are relatively small and their SSDs do not have the critical mass to offer well-rounded provision and some did not fare well in the way resources were carved up during local government reorganisation. Such departments cannot offer the range of foster care that was once available in the larger county councils and some appear to have little choice but to develop a "one size fits all" approach to foster care. While much of the diversity of provision and philosophy identified in the Review still obtains, there seems to be a shared view among several agencies that they have seen a steady increase in children and young people with challenging behaviour entering foster care and that this has placed severe demands on carers and staff, particularly in the smaller authorities.

References

Ahmad B, *Black Perspectives in Social Work*, Venture Press, 1990.

Aldgate J, 'Foster families and residential care for older children: some interpersonal dynamics', *Children and Society*, 3:1, pp 19–36, 1989.

Aldgate J and Hawley D, 'Helping foster families through disruption', *Adoption & Fostering*, 10:2, pp 44–9, 1988.

Banks N, 'Children of black mixed parentage and their placement needs', *Adoption & Fostering*, 19:2, pp 19–24, 1995.

Bebbington A and Miles J, 'The supply of foster families for children in care', *British Journal of Social Work*, 20:4, pp 283–307, 1990.

Berridge D, *Foster Care: A research review*, HMSO, 1996.

Berridge D and Cleaver H, *Foster Home Breakdown*, Blackwell, 1987.

Butler I and Owens D, 'Canaries among sparrows: ideas of the family and the practice of foster care', *Community Alternatives: International Journal of Family Care*, 5:1, pp 25–42, 1993.

Caesar G, Parchment M and Berridge D, *Black Perspectives on Services for Children in Need,* Barnardo's/National Children's Bureau, 1994.

Cliffe D with Berridge D, *Closing Children's Homes: An end to residential child care?*, National Children's Bureau, 1991.

Cooper J, *Patterns of Family Placement*, Allen & Unwin, 1978.

Department of Health Social Services Inspectorate, *Inspection of Local Authority Fostering, 1994–5,* DoH, 1996.

Fox Harding L, *Perspectives in Child Care Policy,* Longman, 1997.

Lowe K, *Teenagers in Foster Care*, National Foster Care Association, 1990.

Millham S, Bullock R, Hosie K and Haak M, *Lost in Care: The problems of maintaining links between children in care and their families,* Gower, 1986.

Mountney J, *Children with Disabilities in Foster Care*, National Foster Care Association, 1991.

Packman J, 'From prevention to partnership: child welfare services across three decades', in Pugh G (ed), *Thirty Years of Change for Children,* National Children's Bureau, 1993.

Pithouse A, Young C and Butler I , 'All Wales Review: local authority fostering services', Children Act Research Group, School of Social and Administrative Studies & Cardiff Law School, University of Wales, 1994.

Rickford F, 'Ringing the changes', *Community Care,* 1129, July18–24, pp 18–9, 1996.

Rowe J, Hundleby M and Garnett L, *Child Care Now: A survey of placement patterns,* BAAF/Batsford, 1989.

Sinclair R, *Decision-making in Statutory Reviews on Children in Care,* Gower, 1984.

Triseliotis J, 'Foster care outcomes: a review of key research findings', *Adoption & Fostering,* 13:3, pp 5–17, 1989.

Triseliotis J, Borland M, Hill M and Lambert L, *Teenagers and the Social Work Services,* HMSO, 1995a.

Triseliotis J, Sellick C and Short R, *Foster Care: Theory and practice,* BAAF/ Batsford, 1995b.

2 A comparative survey of specialist fostering in the UK and North America

Malcolm Hill, Richard Nutter, Donal Giltinan,
Joe Hudson and Burt Galaway

At the time of writing Malcolm Hill was Senior Lecturer, Department of Social Policy and Social Work, University of Glasgow; Richard Nutter was Associate Professor, Faculty of Social Work, The University of Calgary; Donal Giltinan was Consultant/Trainer, BAAF Scottish Centre in Edinburgh; Joe Hudson was Professor, Faculty of Social Work (Edmonton Division), Calgary; and Burt Galaway was Professor of Social Work, University of Manitoba, Winnipeg, Manitoba.

This paper was published in Adoption & Fostering, 17:2, 1993.

The development of specialist fostering in Britain was one of the child-care success stories of the 1980s. The authors report in this paper the main findings of a comparative survey of specialist fostering undertaken in 1992, which provides an up-to-date picture of current trends.

An early evaluation of specialist fostering showed that it could work effectively for teenagers with substantial difficulties (Yelloly, 1979). Later surveys revealed that schemes had proliferated in number, extended the types of children placed and diversified in organisation (Shaw and Hipgrave, 1983, 1989). Yet its very success led to questioning of the basic principles. It was argued that very few foster placements are straightforward and that all foster carers are entitled to training, support and proper remuneration. Hence some people came to think that it was preferable to make the "special" features apply to everyone and do away with separate schemes.

Opportunity to carry out a comparative survey of specialist fostering arose early in 1992. The main findings of the survey presented in this article relate to children and adolescents. The study also included adult family placement schemes which we plan to report on elsewhere.

A questionnaire, previously developed for surveys in North America, was used (Nutter *et al*, 1992; Hudson *et al*, 1992). This was used in the UK with few alterations to make comparability as easy as possible. However, some amendments were made to reflect different linguistic usages. For example, in North America the preferred term for a specialist foster scheme is 'Treatment Fostering Program'.

Questionnaires were sent to all 230 agencies and regional branches listed in the BAAF directory, and three reminders followed at monthly intervals. The responses were:

Questionnaire completed	53
Refusal	10
Responded "no scheme"	109
No reply	58

Many of those with no scheme were specialist adoption agencies with no fostering service. The rest were mostly smaller local authorities, some of whom wrote to explain that they had active plans to introduce a scheme, normally for teenagers. In contrast, there were at least eight authorities who had deliberately dismantled specialist arrangements in order to re-integrate them within mainstream fostering. Whether this represents a minority divergence or the onset of a widespread final stage in the evolution of professional fostering remains to be seen. One agency intended to omit the stage of having a separate system by moving straight to a position where all foster carers had formal contracts and tasks with appropriate payments. The wish to avoid "labelling" or "segregating" foster carers and children was a prominent factor in these developments. Some changes were related to decentralisation of fostering services.

British and North American schemes compared
The statistical analysis was carried out in Edmonton (Alberta). To be included in the study each scheme had to have all six of the following attributes:
- explicit identification as specialist;
- payments above ordinary rates;

- training and support provided;
- formal goal to provide care for children who would otherwise be in residential care;
- care provided in the carer's own home;
- foster carers are part of a service or treatment team.

In the UK there were 37 schemes (out of the 53 who returned questionnaires) and in North America 321 (out of 430 who returned questionnaires) of which 26 were in Canada and the rest in the US. Seven of the UK schemes were in Scotland, two each in Wales and Northern Ireland, 26 in England.

There were significant differences in the auspices and organisation of schemes. Whereas 90 per cent of British schemes were run by local authorities, three-quarters of North American programmes were in the voluntary sector and four per cent were operated by private for-profit agencies. Probably connected with this is the fact that most British agencies, but few North American ones, said they had more than one scheme. A handful of schemes in both cases had started before 1974, but whereas half those in the UK had started between 1975 and 1984, this was true of only one-third of schemes in North America, where a considerably higher proportion had been set up in the last few years.

Table 1
Scheme size (All figures give the mean number per scheme)

	US/Canada (N = 267)	UK (N =34)
Total approved homes	25	26
Homes with children placed	21	23
Total children placed	36	28

Agencies were asked to give a figure for the total budget for their specialist fostering scheme. It is hard to know the accuracy of the information provided and the fluctuating exchange rates add to the difficulties of comparison. Nonetheless, the figures indicated that more UK schemes had smaller budgets (one-half were less than £132,000, compared with half under $450,000 in the US/Canada). This was in spite of the fact that the sizes of schemes were very similar.

Scheme size

Scheme size was assessed by asking about the numbers of children in placement and of approved homes on a specific date. This was 1 February 1992 in the UK. For organisational reasons this was three months later than the North American date, but it is unlikely that this small gap made a significant difference. The results were as in Table 1 above.

Thus, overall there was no great difference, but there was a wide range. The smallest UK scheme had one approved home and the largest 129 – a local authority that regarded all its homes as specialist. Most schemes in both areas had a maximum of two children in any foster home, but a few had up to five.

Reward system

Three-quarters of the foster carers in the US and Canada were paid on a daily basis, only for the days when the child was there. This system did not predominate in the UK. It was used by one-third of UK schemes, but just as common was the practice of paying carers a fixed amount (retainer) with additions for the days when a child was actually present. Monthly payments per child appeared to vary considerably, but in the UK the typical amount was in the region of £500. In the UK the child's age nearly always affects the amount paid, but this was so for only one-third of North American programmes. Conversely, a sizeable minority of agencies in North America vary payment levels according to foster carers' education, training or length of experience. This is rarely done in the UK.

Training and support

Formalisation of planning, training and support has been a key character-istic of specialist fostering and the evidence was that a higher proportion of North American schemes had more stringent requirements in this respect. Written treatment plans specifying goals and tasks were said to be used by four-fifths of British schemes but 98 per cent of North American programmes. Most commonly plans were for three months, but they varied from two weeks to six months. The hours of *pre-service* training required ranged widely in the UK (0–40), but on average were lower (16 against 25). The mean annual requirement for *ongoing* training (11 hours) was half the North American equivalent. In all three countries it was normal to expect attendance at support group meetings. Two British agencies had no such meetings, but at the opposite extreme was a scheme with weekly meetings.

Treatment design and caseload size

One of the most striking contrasts was the greater proportion of North American schemes that teach foster carers specific intervention techniques: nearly two-thirds (62 per cent) as compared to very few (14 per cent) in the UK. Only one-third of British schemes gave any response to a list of six intervention approaches (admittedly derived from North American practice) together with the option of adding "other". This compared with two-thirds of North American programmes. The most popular British method was also the most general, i.e. systems, contextual, ecological.

Table 2

Intervention methods used (singly or in combination)

	US/Canada (N = 203)	UK (N = 12)
Behaviour modification	56%	25%
Social learning	30%	42%
Family therapy	17%	16%
Systems, contexual, ecological	26%	50%
Psychodynamic	13%	25%
Reality therapy	23%	17%
Other	10%	8%

This suggests that in the UK the tendency is that foster carers seek to achieve goals in their own ways with general guidance, whereas in the US and Canada they are more often expected to follow a standard model (see also Hill, 1992). One-third of North American programmes which had a definite treatment approach indicated that behaviour modification was the only approach used, whereas no British scheme was in that position. Even so, there are schemes in North America that adopt ecological perspectives and emphasise developing the particular strengths of individual foster families (Pine and Jacobs, 1989).

In North America the great majority of programmes specified a maximum caseload size for the social workers (89 per cent). In the UK this applied to half the schemes. Moreover, maximum caseload in North America was normally defined in terms of numbers of children (86 per cent), while in this country the criterion was usually the number of foster homes (89 per cent). There were again indications of somewhat poorer resourcing in the UK, since the mean number of foster homes per worker was 13, which contrasts with a mean of seven homes for those North American programmes, basing maximum numbers on homes rather than children.

The children in specialist schemes

The survey also obtained information about individual children, i.e. the ten most recently placed and the ten most recently discharged. This yielded data on 283 children recently placed in the UK and 228 recently discharged. The equivalent figures in North America were nearly ten times greater, which corresponded roughly to the disparity in number of schemes. By and large, the patterns for new placements and discharges were quite similar.

Gender, age and ethnic origin

In all four sets of children, there were rather more boys than girls. Most schemes concentrate on adolescents and in the UK only eight per cent of the children recently placed were aged under five and a further 20 per cent aged six to eleven. This is consistent with the recent study carried out for NFCA by Lowe (1990) which found that half of all local authorities had a special scheme for teenagers.

The British figures also showed more older teenagers placed. For example, 42 per cent of recently placed children were aged 15+ , whereas in North America only 28 per cent were in that age group. Sixty per cent of recently discharged teenagers in the UK were aged 15+ , but only 38 per cent of those in the US. This reflects in part the inclusion of a few remand fostering schemes in the UK sample.

The different ethnic compositions of the national populations was reflected in the foster children:

Table 3

Ethnic group of children most recently placed

	US/Canada (N = 2,304)	UK (N = 283)
Black	26%	7%
White	61%	88%
Other (e.g. Hispanic)	12%	2%

Perceptions of the problem

There were major divergences in the way that children's problems were described. It is hard to know how much this reflects genuine differences in the children and their circumstances, and how much dissimilar ways of defining difficulties. For example, the characteristic of the child selected as the main reason for placement was stated to be "psychiatric or emotional" for as many as two-thirds of the North American children, but only one-tenth of UK children. Conversely, behaviour difficulties of a non-criminal nature applied to one-third of children in the UK but only two per cent of those in North America. We suspect that similar kinds of adolescents are being categorised differently. There is something of a paradox here, when it is recalled that overt behaviour modification is much more common in the US and Canada, yet the problems are more likely to be seen as internal (psychiatric, emotional). In part, this may result from a much greater reluctance in the UK to use what are seen as stigmatising "psychiatric" labels. Also, in the United States many specialist foster care programmes developed from children's mental health services, so that sometimes referrals cannot be accepted unless there is a psychiatric diagnosis.

Relatively fewer children were placed in schemes primarily in relation to physical or mental disability in North America (seven per cent against 20 per cent for the UK). For both areas, about 15 per cent of young people were fostered as a result of criminal or delinquent behaviour, which was one of the targets of the pioneering Kent scheme (Hazel, 1981).

Routes through care and legal status

There were some differences concerning the route into and out of foster care. Thirty-eight per cent of recently placed UK children entered the specialist foster home direct from their parental home, which was twice the North American proportion (16 per cent). In the US and Canada, more had moved from residential care. Turning to the most recently discharged group, more in the UK returned to their parental home (39 per cent against 29 per cent) whereas fewer went to some other family setting (16 per cent against 24 per cent). On average, the adolescents had spent longer in North American programmes (15 months) than in the UK (eight months). Sixty per cent of placements had lasted for less than six months in the UK, 38 per cent in Canada and the US. This may result from the inclusion of some remand and respite placements. However, the length of stay varied greatly, from less than a month to over seven years.

The children's legal position showed marked divergence. In spite of what Parton (1991) has called the shift towards legalism in British child care practice, just under half of the British teenagers had no diminution of their birth parents' rights, but in North America parental rights were temporarily or permanently removed in three-quarters of the cases. Canada had a particularly low proportion with full parental rights retained (13 per cent). This is probably linked to the legal support for early termination of parental rights. For example, in Alberta, there is a two-year limit on voluntary care or accommodation (temporary wardship). Correspondingly, few parents of children recently placed (53 per cent) were said to have been consulted about the child's plan in North America compared with the UK (82 per cent). This did not seem to represent a difference in *planned* family contact, since parental access was planned for similar proportions of youngsters (about six per cent). However, the *actual* visiting pattern in the last month of placement before the survey showed that two-thirds of the UK teenagers had had contact, but only half of the North Americans. This may be an artificial difference, since the North American questionnaire used the phrase "visit with" which is narrower than "contact with". For discharged teenagers, parents in North America were less likely to have met the foster carers to plan the placement.

The reasons that the children and teenagers had left the placement were as follows:

Table 4
Reasons for discharge

	US/Canada (N = 1,898)	UK (N = 229)
Treatment goals achieved	47%	44%
Breakdown — teenager refuses to stay	16%	24%
Breakdown — foster carer(s) request removal	11%	16%
Administrative (e.g. upper age)	10%	6%
Insufficient progress 15%	8%	
Other 1%	2%	

Thus, slightly fewer than half the placements were clearly successful, although some of the administrative reasons (which included legal changes) may also have represented a satisfactory outcome. The British schemes revealed a higher breakdown rate of 40 per cent as opposed to 27 per cent.

Conclusions
This survey has helped to update our knowledge of specialist fostering in the UK at the same time as providing comparative material from North America. It shows that the model of separate schemes is still popular, with several new ones having been established in the last few years. However, some local authorities have moved to reintegrate schemes with the intention of extending the "special" features of better pay, training and support to all foster carers.

Compared with their North American counterparts, UK schemes are more often part of public social services. Typically they have smaller budgets, tend to be less specific in approach and requirements, provide relatively more places for older adolescents and for teenagers with disabilities, place teenagers for shorter periods and have a somewhat higher breakdown rate. The survey thus raises questions about the resourcing of specialist fostering in the UK. There are also indications that more attention should be paid to assessing competences of foster carers, providing more specific instruction and having a structured approach to the evaluation of placements.

Acknowledgements

We would like to thank all the busy people who made time to complete and return the questionnaires. We are grateful to the Laidlaw Foundation which funded the research.

References

Hazel N, *A Bridge to Independence*, Blackwell, 1981.

Hill M, 'Fostering and adoption in Canada: Are there lessons for Britain?', *Adoption & Fostering*, 16:4, pp 39–45, 1992.

Hudson J, Nutter R W and Galaway B, 'A survey of North American specialist foster family programs', *Social Service Review*, 66:1, pp 50–63, 1992.

Nutter R W, Hudson J and Galaway B, 'Survey of treatment fostering programs in Canada and the USA Care and the system of services for children', paper presented to the Provincial Treatment Foster Family Care Conference, Edmonton, Alberta, 1992.

Lowe K, *Teenagers in Foster Care*, NFCA, 1990.

Parton N, *Governing the Family*, Macmillan, 1991.

Pine B A and Jacobs M, 'The training of foster parents for work with adolescents', in Aldgate J, Maluccio A and Reeves C (eds), *Adolescents in Foster Families*, Batsford, 1989.

Shaw M and Hipgrave T, *Specialist Fostering*, Batsford, 1983.

Shaw M and Hipgrave T, 'Specialist fostering 1988 – a research study', *Adoption & Fostering*, 13:3, pp 17–22, 1989.

Yelloly M, *Independent Evaluation of 25 Placements*, Kent Social Services Department, Maidstone, 1979.

3 Developing leaving care services:
tapping the potential of foster carers

Jim Wade

Jim Wade has a background in youth and community work and as a social worker with teenagers. He is now a Senior Research Fellow in the Social Work Research and Development Unit at the University of York. His research interests centre on the transition to adulthood for vulnerable groups of young people, with particular emphasis on care leavers, young runaways from home and substitute care, and young people on the streets. Recent publications include (with Nina Biehal, Jasmine Clayden and Mike Stein): "Moving On: Young people and leaving care schemes" and "Going Missing: Young people absent from care."

This paper was published in Adoption & Fostering, 21:3, 1997.

Introduction

In recent years fostering has become the mainstay of local authority accommodation services for children and young people. Over the decade to 1993 the residential population declined as a proportion of all looked after children from 29 per cent to 16 per cent (Berridge, 1994) and, by 1994, 65 per cent of all looked after children were in foster care (DoH, 1996). Although the proportion of children fostered has increased over this period, the actual numbers of children looked after in foster settings has remained relatively constant due to a declining total population (Berridge, 1994), as have the overall numbers of carers available to fostering agencies – statutory or independent. It is also true that, when the making and ending of placements are viewed over a period of time, residential placements remain an important accommodation resource, especially for teenagers (Berridge and Cleaver, 1987; Rowe *et al*, 1989; Biehal *et al*, 1992). They are more heavily used at various points in young people's care careers than the "static" picture above can convey.

It is perhaps surprising, given the position of fostering, that it remains under researched relative to residential care. Professionals believe it offers the best alternative for young people who cannot be cared for in the family home, but evidence of its effectiveness in relation to other options is quite tentative (Berridge, 1994; ADSS, 1996). This is certainly the case for young people leaving foster care between 16 and 18 years of age to establish independent lives in the community. To date there has only been one study in Britain, a survey conducted under the auspices of the National Foster Care Association (NFCA), with a specific focus on the role played by foster carers in supporting young people through this difficult transition (Fry, 1992).

The findings discussed here derive from a major longitudinal study of the processes associated with this transition or, more precisely, series of transitions to adulthood. The study investigated the impact of different leaving care schemes and approaches to the provision of leaving care services in three local authorities in England. Our aims were to chart the experience of transition for a sample of young people leaving the care of these authorities over their first 18 to 24 months of independent living in the community; to explore the support made available to them from carers, social workers and, in particular, leaving care schemes; and to evaluate the outcomes of scheme interventions for these young people. The aims of this study have been reported at greater length elsewhere (Biehal et al, 1992, 1995).

The study was designed in two stages. An initial survey of 183 young people who left the care of these authorities in a six-month period was conducted during their first three to nine months of independent living. Postal questionnaires completed by social workers enabled us to chart the varied patterns of leaving care and to provide data on outcomes in the first few months of independence (Biehal et al, 1992). The findings examined in this paper are based primarily on our in-depth follow-up study. Interviews were conducted with 74 care leavers, their social workers and, where young people were involved with leaving care schemes (just over half the sample), their leaving care workers. Leaving care was defined as either a move to independence or legal discharge while continuing to live in the same placement (see Biehal et al, 1995, Chapter 1, for a detailed discussion of sampling issues). The interviews were carried out shortly after leaving care and on two subsequent occasions during a two-year period. Data were gathered on young people's care careers – for example, types and quality of placements experienced, patterns of movement, educational progress, involvement in decision-making – and these were related to the progress being made in key post-care transition areas. These included their early housing careers, education and employment options, and their progress in developing life skills and in building a sustaining network of social support. In turn these data provided a basis for evaluating the impact of professional interventions.

All the young people were aged 16–19 when recruited to the research and, of these, 61 per cent were female and 12 per cent were black. Over half (56 per cent) were first looked after as teenagers, although two-thirds of the sample (69 per cent) had been looked after for four or more years. Placement movement was a feature of their care careers, only 16 per cent having made no moves and one-third having made four or more. Two-fifths (41 per cent) moved on from a last placement in residential care and 45 per cent from a foster placement. The fact that only 15 per cent were legally discharged while placed with parents or relatives suggests that, for the majority, a return home was not an immediate option.

In this paper attention will be focused on the implications of our findings for fostering, bearing in mind that many of the needs of young people moving on from substitute care or accommodation are common to all regardless of placement background. I will concentrate on three broad areas important to successful transitions:
- the nature and timing of leaving;
- access to education and employment opportunities; and
- the need to construct a sustaining network of social support.

Some of the difficulties experienced by these young people will be highlighted together with issues that arise from the support that was being made available to them by carers, social workers and leaving care scheme staff. Finally, I will consider the place of foster carers in the development of an integrated approach to delivering leaving care services.

The research did not have foster care as a specific focus and some resulting limitations therefore need to be made explicit. First, last placement can only be a crude indicator of the types of placement experienced by young people during their care careers, as a majority of those looked after experience both residential and foster settings (Rowe et al, 1989; Biehal et al, 1992). Second, the views of foster carers were not directly sought and, given that the first interviews were conducted shortly after young people had moved on, data on past placements were gathered retrospectively. Nonetheless, the interviews gave us important insights into young people's care careers and the influence of these on shaping their transitions from care.

The nature and timing of leaving

Leaving care is a process, not a single discrete event, and involves young people in making a series of transitions. Between the mid-teens and mid-twenties all young people make a series of key transitions in their lives: from school to further education or the labour market; from the family home to independent households; and, for some, the formation of their own families. For most young people these transitions are loosely connected and extend over a number of years. During the 1980s youth policies reinforced young people's dependency upon their families, made leaving home more difficult and consequently made these key transitions more protracted (Banks et al, 1992; Jones and Wallace, 1992; Cole, 1995). In quite stark contrast, transitions for looked after young people, who often lack reliable family support, tend to be both accelerated and compressed. For many in our study, moving from care to independent accommodation, setting up home with a partner and becoming a parent all occurred within 18 to 24 months of leaving care. The assumption of full adult responsibilities in this way suggests that continuity in support from key adult figures in their lives, including carers and social workers, is likely to have an influential bearing on positive outcomes.

Moving on

Looked after young people are expected to move to independent living at a much earlier age than young people in the general population. In relation to our survey sample, 29 per cent had moved on at 16 and 60 per cent before the age of 18 (Biehal et al, 1992), a finding consistent with previous studies of care leavers (Stein and Carey, 1986; Garnett, 1992).

However, there was a significant tendency for those whose last placement was in a residential setting to have left earlier. Of those who had moved on from residential care, 92 per cent did so before the age of 18 compared to 69 per cent of those who had left from a foster home. These patterns contrast with a median age of leaving home of 22 years for men and 20 for women (Jones, 1987).

Young people leaving the family home may leave and return on a number of occasions before finally establishing an independent household (Banks *et al*, 1992). Leaving care tends to be final; respite arrangements are rare. Very few of our follow-up sample were able to return to sheltered accommodation when in crisis. Such opportunities tended to be restricted to those with learning disabilities or young parents where there were clear child care concerns.

Two-thirds of our follow-up sample made planned moves from their final placement. In most cases planning started three to 12 months in advance and involved young people, carers, social workers and, for those referred to schemes, scheme staff. Advanced planning gave young people an opportunity to prepare for the move, to make choices based on the options available and time for a leaving care plan to be drawn up. Joint planning of this type, with a clear division of responsibilities, provided the best foundation for a smooth transition and enabled young people to be reassured about the future sources of support available to them.

A substantial minority of the sample, however, moved on as a result of a crisis, over half arising through the breakdown of a foster placement. Indeed, one-third of those leaving foster homes were propelled to early independence as a result of breakdown – a rate similar to that found in other studies of foster placement breakdown (Berridge and Cleaver, 1987; Rowe *et al*, 1989). In many cases these were long-term placements that foundered when young people reached their mid-teens. This pattern points to the difficulties of maintaining stability for young people at such a crucial time. The profound psychological impact of breakdown was captured by one young woman as she struggled to cope without the continuity of support her foster family could have offered:

They treated me more like a daughter than my own did . . . and I gained sisters and a grandma and grandad you know. Everything that

I didn't have they did, and I had it . . . and I just lost it all. It was awful.

Particular attention needs to be given to supporting foster placements in these vulnerable years if young people are to be given the maximum opportunity of making a planned move out of care and of being able to rely upon continuing support from carers once they have moved. In addition, a recent study found that one-third of foster carers looking after teenagers had received no specialist training in their care and that, when making placements, matching tended to be "hasty or minimal" (Hill *et al*, 1996). It is likely that improvements in these areas could have a positive influence on placement outcomes.

Although some, attracted by the concept of "independence", chose to move on, the assumptions that underpin an expectation that young people should leave at 16 or 17, regardless of their preparedness, need to be questioned. The option to stay on until ready to leave "home" is a rare privilege. Although these expectations about moving on were a particular feature of residential settings, it was also the case that only one in five (21 per cent) of the young people in foster care were able to remain with their carers beyond legal discharge at 18, and all bar one of these had moved on by our second interview some six months later. The proportion staying on is higher than the 5.5 per cent found by the NFCA survey (Fry, 1992) and may in part be due to the development of supported lodgings schemes in two of our three authorities. Staying on was facilitated by converting placements to supported lodgings through the creative use of Section 24 funds.

Recent reports have highlighted acute problems in the recruitment and retention of foster carers (ADSS, 1996; DoH, 1996). Unless greater commitment is given to this area and the pressure for young people to leave is lessened, then the development of a more flexible needs-led approach to the timing of leaving care is unlikely to be realised. For the majority of those fostered, their placement did not provide a substitute home base that could be relied upon in the long term.

Access to education and employment opportunities

For most care leavers, without the security of the parental home, gaining access to intensely competitive youth labour markets is a priority, and success or failure in this field may act reciprocally on other areas of their lives – for example, their ability to manage their accommodation or to sustain friendship networks and an active social life. The key to success tends to be qualifications gained at 16 (Banks *et al*, 1992). Findings in relation to the educational attainment of looked after young people make depressing reading (Jackson, 1988/9; Biehal *et al*, 1992; Aldgate *et al*, 1993), even in relation to those in long-term stable foster placements (Heath *et al*, 1994). Rarely is substitute care able to compensate adequately for pre-care disadvantage.

Attainment was poor for the young people in our study. Two-thirds of our survey sample and over half (54 per cent) of our follow-up sample left school with no qualifications at all and, while one-quarter of the follow-up group attained one or more GCSEs at "A–C" grade, only three young people (four per cent) gained three or more. Allowing for the disadvantaged pool from which looked after young people tend to be drawn, comparison with the attainment levels of 15- to 17-year-olds generally is nonetheless stark. In 1992, 38 per cent attained five or more GCSEs at "A–C" grade nationally (Department for Education, 1992). Given these attainment levels, it is perhaps not surprising to find that the majority failed to establish a stable pattern of education, employment or training upon leaving care. Half were unemployed and two-thirds entered an "insecure" career path, involving periods of casual work or training interspersed with lengthening bouts of unemployment – findings consistent with other studies of care leavers (Garnett, 1992; Broad, 1994; Cook, 1994). Once young people entered this path their careers took on a fixity from which it proved difficult to recover. During the two-year research cycle only three young people managed to recover from unemployment to enter work or training.

For looked after young people the barriers to educational progress are well rehearsed and were apparent for those in our study. The effects of movement and disruption, labelling, feeling "different" and of patterns of truancy all had a negative impact on their educational careers, as did the tendency for social workers and carers to prioritise "welfare" above

educational concerns. In particular, very few of those marked by movement or regular non-attendance were able to avoid unemployment once
they left school.

The minority who did attain some qualifications and start careers –
and these were largely the same group of young people – shared certain
characteristics. Their care careers were more likely to have been stable,
to have enabled a continuous pattern of schooling to be maintained or
renewed. They were disproportionately female and far more likely to
have come from fostering backgrounds in which they were shown
interest, concern and encouragement to attain by carers and social
workers. Their placements provided a secure base from which they could
harness their own motivation. They were more secure and more likely to
have had positive relationships with family and friends. The majority
also started on their career paths from the shelter of supported accommodation – living with family, foster carers or in supported lodgings or
hostels – and most, especially those continuing in education, carried on
receiving practical, financial and emotional support from carers, social
workers and, where involved, leaving care workers.

A number of issues relevant to fostering are raised here. First, our
findings highlight the importance for young people's educational progress of finding a secure and positive home base. Intensive compensatory
inputs are likely to be necessary if young people are to have a chance of
catching up with their peers. Education needs to have a higher priority
and form an integral part of child care planning from the point of entry
to care. In this regard, the age-related schedules developed by the
Looking After Children Project may prove helpful (Parker et al, 1991).
Second, as key attachment figures for young people, carers, working
alongside social workers and others, have a crucial role in helping to
promote their educational and employment careers. These young people
needed to feel they could rely upon the support being offered by carers.
Consistent encouragement and help with motivation were crucial, as
were the links some carers and social workers forged with schools. No
less valued were attempts to help young people negotiate difficulties
encountered in the adult world beyond the family boundary; to offer
advocacy and a buffer as they attempted to find their feet (Downes,
1992). Finally, the importance of a continued stay in supported accom-

modation points to the immense difficulties posed for young people in attempting to maintain or start a career at the same time as coping with the pressures of multiple transitions. It reinforces the need for flexibility in the leaving care process, for a range of supported accommodation options to be made available, and for the recognition and funding of a continuing care role for foster carers. It is unlikely that many of these young people would have been able to cope without continuing support.

The stakes are quite high given what we know about the reciprocal impact of unemployment and poverty on the ability to manage in other life areas, including homelessness (Kirk *et al*, 1991). Equally, going to work or college helps to build self-esteem and confidence, and provides a base for widening networks of social support.

Social support networks
Reappraising and testing out the reliability of support that would be available from family, carers and social workers was very much on the minds of these young people at the point of leaving care. Four-fifths were in touch with family members after moving on, although the quality of support they could expect was more variable as less than one-third had a supportive relationship with a parent at this stage. However, at the close of the study two years later this figure had risen to one-half as young people made continued attempts to renew or repair relationships. The level of contact which young people maintained with their families while looked after was a good indicator of the level of support they could expect from them once they had moved on. However, there were also wider implications. The majority of those who had poor relationships with their parents characterised by rejection, conflict or lack of interest, also had poor friendship networks. They had greater difficulty building and sustaining social relationships in general.

Previous studies have highlighted a tendency for traditional forms of fostering to be "exclusive" of birth families (Millham *et al*, 1986; Berridge and Cleaver, 1987). In contrast, more recent specialist or ecological approaches have tended to emphasise a more "inclusive" relationship (Aldgate *et al*, 1989), involving a care-giving network in which carers, social workers and families attempt to work in partnership to maximise the social support available to young people. Even if reunification with family proves impossible, our findings suggest that this approach is more likely to provide a stable base of support for young people once they have left care. Unfortunately, although family mediation remained an enduring area of need for young people, it represented a declining area of social work activity once they had moved on. Fewer than one-third of social workers were actively helping young people to resolve family difficulties at this stage. Indeed planned social worker support in general tended to decline once young people had been legally discharged – a consistent finding in relation to care leavers (Stein and Carey, 1986; Biehal *et al*, 1992; Garnett, 1992).

Another consistent finding in the research literature has been the low status accorded to foster carers (Sellick, 1992; Berridge, 1996). Without a recognised after-care role, the support they can offer to young people no longer living with them has tended to be informal, self-funded and rarely integrated into leaving care planning (Fry, 1992). In relation to our sample, one-third of those fostered were receiving ongoing support from foster carers when they first left care, but this had declined to a fifth some 18 to 24 months later. The NFCA survey identified almost identical levels of post-care support (Fry, 1992). If our aim is to offer continuity in support to young people through transition, then the potential pool of support available from foster carers needs to be incorporated more effectively into the development of leaving care services.

Developing leaving care services

Despite the new responsibilities placed upon local authorities by the Children Act 1989 with regard to leaving care support and the emergence of a range of specialist leaving care schemes and initiatives, the role of foster carers in relation to these services has tended to be peripheral. In this final section, I intend to consider briefly some issues that arise from considering the place of foster carers in a "through-care" approach to delivering effective leaving care services.

Preparing young people for adult life

Although a pivotal point in young people's lives, leaving care needs to form part of a wider child care strategy that connects prevention, substitute care and after care. Helping young people to prepare for adult life needs to be continuously kept in mind throughout the time they are looked after. It needs to be holistic in approach, giving equal weight to the development of practical, educational, emotional and social skills and resources, and to occur gradually, at a pace young people find appropriate (Clayden and Stein, 1996). A precondition for this – and perhaps the greatest challenge facing the care system – is the need to offer young people a stable and positive care experience; a home base that offers emotional security, positive encouragement and a chance to recover from the stresses of their past lives.

Foster carers, through their daily involvement with young people, clearly have a central role here but their approach, wherever possible, needs to be inclusive of young people's wider networks. The relationships that young people can build at this stage with carers, social workers, families and friends are likely to prove crucial to a successful transition. However, research evidence does point to a tendency for social workers, the unifying figures in these networks, to exclude themselves from direct involvement in foster placements where young people appear settled, often reducing visits to a statutory minimum (DoH, 1996). Given the nature of shared parenting, an active social work role, focused on supporting carers and families, is important and the development of young people's skills needs to be carefully planned, monitored and reviewed as part of the child care planning cycle. Such a role has been shown to have a beneficial effect on placement breakdowns (Berridge and Cleaver, 1987) and could be reinforced if foster carers were offered greater access to specialist training in the care of teenagers.

Planning transitions
Evidence from our study suggests that smooth transitions from care were greatly enhanced by early planning. Written leaving care plans, constructed holistically in the context of all the supports available to young people and delineating clear responsibilities, were helpful. Where leaving care schemes were involved, early referral enabled their specialist knowledge of housing markets, employment options and welfare rights to assist planning and to increase young people's choices, and gave time

for relationships to be built with young people – an important factor in enabling them to feel comfortable returning for help at a later stage. Quality planning enabled young people to feel more confident in the support available to them.

However, despite a planned departure, some of those lacking essential skills were unable to sustain their lives after moving on. It proved no substitute for a flexible and needs-led approach to the timing and nature of leaving. Local authorities need to explore creative ways of funding a continuing stay for those young people in foster – and indeed residential – settings who lack the necessary skills and confidence to live independently. A range of supported accommodation is required, and the schemes in our study had invested heavily in developing a variety of options, including supported lodgings, hostels and floating support schemes. Access to supported options may also be particularly helpful for those whose initial departure is driven by crisis or placement breakdown. Finally, arrangements for respite need to be built into planning if leaving foster care is more closely to approximate leaving home. Over one-fifth (22 per cent) of our sample experienced homelessness within their first 18 to 24 months of leaving care. Shortages in the supply of placements that create a pressure for throughput need to be addressed if these aims are to be realised.

Working in partnership: the place of specialist schemes
In the context of a through-care approach that aims to maximise continuity in support for young people through care *and beyond*, leaving care schemes, as a specialist resource, need to be able to build upon the practical and social supports available to young people, including carers and social workers, and not replace them. Too often in our study, young people's engagement with schemes involved a weakening or withdrawal of links with social workers and, in some instances, with carers – a danger that has been identified in a previous study (Stein, 1990). If young people coping with the pressures of a difficult transition are to be offered a more secure network of support, then the tendency for back-up from carers and social workers to fall away after legal discharge needs to be tackled.

While some young people will choose to transfer to schemes and, for them, that choice should be available, it should neither be required nor expected. Schemes are rarely adequately resourced for this primary care role. Rather they need to be able to use their specialist expertise to work alongside those taking a primary role in an advisory capacity and focus their direct support on those young people who have experienced most instability, those who are more socially isolated, and on older young people returning for help.

If advice, consultancy and resource development are important areas of scheme work, then gaining access to scheme services is a key issue. The origins of three out of the four schemes under investigation lay in developments in the residential sector. Referrals were automatic; scheme staff spent time in units assisting with preparation and leaving care planning, and building informal relationships with young people. Links between the schemes and foster carers were less certain. Involvement depended upon social worker referral and, at the preparatory stage, tended to be restricted to advice and consultancy at reviews. None of the schemes had formal links with foster carer groups and several scheme staff felt that the advice they offered was, in some cases, treated with suspicion by carers who perceived a threat to their role and abilities. There is evidence that some social workers share a similar diffidence with regard to foster carers (Berridge and Cleaver, 1987), although recent reports suggest that, to the contrary, carers would appreciate greater levels of support and involvement (ADSS, 1996). Carers need to be aware of the specialist resources available in their area and of how to access them if they are to obtain the best deal for the young people in their care. Equally, schemes need to explore ways of promoting their services to foster carers more effectively.

Some of the difficulties that carers experience with levels of support and access to specialist training could be helped through a closer partnership with specialist schemes and services. The expertise that schemes develop in supporting young people in the community and their knowledge of housing, education, employment and welfare rights could provide at least one strand of a training input to foster carers. No doubt schemes would also learn much from carers attempting to prepare young people for adult life. In addition, closer partnership may help schemes and foster carers to have more influence over in-care policy and practice developments. All of the schemes in our study had difficulty influencing policies, especially in relation to preparation, the assessment of needs and abilities prior to leaving and, crucially, the timing of leaving care.

A majority of carers also feel that they are not consistently treated as part of a team, nor that they have much involvement in the policy process (ADSS, 1996). The potential contribution that schemes, carers and, indeed, young people themselves could make to policy and practice development needs to be tapped more effectively. Although genuine participation is not easy to achieve, it would help foster carers, among others, to feel that their expertise was more highly valued and, more importantly, it might contribute to the development of better quality services for young people leaving care.

Conclusion

For looked after young people, as we have seen, aspects of their transition to adulthood tend to be both accelerated and compressed. Leaving home and school and, in many cases, starting a family can occur within a relatively short time period; for example, within two years of moving on one-third of the sample were living with partners and one-half of the young women had children (see Biehal et al, 1995). Given that 1990s Britain offers an unfavourable social and economic context for all young people to establish themselves independently in the community, those leaving care seem particularly vulnerable.

The expectation that young people should move on between 16 and 18 years of age is unrealistic. Although two-thirds moved on in a planned way, a large minority did so as a consequence of placement breakdown, including one-third of those leaving foster care. Relatively few young people were able to remain with foster carers beyond legal discharge. Once they had left, arrangements for respite were rare, although stays in supported accommodation did offer a further chance for young people to develop their confidence and skills before taking on a tenancy. For the majority, the failure to attain qualifications and start a career left them at risk of an insecure future, marked by poverty and unemployment; most were struggling at or below benefit levels. The stress of poverty and social isolation were intensified for those who lacked the informal support and services that families can offer.

In this context, continuing support from foster carers, social workers and, where they exist, specialist schemes is likely to prove crucial to successful transitions. However, the levels of professional support indicated in our study tended to decline once the formal responsibility to accommodate had ceased, including that offered informally by foster carers. The potential for continuing care by foster carers is unlikely to be realised without greater recognition and the provision of modest funding to promote an enlarged role for foster carers in the leaving care process – one that reflects their importance to a through-care approach that provides stability and continuity in support for young people through transition.

A closer partnership between specialist services and foster carers could help to reduce problems of access to scheme services, improve the level of support and training available to foster carers, and help both to be more effective in influencing the development of leaving care policies and services. Effective leaving care planning also requires, wherever possible, close working relationships to be established between young people, social workers, carers, schemes and families in order that plans can be drawn up in the context of all the potential supports available to young people. However, while planning and joint working are important, they remain a poor substitute for a more flexible approach to leaving care which enables young people to remain with carers until they and others feel that they are ready to leave home.

References

Association of Directors of Social Services, *The Foster Carer Market: A national perspective*, ADSS, 1996.

Aldgate J, Maluccio A and Reeves C, *Adolescents in Foster Families*, BAAF/ Batsford, 1989.

Aldgate J, Heath A, Colton M and Simm M, 'Social work and the education of children in foster care', *Adoption & Fostering*, 17:3, pp 25–34, 1993.

Banks M, Bates I, Breakwell G, Bynner J, Emler N, Jamieson L and Roberts K, *Careers and Identities*, Open University Press, 1992.

Berridge D, 'Foster and residential care reassessed: a research perspective', *Children and Society*, 8:2, pp 132–50, 1994.

Berridge D, *Foster Care: A research review*, HMSO, 1996.

Berridge D and Cleaver H, *Foster Home Breakdown*, Blackwell, 1987.

Biehal N, Clayden J, Stein M and Wade J, *Prepared for Living?*, National Children's Bureau, 1992.

Biehal N, Clayden J, Stein M and Wade J, *Moving On: Young people and leaving care schemes*, HMSO, 1995.

Broad B, *Leaving Care in the 1990s*, Royal Philanthropic Society, 1994.

Clayden J and Stein M, 'Self-care skills and becoming adult', in Jackson S and Kilroe S (eds), *Looking After Children: Good parenting, good outcomes*, HMSO, 1996.

Cole B, *Youth and Social Policy*, UCL Press, 1995.

Cook R, 'Are we helping foster care youth prepare for their future?', *Children and Youth Services Review*, 16:3/4, pp 213–29, 1994.

Department for Education, *School Performance Tables: Public examination results 1991*, Department for Education, 1992.

Department of Health, Social Services Inspectorate, *Inspection of Local Authority Fostering 1994/5*, DoH, 1996.

Downes C, *Separation Revisited*, Ashgate, 1992.

Fry E, *After Care: Making the most of foster care*, National Foster Care Association, 1992.

Garnett L, *Leaving Care and After*, National Children's Bureau, 1992.

Heath A, Colton M and Aldgate J, 'Failure to escape: a longitudinal study of foster children's educational attainment', *British Journal of Social Work*, 24, pp 241–60, 1994.

Hill M, Triseliotis J, Borland M and Lambert L, 'Fostering adolescents in Britain: outcomes and processes', *Community Alternatives*, 8:1, pp 77–92, 1996.

Jackson S, 'Residential care and education', *Children and Society*, 4, pp 335–50, 1988/9.

Jones G, 'Leaving the parental home: an analysis of early housing careers', *Journal of Social Policy*, 16: 1, pp 49–74, 1987.

Jones G and Wallace C, *Youth, Family and Citizenship*, Open University Press, 1992.

Kirk D, Nelson S, Sinfield A and Sinfield D, *Excluding Youth: Poverty among young people living away from home*, Bridges Project/University of Edinburgh, 1991.

Millham S, Bullock R, Hosie K and Haak M, *Lost in Care*, Gower, 1986.

Parker R, Ward H, Jackson S, Aldgate J and Wedge P (eds), *Assessing Outcomes in Child Care*, HMSO, 1991.

Rowe J, Hundleby M and Garnett L, *Child Care Now*, BAAF/Batsford, 1989.

Sellick C, *Supporting Short-term Foster Carers*, Avebury, 1992.

Stein M, *Living Out of Care*, Barnardo's, 1990.

Stein M and Carey K, *Leaving Care*, Blackwell, 1986.

Section II
Recruitment, assessment and training

Recurrent concern has been expressed that the supply of foster carers is either drying up or will do so in the near future. Bebbington and Miles (1990) reported that many families were giving up fostering 'because they felt undervalued and unsupported' (p. 301). It has also been suggested that changes in women's roles and employment patterns mean that fewer wish to care for others' children full time than formerly. Even if the numbers of foster homes in many areas continue to equate roughly with the numbers of children in need of fostering, the absence of any surplus means that choice and matching may be difficult or impossible, with children simply going to the only home available (Millham *et al*, 1986; Triseliotis *et al*, 1995a, 1998).

The supply of foster homes is closely related to recruitment strategies, which affect the acquisition of new fostering resources. Equally important is the matter of retention. If more people leave quickly, then more new recruits are needed. Good preparation, support and recognition are not only foster carers' entitlements; they are also vital to ensure adequate availability of homes for children.

It probably is not a coincidence that the articles in this section come from Scotland where particular concern has been evident about the supply of carers. This prompted the Scottish Office to fund a study of foster care services. It showed that the "wastage" rate of foster carers was in fact quite low. Nevertheless, many carers had significant dissatisfactions with aspects of the service, while recruitment campaigns by different agencies were not co-ordinated and were sometimes deficient in their messages and targeting (Triseliotis *et al*, 1998).

Ramsay (1996) described how one Scottish local authority investigated foster carers' views on issues connected with recruitment and retention. Like some others, this authority had universalised fee-payment and professionalisation of its whole fostering service five years before, to replace the previous mainstream/specialist distinction (See Section I). The introduction of the fee did not appear to have altered the profile of carers, whose characteristics were typical of those elsewhere. Over half indicated that the fee was a vital consideration in their capacity to continue fostering. Adverts and information in newspapers and on TV were important stimuli to consider fostering, but so was the influence of relatives and friends who already foster. The importance for recruitment of word-of-mouth recommendations or suggestions means that satisfaction with payments and other supports will not only sustain existing carers but also act as an encouragement to others. In this survey, satisfaction levels were high, but many carers wanted more frequent contact with children's social workers and greater involvement in care planning (see also Sellick, 1992).

Once individuals or couples have registered an interest in fostering, the next step is to go through a process that nowadays combines elements of assessment and preparation (McColgan, 1991). Applicants are given information about the fostering role and the kinds of children who need homes. Not uncommonly, people realise for themselves that fostering is not for them. However, it remains essential for a careful assessment to take place, including police checks, in order to try and ensure the safety and welfare of children. **Brown (1992)** observed that assessment has two interrelated aspects:

- evaluation of prospective carers' strengths and weaknesses; and
- assessment of the capacity to learn, adapt and change.

For many years it was usually assumed that foster carers should be heterosexual couples. It is now recognised that this was not only discriminatory, but restricted the pool of carers. It has become generally accepted that single people can be excellent foster carers. Attitudes to openly gay individuals or couples remain more varied, but most agencies recognise that the important considerations are people's capacities to nurture, respect and help children rather than sexual orientation or household pattern. Research indicates that no major differences can be detected in the development of those brought up by heterosexual mothers and those reared by lesbian mothers (Schaffer, 1990; Brown, 1991). Knowledge about gay male carers is scant.

Recruitment mechanisms and assessment processes also need to be sensitive to cultural backgrounds and experiences of racism. **Singh (1997)** argued that assessment should be individualised and avoid stereotypes, while taking account of some general differences. For instance, religion plays a major part in the lives of most families of Asian background. Expectations about gender and marriage tend to differ from current white European norms. As others have observed, most Asian traditions tend to put stress on family and community identity, and less on self actualisation. The recruitment of black foster carers needs to recognise not only cultural differences, but also the importance of power, racism and economic discrimination (Rhodes, 1992).

As fostering has come to be seen in more professional terms, so the need for training has been acknowledged. This is now provided as part of the preparatory processes and as a component of ongoing support. Many agencies require some or all of their carers to undertake continuing training. **Gilchrist and Hoggan (1996)** discussed an innovatory programme that included birth parents. This was intended to heighten foster carers' sensitivity towards birth parents and empathy for them. The birth parents were understandably anxious about taking part, but were able to share some of their feelings and thoughts about communication and contact. It became apparent that parents and carers should discuss openly their expectations and routines, so that each can take account of emotional and practical constraints experienced by the other. The process improved mutual understanding and increased birth parents' sense of having a positive contribution to make. A great deal of staff time was required and this may often not be available. Nevertheless, the early inclusion of birth parents in preparation and training offers a good model to aid contact and partnership (See Section V).

4 Recruiting and retaining foster carers: implications of a professional service in Fife

Donald Ramsay

Donald Ramsay is a Research Officer for Fife Council's Social Work Service. A former senior social worker, he has worked in the Planning and Evaluation Team since 1990. His main areas of research interest are child care, juvenile justice and home care services.

This paper was published in Adoption & Fostering, 20:1, 1996.

The development of foster care began in Scotland in the mid-19th century (Triseliotis, Sellick and Short, 1995), although different forms of boarding-out existed as far back as the 17th century and beyond (Reeves, 1980). Its original aim was to provide substitute parents for children requiring public care. Some maintenance allowances were paid for looking after children but there was an historical view which persisted well into the following century that self-sacrifice was an 'essential ingredient of the mother–child relationship', and that 'payment for the work cut at the roots of [that] relationship' (Care of Children Committee 1946, cited by Smith, 1988).

The traditional role of foster carer was to act as substitute parent, so very often contact between the child and the birth family was discouraged in an attempt to strengthen the fostering relationship. Short-term care and reunification came to be seen as complementary goals only after the 1948 Children Act (Triseliotis *et al*, as above). Different skills were required as the role developed from foster parent to foster carer, eg. working with birth families and contributing to case planning. The speed and scope of these changes were increased by the philosophical and economic movement away from residential care towards community-based care in the 1980s: specialist foster carers or community carers were recruited to look after children with particular disadvantages who were previously thought to require children's homes or other residential care.

As a consequence of this change in direction, children entered foster care with a wider variety of needs, and made additional demands on foster carers (Bullock, 1990). Bullock argued that if foster carers were wanted to take disturbed or disabled young people they would have to be partners rather than agents of social workers. Indeed, Bebbington and Miles (1990) wrote that many carers were leaving fostering because they felt undervalued and unsupported. Triseliotis *et al* cite an American study which found the attrition rate of foster carers reduced when they were better paid, better supported and better trained by the agency (Chamberlain *et al*, 1982).

Nonetheless, attitudes towards the financial reward of foster carers still vary across the country, both among agencies (NFCA, 1990) and among carers (Smith, 1988). The National Foster Carers' Association reported wide differences in allowances paid by authorities – over and above whether or not a financial reward element was included; this despite NFCA campaigns for increased standard allowances, predicated on the greater demands on foster carers to attend reviews and operate as quasi-professionals. Foster carers themselves, however, have shown ambivalence about payment, on the one hand not wanting to see themselves or be seen as mercenary, but also not wanting their commitment to be taken for granted or exploited.

In Fife, two types of foster carer existed during the 1980s: "traditional" foster carers/parents and "community carers". The "traditional" foster carers/parents received maintenance allowances based on the age of the child and any particular needs which caused extra expense. They were recruited, trained and supported by local field-workers. Community carers, on the other hand, were paid a professional fee plus maintenance allowances; they were contracted to take teenagers for up to two years. Initially, community carers were recruited, trained and supported by specialist social workers from the Adolescent Placement Scheme whose remit was to offer child care placements as an alternative to residential care.

While older children often presented different types of care needs from younger children, it was convincingly argued that carers looking after younger children expended just as much energy as those looking after teenagers. Furthermore, all foster carers were expected to take part in child in care reviews so there was no differentiation between the "professional" tasks expected of them. Consequently it was decided to rationalise the financial and professional support for carers by making conditions for all foster carers the same. Following departmental re-organisation in 1990, all carers were paid one professional fee per household as well as age-related allowances for each child. Professional support is now concentrated in two teams of specialist foster care social workers, amalgamating the area-based homemakers and the Adolescent Placement Scheme staff. Each foster carer household is allocated a link social worker from one of two foster-care teams.

The white paper 'Scotland's Children' (Cmnd, 2286; HMSO, 1993) suggested that local authorities obtain a comprehensive picture of fostering resources in their area. Prompted by this, the foster care teams in Fife requested a survey from the social work department's research station. Its three aims were:

- to obtain an overall picture of fostering resources, complementing the information on individual files;
- to obtain a general picture of the rewards and difficulties foster carers experienced;
- to discover what made people interested in fostering, in order to guide future recruitment.

Ninety-two structured questionnaires were sent out and 72 were completed, a return rate of 78.3 per cent. Anonymity was offered to the foster carers to encourage candour in their replies and a high response rate. While these two objectives appear to have been met, it was not possible to identify any non-response bias accurately, although foster care social workers thought long-term carers of children from their own extended families were least likely to have replied.

Foster carer population
Sixty-three of the foster homes covered by the survey were provided by a married couple, the other nine by sole female carers. The lone carers were either divorced or widowed, ie. none was never married.

The majority of carers were in their forties (42 per cent) which is close to the finding of Dando and Minty (1987) who found the mean ages of female and male foster carers were 44 years and

47.5 years, respectively; and the 80 per cent of foster mothers in the study by Bebbington and Miles (1990) who were between 31 and 55 years old.

Twenty-three of the 126 married carers had been married previously and 40 per cent of those had children from their previous marriage. This figure comes very close to the 1987 figure obtained by Bebbington and Miles.

In two of the dual-carer foster homes both partners were unemployed; in the others at least one partner was in employment. In 13 homes one carer was employed full-time and the other was either self-employed or employed part-time, similar to the findings of Dando and Minty (1987).

Ninety-two per cent of homes had three or more bedrooms (compared with 90 per cent in Bebbington and Miles' study). Ninety-three per cent of foster homes had use of at least one private car, which is not a requirement of foster caring but confers a degree of mobility which helps them, among other things, to attend child-in-care reviews, meetings, etc.

Forty-six per cent of foster homes had a smoker in the household. This figure is similar to the proportion of smokers in the general population (Scottish Abstract of Statistics, 1993). It is not clear from the data whether the smokers are the foster carers themselves or other members of their family; this distinction may be relevant in respect of the role models foster carers and their own families present for children, although the risks of passive smoking apply whatever the age of the smoker.

Dando and Minty found 90 per cent of foster households had at least one pet – often two or three. The figure was slightly lower in Fife, 75 per cent of homes having at least one pet.

Foster carers in Fife therefore share many of the characteristics of foster carers in other recent surveys, irrespective of the service having been fully professional for five years. Where they may differ from carers in other authorities is in the role they are given in child care provision. Fife greatly reduced its residential provision for children between 1980 and 1988, leaving only one social-work run residential establishment whose primary aim was assessment. Children received into the physical care of the department are, typically, placed with emergency foster carers. Then, if they require further care, they are matched with longer-term carers.

Support to carers

The survey was also used to gauge the value foster carers attached to the financial and professional support they received; and it was particularly important to assess the role of the professional fee. Rather than ask a direct self-report question about dependency on the fee, carers were asked whether they thought the fee had become part of foster carers' household budgets in general. They were then asked whether their own continued service as foster carers was dependent on receiving a fee.

Almost two-thirds of carers said they thought the professional fee had become an integral part of the household budget, and one-third said they thought it had "possibly" become an integral part of household budgets "for some carers". Only 5.6 of carers said the fee was "not usually" part of the household budget.

Over half of carers (59 per cent) said they would not be able to continue fostering if only maintenance rates were paid and the professional fee were withdrawn (though that was expressly not presented as a future proposal). Carers most likely to continue without a fee were those who had already fostered for more than ten years (55 per cent of this group).

It appears, therefore, that the professional fee has become a widely accepted, and indeed necessary, part of foster carer conditions of service. The spirit of voluntarism has not been eroded since, as Smith (1988) points out, 'a fair wage would far exceed current payments'. There is no evidence from the Fife survey that payment of a fee has been effective in attracting 'carers from previously under-represented groups, eg. black people, low income, unemployed' (Rhodes, 1993). On the other hand, a professional fee has enabled carers, primarily women, to resist the lures and opportunities of the labour market, either by not seeking paid employment or taking part-time employment instead of working full-time.

Besides its financial support to carers, the social work department also provides professional and group support. Preparation and training groups are run for people applying to foster; and foster carer support groups are run for all approved foster carers. Additional courses have been run for carers on relevant subjects, for example, sexual abuse and HIV/AIDS. Each foster home has a link social worker, normally the worker who carried out their assessment. The link worker's main tasks are to ensure the carer's training and practical needs are met; to offer ongoing support and guidance; and to ensure placement contracts are drawn up which meet the needs of both child and carer.

A clear majority (69 per cent) of carers said they were satisfied with the support from their link worker 'all of the time' and a further 29 per cent said they were satisfied 'most of the time'. Carers with more than ten years' experience were slightly more likely to say 'most of the time' than 'all of the time' while less experienced carers were most likely to say 'all of the time' (see Table 1). This may mean that experienced carers are less reliant on their link worker and are more able to evaluate critically the support they provide; it may also mean that link social workers do not feel they have to give the same degree of support to the most experienced foster carers. Nonetheless, these figures represent a very high degree of satisfaction with professional support from the link social workers.

The same questions were asked of carers about support from the social workers of children currently placed with them. Although one of the link social worker's tasks is to effect liaison between the foster carer and the child's social worker, a lower degree of satisfaction was anticipated with support from the latter since lack of awareness of carers' needs, missed appointments and a too-hectic schedule are commonly thought to characterise the field-worker's lot. Encouragingly, over two-thirds of carers said they were either satisfied with the support from their foster child's social worker 'all of the time' or 'most of the time', and only 5.6 per cent said they were satisfied with their current child's social worker 'none of the time'.

Table 1

Comparison of satisfaction with support from (1) 'link' workers and (2) foster children's social workers

	All of the time	Most of the time	Some of the time	None of the time
(1) Satisfaction with support from 'link worker'	66.6%	27.8%	1.4%	0
(2) Satisfaction with support from child's social worker	35.2%	32.4%	23.9%	5.6%

Note: Total percentages are less than 100% because of two missing cases.

As with support from link workers, the carers who were least likely to be satisfied with their child's social worker 'all of the time' were those who had been fostering for more than a decade, perhaps drawing on their years of experience to assess the support they were receiving. That said, two-thirds of the most experienced carers said they found the support from the child's social worker satisfactory most or all of the time.

Recruitment

It is likely that people are attracted to fostering by a combination of general factors, eg. knowledge of foster carers, childhood experience, a desire to contribute. It is worth noting, however, the things which foster carers identified as the trigger for applying to the social work department since these have implications for future recruitment. Twenty-five per cent were prompted to apply having seen an article or advert in a newspaper; 11 per cent said they were attracted to fostering by a television programme or advertisement; 25 per cent said their interest was prompted by a friend or relative who was fostering; and 33 per cent did not identify a particular event which triggered their interest but said it had been long term.

Advertising cost is a major consideration in recruitment so adverts in the local press have provided the mainstay of recruitment campaigns. However, the local press had a relatively low circulation among foster carers with only 16.5 per cent buying a local paper. Indeed only six foster homes whose interest was prompted by a press advert bought a local paper. The national press and television are seen to be too expensive and inappropriate media for local recruitment although national campaigns have also stimulated interest in fostering at local level. (Data are not available on the number of applications received from different forms of recruitment; nor are the numbers known of people who sustain their interest and who are subsequently approved.)

Given that one-quarter of foster carers were motivated to apply from an acquaintance with friends or relatives who fostered already, the reward and recognition carers receive from the fostering agency are likely to be an important influence on the image of fostering acquired. As Reeves (1980) points out, foster carers are less likely to recruit others if they feel the fostering agency's organisation is poor. Conversely, foster carers are more likely to attract new recruits if they feel valued by the agency and find the work rewarding.

Retention of foster carers
High levels of satisfaction with social work support are important in retaining the services of foster carers. In turn, stability in the foster care population offers greater continuity of care for children and adds to the sum of fostering skills in the area. Three-quarters of carers in the survey said they intended to continue fostering for more than five years. Sixteen per cent said they would continue for three to five years, and less than six per cent intended to give up within three years. All but one of those who anticipated giving up within three years were aged over 50, indicating that changes in personal circumstances were more influential than the degree of satisfaction with social work support in determining turnover of foster carers. Changes in life-stage and preferred life-style aside, these figures suggest a low turnover of carers can be expected.

Local foster carer groups provide a valuable conduit for suggestions for improving the service, as well as providing mutual support and a forum for training. These groups notwithstanding, suggestions for improvement of the service were also invited in the survey. Many suggestions not only serve as reminders of good social work practice, they are also indicative of the contribution foster carers wish to make and the role they seek as partners of the social work department.

The most frequent plea from carers was for more frequent visits from the children's social workers and an increased involvement in case planning. A small number of carers asked for better information on the background and lifestyle of children prior to placement; and three carers also wished for follow-up information on children's progress after moving on from their placement. One suggestion, echoed in two of the completed questionnaires, was for an itemised payslip detailing the composition of the allowances being paid for children in care. Another suggestion was for identification cards for foster carers to use when taking children to hospitals, schools, etc. Work has already been undertaken to implement these suggestions.

Conclusions

Foster carers in Fife share many of the socio-demographic characteristics of foster carers in general. They exhibit considerable stability and satisfaction with their role despite changes in the nature of their task, particularly in the last ten years.

The evidence from the Fife survey clearly indicates that an element of financial reward, and the support infrastructure which link social workers and foster carer groups provide, play an important part in attracting and retaining a stable number of foster carers. The professional fee reduces the need for people to find alternative paid employment and allows them a degree of financial freedom to put into practice their wish to contribute to the care of children.

Foster care teams provide valued professional support to carers which acknowledges their role in child care and enhances the quality of the care they provide. As local authorities reorganise in 1996 and develop new structures with which to deliver services, a clear opportunity arises to ensure that adequate support systems for foster care services are established.

References

Bebbington A and Miles J, 'Supply of foster families for children in care', *British Journal of Social Work*, 20, pp 283–307, 1990.

Bullock R, 'Implications of recent child care research findings for foster care', in *Adoption & Fostering*, 14:3, pp 43–5, 1990.

Dando I and Minty B, 'What makes good foster parents?', 17:4, pp 383–400, *British Journal of Social Work*, 1987.

NFCA, 'Foster care finance: advice and information on the cost of caring for a child', NFCA, 1990.

Reeves C S, Chapter in Triseliotis J (ed), *New Developments in Foster Care*, Routledge & Kegan Paul, 1980.

Rhodes P, 'Charitable vocation or "proper job"? The role of payment in foster care', *Adoption & Fostering*, 17:1, pp 8–13, 1993.

Smith B, 'Something you do for love: A question of money and foster care', *Adoption & Fostering*, 12:4, pp 39–9, 1988.

Triseliotis J, Sellick C and Short R, *Foster Care: Theory and practice*, BAAF/Batsford, 1995.

5 Gender, sex and sexuality in the assessment of prospective carers

Helen Cosis Brown

Helen Cosis Brown is a Principal Officer, Research and Development at Barnardo's. Before this she was Head of the Department of Health and Social Care at the University of Hertfordshire, and worked for nine years in social work in an inner London borough. She has written widely about social work and sexuality and her book, "Social Work and Sexuality: Working with lesbians and gay men", was published in 1998. Her chapter, 'The knowledge base of social work', in Vass A (ed), "Social Work Competences: Core knowledge, values and skills", is also pertinent to this article.

This paper was published in Adoption & Fostering, 16:2, 1992.

Introduction

Sex and sexuality are integral parts of the way we see ourselves and are perceived by others, but they are also highly privatised areas and sometimes split off from the rest of our lives. For social workers, addressing this area in their work can feel like crossing an inappropriate boundary. As a newly qualified worker undertaking an assessment of prospective foster carers, I realised that "the sexual relationship" was something I had to cover on my assessment schedules, but I did not know why. I felt isolated and stupid, and I certainly wasn't going to ask. It never occurred to me that it might have direct implications for children placed with the prospective carers. In retrospect, we were unclear about why these questions *were* asked.

Since that time the area of sex and sexuality has appeared and disappeared on and off the assessment agenda. In this article I wish to argue that the subjects of gender, sex and sexuality need to be firmly and permanently placed within the assessment process. These are areas of human emotion and activity that have direct implications for children we place with carers; and we have a responsibility to ensure that the carers with whom we are working will have the ability to offer a comfortable framework in which children and young people can develop. I will try to offer some pointers and ideas to develop during the assessment process.

Assessment

The Department of Health (HMSO, 1991) has identified areas in which an agency must satisfy itself when assessing prospective carers. This offers us a baseline below which practice should not fall. Many agencies, however, have been operating sophisticated assessment guidelines for some time. The assessment process is crucial as the quality of a child's life and life-potential are partly dependent on its accuracy and success.

Assessment has two interrelated aspects: firstly, an evaluation of what prospective carers can offer, their suitability, strengths, weaknesses, etc.; secondly, an assessment of their capability to develop through the assessment process itself and after, plus their ability to work together with the social worker in partnership to develop and further their potential – in other words, assessing their capacity for change.

The prospective carer's potential for facilitating the comfortable (enough) development of each individual child's complete self is what is being assessed. What is meant by "complete self"? It means three things: a good enough sense of themselves, good enough relationships with others and good enough relationships with the outside world/society. Gender, sex and sexuality are integral parts of all three aspects. To ask prospective carers to facilitate this for children is a huge demand. We live in communities and a society where gender power relations distort our relationships to sex, sexuality and gender. Being a man or woman, lesbian or gay, has a socially constructed meaning beyond the power and control of the individual. Carers cannot be asked to be responsible for changing the world and obliterating oppression, but they can be expected to help young people make sense of the communities and the society in which they live, and to find a place within it.

Social workers are being asked to take part in a difficult and complex process. Having a framework to structure our ideas can be helpful.

Figure 1

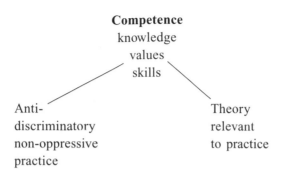

Practice framework

The Diploma in Social Work (CCETSW, 1989, 1995) has enshrined the notion of competence within social work practice. Competence can offer us a practice framework to focus our thinking when assessing prospective carers.

When approaching an assessment we could usefully ask ourselves the following questions, using the above framework.

1. What knowledge do I need/am I drawing on? Is it relevant? Is it discriminatory or oppressive?
2. What values should I address, in myself and the prospective carers? Are these values relevant to the assessment? How might these values be discriminatory? What are my values and how do they affect my work? How may these differ from the carer's? How do both sets of values fit with the task in hand and what implications do they have for children?
3. What skills do I need and do I have them? Are my skills relevant for this task? Do I need to rethink my skills to enable me to offer an anti-discriminatory, non-oppressive service?

To enable this practice framework to be of use, some of this questioning needs to be part of social workers' self-evaluation and the supervisory process.

Social workers' use of knowledge

The interrelationship between knowledge and practice in the area of gender, sex and sexuality has historically been problematic (Wilson, 1977; Hart and Richardson, 1981; Brown, 1992).

In the period of social work's metamorphosis into a profession, it sought an applicable body of theory. From the 1920s, both in America and Britain, social work turned to psychoanalysis as the most relevant area of knowledge from which to draw (Yelloly, 1980).

Social work's adaptation of psychoanalytic ideas between the 1920s and 1960s led to some problematic developments in relation to gender, sex and sexuality. There evolved a normative view of the family, gender relations, masculinity and femininity and "normal" psychosexual development. The consequent social work practice drawing on these ideas was often overtly oppressive to clients (Wilson, 1977).

These ideas and their misuse have been particularly influential in the area of fostering and adoption. This was inevitable as many believe that it is within the family itself that psychosexual development takes place, where masculinity and femininity are formed, and where gender relations are first experienced. Historically carers were recruited because they were likely to reflect the normative ideas of "the family". Since the 1960s this "knowledge" has been reviewed with a growing awareness of how it discriminated against, and oppressed, many families/households and communities that did not fit within its norms.

Social workers today have the benefit of many more theories to inform their practice. The process of the deconstruction and the reconstruction of social work knowledge has begun to enable us to offer our clients a better quality of practice (Phoenix, 1990; Brown, 1992).

The practice framework described above portrays knowledge and values as if they are discrete categories. In practice this is sometimes not the case. Practitioners can draw on selected pieces of theory to back their own values. A foster placement panel in which I was involved ten years ago looked at a report on a prospective single carer. This was still uncharted territory. The lines were drawn between those who felt individuals had to be assessed on their own merits and those who felt children should only be placed in "normal" two-parent families. Both sides were searching for theories to back their positions. One participant intervened: 'What about the Oedipal complex, how could there possibly be a healthy resolution of the Oedipal phase?'. The intervention was successful. We didn't know. No one challenged this intervention as being outside the capabilities and expertise of those present. We were just silent. If knowledge is to be used in a way that informs practice usefully, we cannot remain silent. Ill-informed assumptions need to be challenged, to enable us to work competently.

Assessment of prospective carers

Gender relationships within families/households

People organise their lives, their relationships and their roles within their families and households in many different ways. Social workers are not ideological police, there to dictate how individuals should construct their thoughts and behaviour. However, how people organise themselves, and experience their gender and gender relationships, will have implications for children placed with them.

It has been argued (Shaw, 1989) that when thinking about assessment of foster carers we should be addressing whether or not the family system is "closed" or "open". By closed, Shaw is referring to a family system that has over-rigid roles, little possibility of movement, one that resists and rejects change. This is opposed to open, which refers to a family system that is able to negotiate roles, and is open to change. Shaw argues that open family systems are more likely to offer successful placements. The question of "open" or "closed" seems particularly pertinent to assessing gender relationships. If a couple are being assessed, they need to feel comfortable with the roles they have within their household, and have the capacity to negotiate change if and when that is required. The placement of a child within a family is a crisis. It is likely to be a positive one, but still a crisis. The prospective carers need to be able to respond in ways that help them adapt to this new situation (Parad, 1965). This will include having a degree of role flexibility.

Families have their own life-cycles (Gorrel Barnes, 1984) which involve their own maturational crises. Carers often experience this most acutely during their children's adolescence. This is a time when carers need to feel secure in their own relationships and sexuality, to be able to offer adolescents a secure and flexible enough framework within which to develop. A colleague and I were recently involved in a piece of consultative work with a local authority (Brown and Pearce, 1991) examining preventive work with girls and young women and their families. We examined both birth families and foster families. A frequent cause of relationship breakdown for these families was a breakdown of the mother–daughter relationship, the mother seeming unable to adapt to her daughter's developing sexuality. Similar findings have been described by others (Apter, 1990). For assessment purposes, it would therefore seem important to examine with applicants how they perceive their ability to adapt to the changing challenges children will place on both their relationships, and on themselves as individuals.

Single carers
Many agencies have, until more recently, refused to assess single carers. This practice has changed as agencies have successfully used single carers, both male and female, for foster and adoptive placements. Some descriptions of single carers' assessment experiences give cause for concern (Blunden, 1980). Some of the theory drawn on by social work, discussed above, has prejudiced agencies and individual social workers against them. These applicants have sometimes had to prove their worth in ways beyond what would be expected from a heterosexual couple.

When, in the past, social work has pathologised a particular group, the reaction has been to adopt an over-liberal response. *All* prospective carers need thorough assessments. For example, the processes involved in assessment discussed in relation to single carers are as relevant to the assessment of lesbians and gay men. These assessments need to be as rigorous as all other assessments. If the applicant is single the same areas apply as for all single carers. Where the assessment is of a couple, it needs to address, as with heterosexual couples, whether or not the system is closed or open. (For a fuller discussion of this area see Brown, 1991.)

There has sometimes been a tendency to shy away from certain areas. For example, how are the applicants' needs met, emotionally, physically, sexually; what are the implications of these areas for children who might be placed with them? This last question is the crucial point; the areas we cover with applicants are only pertinent if they relate to this.

Sexuality and sex

How we feel about ourselves physically and sexually is likely to have profound implications for the development of children in our care. How children feel about themselves physically and sexually will also have implications for how they relate to others and society. This is all part of developing a good enough sense of self, and helping this development is one of the major tasks for prospective carers.

Sex has many different functions and aspects (Christopher, 1987). I will only refer to two aspects relevant to the assessment process. Firstly, sex is a form of communication. Many couples that are assessed may no longer be sexually active. If this is the case, is this symptomatic of a wider breakdown in communication, or not? Secondly, sex is an important source of pleasure. Do the applicants experience sex as pleasurable? The answer to this question is likely to have important implications for children, particularly during adolescence.

For many heterosexual couples who are assessed (especially adoptive parents) sex has for many years been intricately linked with fertility. Some couples have had to face the loss of not being able to conceive. The process and stages of loss have been well documented (Worden, 1983). For couples to be able to move on in their relationships, they will have needed to have reached some resolution to this area of loss. There needs to be an exploration of this as it has serious implications for children. How has the inability to conceive affected the two aspects of sex mentioned above – communication and pleasure?

Adolescent sexuality challenges most adults. Carers have to feel comfortable and secure enough in themselves to stay in dialogue with their children during this time. This dialogue needs to be practical as well as emotional. Parents have a responsibility to help young people think about and act on safer sex, for example. When we place children we do not know what their eventual sexual orientation will be. Prospective carers should be helped to address this area, as this has serious implications for future children placed with them.

Many children needing placements have been sexually abused, and this is not always known at the time of placement. Assessing social workers should be assured that prospective carers have a clear enough sense of their own sexuality and sexual boundaries to help children with their difficult emotional experiences, which may manifest themselves in quite problematic ways.

Prospective carers, facilitating in children the development of a good-enough sense of self as sexual adults, need to have internalised a good-enough sense of themselves as well.

Future directions

The ability to assess an applicant's potential as a carer will partly depend on the social worker's ability to establish a positive relationship with the applicant. I have already argued that gender, sex and sexuality need to be part of the assessment process. Below is a list of simple points to be kept in mind when approaching these areas with prospective carers.

- It is useful to focus preparation and planning of the assessment around the practice framework of competence, mentioned above.
- The skills of engagement (Egan, 1990) are essential in establishing a good enough relationship between social worker and applicant.
- There needs to be complete clarity about the assessment process with the prospective carers. Why is this information necessary? What is its relevance for children needing placements?
- Both parties need to be engaged in a child-focused exercise.
- Applicants need to be helped to understand that families have life-cycles of their own, and what seems of little relevance today, may be crucial tomorrow.
- The assessment is a two-way process. It is the beginning of a partner-ship developing the potential of applicants, as well as formulating an evaluation.
- The social worker is part of the assessment and affects its outcome (Ryburn, 1991).
- Evaluation should be based on professional judgement, not on per-sonal prejudices.
- The assessment should be experienced as a process of empowerment for prospective carers.

Gender and sexuality are integral aspects of us all. Children for whom carers are sought have the right to good enough placements, part of which is enough safe space and clear boundaries to develop their own unique sexualities securely. The assessment process is the time to focus on the ability of prospective carers to provide that space and establish those boundaries.

References

Apter T, *Altered Loves: Mothers and daughters during adolescence,* Harvester Wheatsheaf, 1990.

Brown H C, 'Competent child-focused practice: working with lesbian and gay carers', *Adoption & Fostering,* 15:2, pp 11–17, 1991.

Brown H C, 'Lesbians, the state and social work practice', in Langan M and Day L, *Women, Oppression and Social Work,* Routledge, 1992.

Brown H C and Pearce J J, *Careful with Care: Improving social work policy and practice with girls and young women in relation to implementation of the Children Act 1989,* London Borough of Camden/Middlesex Polytechnic, 1991.

CCETSW, *DipSW requirements and regulations for the diploma in social work,* Paper 30, CCETSW, London, 1989, 1995.

Christopher E, *Sexuality and Birth Control in Community Work,* Tavistock, 1987.

Department of Health, *The Children Act 1989: Guidance and Regulations, Volume 3, Family Placements,* HMSO, 1991.

Egan O, *The Skilled Helper: A systematic approach to affective helping,* Brooks/Cole, 1990, USA.

Gorrel-Barness, *Working with Families,* Macmillan, 1984.

Hart J and Richardson D, *The Theory and Practice of Homosexuality,* Routledge & Kegan Paul, 1981.

Parad H G, *Crisis Intervention: Selected readings,* Family Services Association of America, 1965, USA.

Lovell T (ed), *British Feminist Thought,* Blackwell, 1990.

Ryburn M, 'The myth of assessment', *Adoption & Fostering,* 15:1, pp 20–7, 1991.

Shaw M, 'Thinking about assessment of foster parents', in Aldgate J, Maluccio A and Reeves C (eds), *Adolescents in Foster Families,* Batsford/BAAF, 1989.

Wilson E, *Women and the Welfare State*, Tavistock, 1977.

Worden J W, *Grief Counselling and Grief Therapy*, Tavistock, 1983.

Yelloly M A, *Social Work Theory and Psychoanalysis*, Van Nostrand Reinhold Co., 1980.

6 Assessing Asian families in Scotland: a discussion

Satnam Singh

Satnam Singh is a Senior Practitioner with Barnardo's Family Placement Services in Edinburgh with lead responsibility for the Khandan Initiative, a development designed to promote policy and practice in relation to the provision of same-race placements as placements of choice. He is also an Associate Lecturer on the Open University's diploma course in Health and Social Welfare.

This paper was published in Adoption & Fostering, 21:3, 1997.

Introduction

A holistic assessment of the needs of children requiring substitute families is paramount not only for a successful placement, by which I mean a placement that does not disrupt, but also for ensuring the psychological well-being of the child.

In Scotland an important aspect of the child's needs has been largely ignored or underplayed by adoption and fostering agencies. I am referring to the identity needs of black[1] children arising from the child's heritage[2].

As early as 1979, identity formation and identity maintenance were seen as significant tasks for all children in substitute care. In the words of Germaine (1979):

> *The child who must be placed in substitute care at any age, and regardless of the reason, is torn from the biological and symbolic context of his identity. No matter how nurturing the substitute care, the child's ongoing task will always be to reweave the jagged tear in the fabric of his identity, to make himself whole again.*

---

[1] By black I mean all people who share the common experience of racism, and this includes people from all ethnic minorities.

[2] By heritage I mean the child's racial, cultural, religious, social and linguistic background.

For black children however, the denial or whitewash [sic] of the child's heritage has resulted in black children being placed transracially into white substitute families. Consequently the task of reweaving the fabric of their identity is made all the more difficult.

The "colour-blind" approach to social work which precipitated many of these transracial placements of black children owes much to the prevalent ideology of the late 1970s and early 1980s, when it was believed that black children who identified more closely with white people were actually assimilating successfully and, as such, this was seen as a sign of psychological well-being. This assimilationist philosophy was derived from a "cultural deficit" model of social work which viewed black people as lacking, abnormal or deviant. In a critique of this view, Rhodes (1992) made explicit the assumptions which were so pervasive throughout the above period:

> ... *Black people's life-styles, family patterns and child-rearing practices are deemed inappropriate to life in the modern, advanced Western society ... Social workers' role is to preserve the integrity of British cultural values and to facilitate assimilation.*

These melting pot theories also propagated a belief that racism, prejudice and discrimination amounted to a normal and logical reaction to such shortcomings and would necessarily decline once black people fully assimilated into the dominant culture.

Since the 1980s, however, there has been a gradual but significant shift in this thinking due to the influence and struggle of an increasing number of black professionals. This epistemological shift can be traced back to the Association of Black Social Workers and Allied Professionals (ABSWAP) who, in their submission to the House of Commons Select Committee in 1983, wrote that 'Bonding without a sense of racial identity is pathological and is against the best interest of the black child'.

Other writers and researchers were also finding evidence to contribute to this emerging ideology. A controversial 1983 study by Gill and Jackson found that transracially placed children only

> ... *coped by denying their racial background and had not developed*

a sense of racial identity – they saw themselves as white in all but skin colour.

Maximé writing in the mid-1980s and drawing on her work with black children and adults in care, asserted that black children's misidentification or over-identification with white people was in fact pathological. In a letter to *The Caribbean Times* (18 March 1983), David Divine wrote passionately that this one-way trafficking of black children into white families was the modern-day equivalent of slavery. These children, he stated, are:

> *... lost to our communities ... No community can afford hundreds of such casualties each year, no community can be so profligate with its most precious resources – its children.*

There is – and has been for some time – a clear imperative for action, both from academic sources and from the black communities themselves. This imperative is now further legitimated in Scotland by the requirements of the 1995 Children (Scotland) Act, to take account of a child's racial, cultural, religious and linguistic needs.

The Khandan Initiative

It was in response to these imperatives, coupled with a realisation that in Scotland the needs of black children were remaining unmet, that in 1996 Barnardo's Family Placement Services, an adoption and fostering agency based in Edinburgh, developed the Khandan Initiative. "Khandan" means "family" in Punjabi, Hindi and Urdu, and as such reflects very clearly the nature of the work. Put simply, the Khandan Initiative is trying to attract, recruit and support adoptive and foster carers from the Asian population in the central belt of Scotland.

The primary aim of the Initiative is to ensure that same-race placements are the placements of choice for all children referred to the project for placement in a substitute family. In order for this same-race commitment to become a reality, there are many areas of policy and practice that have changed and continue to change. In the rest of this paper I want to look critically at only one aspect of this process, that of the assessment of Asian families.

Towards an integrated model for the assessment of Asian families

Any discussion about work with black families must give regard to the context in which that work takes place. Dutt (1991) argues that for black people in Britain the context is always of racism. Racism is such an indelible part of our lives, it permeates everything we do and it affects every interaction and relationship we have.

It was in this context of racism that Nobles (1978) identified that the history of the study of black families is one which has focused primarily on three themes: poverty, pathology and victimisation. Clearly assessment of black families needs to steer away from these myths which seriously undermine black people and devalue their contribution. Valid assessment of black people needs to move towards a richer understanding of the unique and diverse nature and functioning of black families.

Nobles warned of the danger of "transubstantiation" through a process of "conceptual incarceration" when undertaking assessments of black families. He described transubstantiation as a process 'wherein one defines or interprets the behaviour and/or medium of one culture with the "meanings" appropriate to another culture'. For example, one aspect of a typical assessment of any family might be to try to establish the quality of the relationships within that family, particularly between the husband and wife. A typical worker might then try to assess this by trying to identify the "behaviours" of the family which relay the "meanings" that the worker is seeking. In a typical white family this might mean such things as holding hands, linking arms, cuddling and spending time in shared leisure activities. It would be fair to say that a typical Asian family would probably not display these behaviours. Being unable to identify the "behaviours" which carry the required "meanings" sought by the worker, the Asian family would then certainly fail the assessment.

Another example of possible misinterpretation could arise from the actual structure and process of the interview itself. In a traditional Asian family the gender roles are very clearly defined. This often results in the wife adopting a much more deferential role in public situations. The interviewer might then find that throughout the interview the wife says very little, perhaps even avoids eye contact, often sitting some distance away from her husband or occasionally with her head slightly down. This behaviour in a traditional interview would probably sit uncomfortably with most social workers. It appears to represent an unequal relationship, where the husband holds and wields the power in the family and where the wife is seen as weak and unassuming. The reality, however, would in most cases be very different with the wife having much more responsibility, autonomy and authority within the context of family, extended family and community. What is being observed is not a negative expression of the quality of the husband's relationship, but rather a manifestation of the values of the family's traditions and culture, in other words, positive attributes.

The process of "conceptual incarceration" is not dissimilar to that of transubstantiation, and is described by Nobles as a process which 'inhibits people from asking the right questions'. Nobles argues that this so-called inhibition occurs as a result of workers having internalised the dominant culture. I would take Nobles' point a stage further and suggest that, even if the right questions are asked, there is a danger of the worker not having the cultural specificity to understand the answers received. For example, most assessment forms ask for information about religion. A recent review of a random selection of assessment forms within our own project showed that the information about religion was either missing, or was so sparse as to be of no value.

Religion may no longer play an important role in the dominant culture, but for many Asian families and communities it is still a significant factor in the ways in which their lives are ordered. A typical social worker may not give this area much significance throughout the assessment process, and thus be culturally inhibited from asking the right questions. Even if questions are asked about the family's religion, what will the social worker do with a response that the family is, for instance, Sikh, Hindu or Muslim? She or he is not likely to have the conceptual framework to interpret the information being received in any meaningful way. As Nobles (1978) puts it:

> One's ability to understand black reality is limited if the 'interpretive framework' for the analysis of that reality is based on assumptions associated with a non-black reality.

An effective assessment of black families which is both reliable and valid requires a reorientation away from the traditional structures of

91

assessment towards one which seeks to focus on each family's strengths. It is this position, that assessments should focus on a family's strengths, drawn from their social and cultural milieux, which will form the backcloth for the rest of this discussion. (For a useful discussion and checklist of the strengths of black families which provides a reliable tool around which to build an assessment see Small, 1989.)

Elements of assessment

The traditional assessment focuses on a wide variety of factors, usually including at the very least: childhood, education, health, relationships, work and family. Each of these areas are also of significance in an assessment of Asian families. However, it is my assertion that a valid assessment of Asian families must at the very least take cognisance of four more specific factors:

- the experience of racism;
- marriage as an institution;
- religion and its impact on family functioning; and
- the balance between the family and the self.

The experience of racism

It is important to recognise the impact that the experience of racism has in the way the family functions, about the attitudes and values the family expresses, and the way family life is generally structured on a day-to-day basis. Without a recognition of the centrality of these experiences it is not possible to produce a valid assessment. Without a doubt, the experience of racism will be the single most common feature of every Asian family. This common experience will impinge on every aspect of life, on every member of the family and on every system and sub-system within that family.

For many individuals the experience of racism will be an inextricable part of their growing up, education, work and leisure throughout their lives in Britain. For others this experience will be amplified by the experiences of loss and change associated with the process of migration. It is important then to ensure that, as these experiences are so central to the existence of Asian people and families, they are not marginalised, side-lined or denied. Instead it is important to recognise the strength, stamina and capacity to flourish and develop in adversity as being positive attributes.

Marriage as an institution

It is probably true to say that the institution of marriage is still of fundamental importance to Asian families and communities, to the extent that its corollary of divorce, separation, adultery and infidelity all exist but are either repressed, denied or not spoken about. Such issues as same-sex relationships are strictly taboo.

The crucial point for an assessment is the recognition that although marriage is "universal", the actual structure, form and meaning vary dramatically across cultures. Most Asian marriages have in the past been arranged, as are many today. These simple words "arranged marriage" carry many racist connotations of young girls being forced against their will to marry older men. The truth of the matter is that "force" and "against their will" are social constructs imposing a reality that does not exist. Marriage within Asian communities, as anywhere else, is a complex social arrangement with subtleties inextricably rooted in culture and history. Marriage is seen not just as a union of two people, but a union of two families. For this union of families to be successful, meticulous planning and preparation are required, much of it shrouded in ritual and custom. It is this planning that gives rise to the myth of "arranged".

Marriage is rarely the end product of a long romance, rather the beginning of one. Indeed, romance is rarely seen as a pre-requisite for a successful marriage. In many cases marriages will have taken place abroad, or where one partner is from abroad. Marriages nearly always exist within the context of an extended family and, even where the extended family is fragmented across geographical space, its unity and sanctity remain paramount.

It is clear that in assessments of Asian families we need to be aware of the many extra dimensions to marriage for it is this richness of marriage as an institution that provides the positive substance and material of assessment.

Religion and its impact on family functioning

Although in the West we live in an increasingly secular society, this contrasts sharply with the role of religion in Asian families for whom it provides many things. Against the backdrop of racism, religion provides a mechanism for affirming and reaffirming identity, not only with other Asians but also with Asian culture and history.

Religion can then be seen as providing meaning, security and continuity in the lives of most Asian families. It also shapes, informs and structures much of their daily lives, by providing rules of conduct, codes of ethics and moral frameworks for interpreting life events. Therefore any proper assessment of Asian families must consider the role of religion in the family's life and how it shapes or influences family functioning. Religion is a central concept to the assessment and should not be confined to a peripheral question to be ticked off on an assessment checklist.

Balance between family and self

The modern world has been described by Lasch (1977) as narcissistic, based as it is on the "cult of the individual". He describes the modern personality as shallow, self-centred and lacking emotion. The Asian family, in contrast, does not necessarily place so much importance on the individual. In many cases it is the family or community that is considered to be supreme. It is assumed that either the needs of the individual are one and the same as the needs of the family or group, or that the needs of the individual will be fulfilled when the needs of the family or group are met.

This shift in emphasis in the balance between self and others sits uncomfortably with social work values of promoting independence or empowerment. It is important that assessments take into account that individuals and families do function differently and that at times these may be based on different value systems. Cognisance needs to be given to the way this strong family orientation manifests in the daily functioning of the family and how it is expressed in the family's value system.

Conclusion

It is not possible to be conclusive about what should and should not form part of an assessment. As every worker knows, assessments are as individual as the families being assessed, and we need to be alert to this fact. I have, however, tried to bring together four key elements which must inform any valid assessment of Asian families. Only then can we be sure of identifying the real potential of Asian families in a way that is both relevant to their experiences and that focuses on their particular strengths in a much more meaningful way.

Note

Since the publication of this paper in 1997, the Khandan Initiative has assessed and approved a number of Asian families, and indeed made placements of children. The majority of these assessments and the post-placement support has been and will be provided to the Asian families by white workers, raising new challenges to our practice. It is useful to consider the perspective of white workers and a white colleague writes (Singh and McFadyen, 1997):

> *In the two previous assessments I had undertaken of black and Asian applicants I had found myself floundering. I was both paralysed by an acute awareness of the cultural bias in much of the process and content of a conventional fostering assessment and at the same time I was uncertain as to how to integrate different perspectives, values and norms into the usual criteria of a Form "F". The framework being proposed in this article has helped me with both dilemmas, and it has provided another and very significant guide to the assessment structure process. Focusing on these four (and there may be others) themes within each conventional area of the Form "F" has opened up territory that might otherwise have remained unexplored or misunderstood on my part. It has also helped me to shift my own thinking and perspective as well as my intention, beyond what is over familiar and culturally biased and thus discriminatory.*

> *Finally, my experience of this assessment has been radically affected by sharing it with an Asian colleague. This joint work has challenged and encouraged my own learning and sensitisation. The value of such an opportunity should not be underestimated.*

References

ABSWAP, 'Black children in care', Evidence to the House of Commons Social Services Committee, 1983.

Ahmed S, 'Children in care: the racial dimension in social work assessment', in Cheetham J, Loney M, Mayor B and Prescott W, *Social and Community Work in a Multi-racial Society*, Harper & Row, 1981.

Cheetham J, 'Problems of adoption for black children', in Cheetham J (ed), *Social Work and Ethnicity*, National Institute of Social Work, 1982.

Divine D, 'Time for decision', *The Caribbean Times*, 18 March 1983.

Dutt R, 'Open adoption – a black perspective', *Adoption & Fostering*, 15:4, pp 111–15, 1991.

Gaber I and Aldridge J (eds), *In the Best Interests of the Child: Culture, identity and transracial adoption*, Free Association Books, 1994.

Germaine C B, 'Social work practice: people and environment', in Maluccio A, Fein E and Olmstead K, *Permanency Planning for Children: Concepts and methods*, Tavistock, 1986.

Gill O and Jackson B, *Adoption and Race: Black, Asian and mixed-race children in white families*, Batsford/BAAF, 1983.

HMSO, *The Children (Scotland) Act*, London: HMSO, 1995.

Lasch C, *Haven in a Heartless World: The family besieged*, Basic Books, 1977, USA.

Maximé J, 'Some psychological models of black self-concept', in Ahmed S, Cheetham J and Small J (eds), *Social Work with Black Children and their Families*, Batsford/BAAF, 1991.

Maluccio A, *Permanency Planning for Children: Concepts and methods*, Tavistock, 1986.

Nobles W, 'Toward an empirical and theoretical framework for defining black families', *Journal of Marriage and the Family* 70, pp 679–88, 1978.

Rhodes P, *Racial Matching in Fostering*, Avebury, 1992.

Singh S and McFadyen S, 'Assessing Asian families as substitute carers: a case study', *Journal of the Scottish Anti-Racist Federation*, October 1997.

Small J, 'Transracial placements: conflicts and contradictions', in Morgan S and Righton P (eds), *Child Care: Concerns and conflicts*, Hodder & Stoughton, 1989.

Small J, 'Ethnic and racial adoption within the United Kingdom', *Adoption & Fostering*, 15:4, pp 61–9, 1991.

7 Involving birth parents in foster care training

Anne Gilchrist and Pauline Hoggan

Anne Gilchrist is Senior Social Worker in the East Lothian Resource Team, Lothian Regional Social Work Department. When this article was written Pauline Hoggan was a Principal Officer (Children and Families) in the same Department. At the time of the creation of unitary authorities in Scotland in 1996, she became Head of Service (Children and Families) in the now Argyll and Bute Council. She has recently become Director of the Independent Adoption Service, based in London.

This paper was published in Adoption & Fostering, 20:1, 1996.

Lothian Region Social Work Department has run a large foster care service since its establishment in 1975. In mid-1995 there were 330 foster families contracted by the Social Work Department, caring for around 520 children and young people at any time. Since the early 1980s, the Department has had a growing commitment to promoting a high standard of care for children and concern for their birth families by providing effective training and ongoing support to substitute family carers, e.g. by payment of monthly fees as well as boarding out allowances, by having specialist local staff teams dedicated to carer support and recruitment, and by the provision of planned training programmes and events.

For many years, prospective foster carers have been required to participate in a series of basic group preparation sessions before their approval as carers. Although workers have used a number of sources for the style and content of these sessions, including their own ideas, much material has been drawn in recent years from the NFCA training packs, particularly *The Challenge of Foster Care* (1994). Following the basic seven-session programme, staff in the carers' local district resource team offer regular support group sessions as well as topic based training. For example, one district has commissioned the Barnardo's Skylight Project, which offers a post sexual abuse support service for children and young people in care, to deliver a series of four-day sessions for foster carers on safe caring practice and helping abused children.

This article describes and discusses a recent initiative by one district resource team to involve birth parents in ongoing training for approved foster carers. The objective was to enhance the existing carers' sensitivity to birth parents' feelings and difficulties, and their ability to empathise with them.

Preparation

The resource team staff broached the idea of involving birth parents in a training session with their colleagues in the local practice teams which work directly with children and families. Workers within the teams responded positively to the idea and were able to obtain the involvement of five birth parents with children who were currently or previously in the care of the Department. It was agreed that the parents' workers should attend the training session with them, particularly as this was a pilot venture and it was difficult to predict the level of protectiveness vis-à-vis independence which would be needed and wanted by the individual parents. In pre-discussion with the workers certain issues affecting particular parents were identified, thus enabling some of the possible implications of these issues to be explored at the training session. Among the issues were:

- alcohol dependency;
- lack of self-confidence;
- recurring severe depression;
- feelings of failure as a parent; and
- feelings of being judged negatively.

The birth parents' experiences with carers ranged from very positive, through mixed to very negative – sometimes all these feelings being around for one person! The birth parents included men and women, all of whom had had experience of being a single parent. Care was taken to avoid involving birth parents and carers who already knew each other.

In the light of the sensitivity of the above issues, the workers attempted to structure the session in a way that minimised the vulnerability of the parents, for example, by using small groups and ensuring that each parent's worker, who had a clear remit to support that person, remained alongside them throughout all the discussions. It was recognised that there was a risk of discussion focusing on negative experiences and perceptions in a way that might feel disabling, or even destructive. The workers provided a framework for the parents during their preparation session and during the introductory part of the evening by focusing on "what was" or "would have been" helpful when your child was in care, rather than "what was awful" about it. Workers from the resource team had the role of leading the small group discussions and part of their remit was to maintain this constructive framework. It was acknowledged that one of the drawbacks of this particular session was the unusually large number of social work staff present (ten).

Programme
The event was held one evening during the middle of the week. The venue was a comfortable community room adjacent to a social work department office.

7.30 p.m. *Introduction* highlighting the importance of carers' sensitivity to feelings and issues which might be around for parents at different stages of the placement. These stages could be:
• when the decision is taken to place the child in care;
• the actual move;
• the first visit after the move;
• subsequent face-to-face contact;
• participation in reviews; and
• when the child goes home or moves to another placement.

7.50 p.m. *Small group discussion* about how these different stages were experienced and the feelings around. Each group consisted of a birth parent, the parent's worker, carers and a resource team worker. The latter was responsible for encouraging group discussion, promoting participation and sustaining a constructive framework, as well as providing feedback to the larger group at the end of the session.

8.40 p.m. *Coffee and social chat*

9 p.m. *Drawing the threads together*, based on feedback from the small groups (five in all, with 25 carers)

Feedback
The initial stage of placement
The discussions highlighted parents' feelings of anxiety, "uptightness" and the fantasies they had about the consequences of their child being in care. As Triseliotis and colleagues (1995) comment, 'Parents may have all sorts of misconceptions about fostering and varying degrees of guilt, anxiety and suspicion about foster parents looking after their child.' They spoke of the helpfulness of introductory visits and meetings and the vital importance of being involved in the planning. The value of good communication between all parties (carer, social worker and parent) was emphasised, for instance, the importance of returning phone calls to give straightforward practical information about times of meetings. It was clearly much easier for parents when they felt comfortable with a carer and their setting. Attention was drawn to the feelings parents have of fear, guilt, jealousy and lack of self-respect. One parent spoke of how difficult it was, in the face of her huge feelings of failure and inadequacy, to have to meet carers for the first time in their own comfortable, well-run home. She thought it might have been easier if the initial meeting had taken place in a more neutral setting, such as the social work office. However, subsequent discussion with workers suggested that the carer's home was felt by other parents to be a more relaxed venue.

First and subsequent visits and contacts
Again attention was drawn to how "judged and threatened" parents can feel and the value of feeling welcomed by carers. This can be helped by focusing on the child, i.e. talking about how they are doing and what has been happening in his or her day-to-day life. One practical issue which emerged was that, because our Department always has an initial 72-hour review, it often coincides with the birth parent's first visit. The business-like focus necessitated by the review and the presence of other staff such as the senior social worker makes it more difficult for the carers to

provide a relaxed and welcoming ambience for parents. This points to the importance of workers making greater efforts to ensure that the parent's first visit to the carer's home happens before the 72-hour review and/or that review meetings do not take place in the carer's home, if for some reason it is inappropriate for a visit to take place so soon.

The role of good communication between carers, parents and social workers in promoting a positive visiting pattern was stressed, as was the need to be "upfront" in sharing information. The lack of a phone on the part of either party (usually the parent) makes it more difficult to sustain regular informal communication. The importance of being given detailed information about what the child was doing was emphasised, as was the need to be given sufficient time and space to do something with the child independently. The difficulties inherent in supervised access arrangements were noted, but time (and probably the public nature of a group setting) did not allow for this topic to be explored in any depth.

Birth parents valued a welcoming approach on the part of carers, which gave reassurance about their role as parents and about their child's attachment to them. One parent referred to the courteous approach of her child's carer who not only provided coffee but also home baking, 'as if I was somebody important'. Parents also appreciated their opinion being sought in relation to the child, for example about their ways of dressing, expectations about them and their behaviour at school. One parent valued the straight approach of a carer who could clearly explain to her why arrangements for weekend visits needed to be made so that the carer and child would be at home when the parent came, and to ensure space and privacy for the visit.

Another learning point related to a parent feeling that a flexible, open-ended invitation to visit was insincere and that it was important for carers and workers to check out with parents their preferences. Some might find it easier to have specific times and set arrangements for visiting and other contact. Another parent explained the difficulty of having her children placed geographically near her home, despite this being against her explicit wishes. This was very uncomfortable for her and, she felt, made it much more difficult to sustain helpful boundaries between the two homes. It also made the situation much more visible to the local community, which she experienced as humiliating. The importance of checking out lifestyle patterns for the child and new carers was highlighted. This included such matters as eating habits and meal-times, bedtimes and style of family communication, so that some kind of continuity or bridging could be consciously built in for the child's benefit.

The observations and feelings expressed by the parents reflect and reaffirm much of the good practice guidance offered in recent years in the literature published by BAAF, particularly in *Contact: Managing visits to children looked after away from home* (Hess and Proch, 1993) and *Foster Care: Theory and practice* (Triseliotis, Sellick and Short, 1995).

Participation in reviews

All five parents had attended reviews and saw this as an important entitlement. They commented on the frequent use of jargon by pro-fessional staff. Another complaint related to overloaded discussions where too many issues were addressed. Both carers and parents spoke of having no say as to what was to be discussed. Some parents were unhappy that certain issues were addressed in the presence of their children – not always appropriately, they felt.

The role of the chairperson of Child Care Reviews and Child Protec-tion Case Conferences has recently been highlighted in updated depart-mental training and guidance, and chairs are now expected to make time before meetings to discuss the proposed process and content with parents and children.

Moving back home

There was considerable awareness of how difficult and confusing this process can be for the child, attention being drawn to the need for conscious and detailed work with them at this stage. Comment was made about the range of feelings experienced by parents, for instance, appre-hensiveness as well as eagerness for the child's return, and the usefulness of maintaining contact between carers, parents and the child in order to provide continuity of relationships for the latter.

Outcome of the session

While much that was shared and referred to was reasonably familiar to carers and staff, they all recognised the value of highlighting again and in more explicit detail the extremely painful and difficult feelings of parents. The parents' workers underlined the importance of continually reminding themselves of the rawness of such pain, in order to ensure that our sensitivity to it, as workers and carers, is not dulled.

Perhaps most significant was that all the parents commented on how positive they had found the experience of taking part in the training. There were a number of different strands to this:

- a sense of being accepted and perceived as having a contribution to make;
- a greater sense of partnership or parity with carers and professionals, an offshoot of which was the "demystifying" of what carers had to offer; and
- a sense of relief and comfort from knowing that carers, too, feel anxious and vulnerable.

The workers also expressed the view that the session had been positive and enjoyable for them.

The importance of aspiring to this sense of mutual learning and respect is reflected in many studies which include consumer feedback, such as June Thoburn's recent (1995) findings on parents' experiences of child protection investigations:

All family members stressed the importance of being cared about as people. They could understand that the professionals had a job to do . . . but strongly objected to workers . . . who did not appear to listen, did not show warmth and concern, and just did things by the book.

The workers' experience of this event has been shared with the other district resource teams and similar events could become standard post-approval training. While it is possible that, with increased confidence in the process, training organisers might be able to have less intensive involvement by such a high number of staff, it is essential to heed the lesson from this experience, about the benefits of careful planning, debriefing and attention to detail in achieving a successful outcome.

Conclusion

The event we have described took place in the context of the radical shift in perception there has been since the establishment of social work as a profession which was dominated by a culture in which decision-making by and about clients was made in secret by so-called experts with little, if any, commitment to encouraging the participation of non-professionals. Over the last 15 years, there have been substantial moves towards involving substitute family carers in practice development; for example, since the early 1980s our agency has routinely deployed (and paid sessional fees to) experienced foster carers and adopters to contribute to training. The move towards more openness in adoption means that, in many areas, it is now more common than not for birth parents to meet with prospective adopters before their child's placement. In the child protection context, several years ago many professionals would never have envisaged that social work managers, medical consultants and police officers would have found it acceptable, and indeed desirable in the interests of effective decision-making, to have parents participating throughout a child protection case conference. However, the outcome of the introduction of such practice consistently shows benefits for the quality of the service, particularly if professionals tackle potential difficulties in a constructive manner and if policy implementation is not flagrantly tokenistic. For instance, little purpose is served in setting up events such as case reviews at which parents may be physically present but not genuinely enabled to participate, thereby making it likely that the real decision-making will still take place elsewhere.

Another aspect of our local and national context is the change in Scotland this year to mainly smaller local authorities, combined with pressure to move towards private or voluntary sector provision of services traditionally provided directly by the public sector, such as the large mainstream fostering services. This training event provided a good example of specialist staff with dedicated time, working within a local authority, being able to carry out innovative work and benefiting from their ease of access to decision-makers and to the relevant resources (in this case, family social workers and the birth parents). If there is a move towards non-public sector agencies providing more of these services, it is essential that they have the kind of close professional relationships and credibility with key staff responsible for work with children and families, so that practice development such as this can be initiated from a point at which the child and family are the centre.

On the other hand, it is important not to be tempted to see public sector delivery of service as being automatically the most effective or best value for money. Although the staff in this resource team had relatively straightforward access to the resources they required, the event was by no means cheap. In order to carry it out effectively, it required a higher than normal number of resource team staff to work in an evening running a group, and there were also expenses to cover the birth families' workers' time and for the parents themselves, in addition to the preparation and de-briefing time required to ensure that the event could be meaningful for all concerned. As David Berridge (1994) has observed, 'Foster care is only cheap if it's done on the cheap'.

References

Berridge D, 'Foster and residential care reassessed', in *Children and Society*, 8:2, pp 132–50, 1994.

Hess P and Proch K, *Contact: Managing visits to children looked after away from home*, BAAF, 1993.

National Foster Care Association, *The Challenge of Foster Care*, NFCA, 1994 (updated 1998).

Thoburn J, *Child Placement: Principles and practice*, Wildwood House/Gower, 1994.

Thoburn J, Louis A and Shemmings D, *Paternalism or Partnership? Family involvement in the child protection process*, HMSO, 1995.

Triseliotis J, Sellick C and Short R, *Foster Care: Theory and practice*, Batsford/ BAAF, 1995.

Section III
Short-term placements

Although the majority of foster placements last only a few weeks or months, relatively little information was available about short placements at the beginning of the 1990s, with earlier research having focused on intermediate and longer-term placements. During the first half of the decade the position reversed, with a number of important studies concentrating on short-term placements (e.g. Sellick, 1992).

One of the ways in which the Children Act 1989 both reflected and prompted changes in thinking was about the role of short-term care as a contribution to family support. Formerly, moving a child from home had often been seen as a last resort or failure, now a *planned* brief spell away from home was viewed as helping families to cope with crises. As **Bradley and Aldgate (1994)** noted, such breaks 'can offer a vital breathing space and the chance to strengthen and build on family coping strategies' (p 24).

The notion of respite originally developed in relation to periodic stays away from home by disabled children. Implicit was the idea of parents needing relief from the "burden" of care. The term has been developed and applied to providing one or more short-term placements as a response to family conflicts or crises, giving parents, children or both time to recuperate, reflect and regroup before coming back together again. Respite placements are also made available nowadays by some agencies for foster carers dealing with particularly demanding children or families. A related function is that of refuge, where a young person is accommodated at their own request and perhaps contrary to parental wishes in circumstances of intense family conflict.

Webb (1990) observed that respite could be made available as an *ad hoc* response to a crisis or as a contingency option within a longer-term plan. It can also be an integrated element of a planned family support programme.

A piece of action research was carried out by Webb and Aldgate to see how existing services in one local authority in the English Midlands could be developed into a more flexible supportive service for children and families. Practitioners saw respite as consisting of one or more periods of care lasting up to a week or so. Imaginative arrangements were already in place, for example, providing voluntary accommodation of children to avoid breakdown of lone parent households. Most workers could see the value of extending respite care to families with relationship and behaviour problems, but doubted its applicability to situations of abuse or extreme crisis, though such uses had been pioneered in the USA. Workers believed that respite could normalise sharing care between birth families and foster carers, so that parents felt less stigmatised and powerless in using this form of help. They were in favour of specialised and decentralised structures of joint decision-making to implement a new model of respite care.

Following on the earlier work undertaken by **Webb and Aldgate (1990)**, a study of short-term carers providing family support was undertaken by **Bradley and Aldgate (1994)** to obtain the perspectives of those directly involved in the placements. This revealed that most carers were themselves parents and many had previously worked with children too. They usually lived quite nearby the service users, but not 'too close'. Parents found the carers to be helpful and non-judgemental. The carers saw their role as combining support to parents with giving children individual attention and relief from worries and responsibilities at home. Most of them also participated effectively in planning and review. In nearly all respects, this scheme was working well, though it was noted that minority ethnic families were under-represented among both carers and users.

In a later report Aldgate *et al* (1996) provided feedback from children about their experiences of family-based respite accommodation. Generally the children's perceptions of why they were there corresponded with social work plans (e.g. to give Mum a rest or themselves a break). Normally preparatory visits took place to the foster home, which is a rare luxury for many emergency admissions. The children found these visits very reassuring. They enjoyed the kindness, consideration and play offered by carers. Overall the experiences of carers, parents and children provided a good model of partnership in which worries and expectations were shared with a high degree of openness and mutual understanding.

The model of planned short-term care with flexible sharing of care described by Aldgate and colleagues appears to offer a helpful way forward. Indeed Berridge and Brodie (1998) recommended a similar framework for the development of residential care. Ideally this means that parents, foster carers and older children all contribute to decisions about the nature and timing of care arrangements. However, all too often placements are still made in an emergency with few available options. Much less consideration is given to children's "race", culture, religion and language, when placements are made for briefer periods compared with long-term planning (Barn *et al*, 1997).

Whereas the above linked studies portrayed innovative developments in brief placements, **Stone (1991)** undertook a broader survey of 183 short-term fostering placements in Northern England. She began by noting that earlier research had shown that about half of all foster placements lasted less than three months, though it was also not uncommon for placements that were intended to be short-term to last considerably longer than planned (Rowe *et al*, 1989). Stone observed that short-term foster care embraced a wide range of tasks. The majority of placements involved pre-school children who returned home within a matter of weeks. Usually the reasons for admission were related to parental care, ill health, adult relationships, housing and poverty. Few of the children had identified behaviour difficulties. Short-term fostering was rarely used for teenagers. Rates of admission seemed to depend to a considerable degree on individual and office practices, since the use of short-term fostering was quite different among teams with similar catchment areas. As noted in Section I, agency policy and practice have been identified as key influences on services and admission patterns for many years (see e.g. Packman, 1968), but the precise mechanisms remain poorly understood.

Stone concluded by recommending that the 'tangled web' of short-term foster care be unravelled into four main strands:
1. time-limited family support placements for children aged under ten who have a very good chance of quick return home;
2. more flexible intermediate length placements for children aged under ten, where abuse, neglect or significant emotional/ behavioural problems are present. Return home is desirable but less certain. For some children it may sooner or later become necessary to prepare for an alternative permanent substitute family. The notion of concurrent planning, later popularised by Katz (1996), may be relevant, whereby foster carers work

intensively towards restoration but are prepared to keep the child for good if return home does not work out.

3. specific packages for adolescents (see also Downes, 1992; Triseliotis *et al*, 1995a; Hill *et al*, 1996); and

4. pre-adoptive services.

8   Using respite care to prevent long-term family breakdown

Stephen Webb and Jane Aldgate

At the time of writing Stephen Webb was Lecturer in Social Work at the University of Dundee. Jane Aldgate was Fellow of St Hilda's College and Lecturer in Applied Social Studies at the University of Oxford and is now Professor of Social Care at the Open University, Milton Keynes.

This paper was published in Adoption & Fostering, 15:1, 1991.

Introduction

This article reports on the findings of a study which tested the feasibility of using respite care in a local authority social services department, firstly to see whether this type of provision might be incorporated into existing, more conventional forms of preventive child care policy and practice, and secondly, how authorities might prepare for changes in practice in anticipation of the Children Act 1989.

Changes in child care law, the use of alternative types of provision and the development of more flexible child care policies are not unconnected. Indeed, key concepts in the Children Act include maximising parental responsibility, even in compulsory care cases; the promotion of the welfare of children in need in the community, and the blurring of the boundary between being "in" , or "out" of care. As suggested in previous papers (Webb, 1990; Aldgate *et al*, 1989) respite care can be an integral part of supportive services to families under stress and, in the future, will certainly be included in the definition of accommodation of children away from home to prevent long-term family breakdown.

What is respite care?

At the most basic level respite care in child and family work means providing a short period of care away from a difficult or stressful situation. Relief is for both the carers and the cared for. A more flexible definition, which we prefer, allows respite to be part of a "package of services" to achieve a given aim. Respite can respond to an emergency, but preferably can be planned over periods of time on a contingency basis within or outside the child's home, and will incorporate a range of individuals (see Webb, 1990) including family members, extended kin, neighbours, foster carers, family aides, home helps, volunteers, residential and field social workers in settings such as a family home, day-care or family centre, residential homes, boarding-out lodgings, independent living units and even seaside holiday accommodation. If planned, it can be provided by both statutory and voluntary agencies and be used in conjunction with a variety of social work methods and interventions to achieve a set goal. Periods of respite care can last from a few hours to a few days, over several months or even years.

Planned respite care is founded on the principles of partnership, shared care and a wider definition of prevention. Each of these imply involving clients in the decision-making process, providing easily accessible, locally-based services and working towards the empowerment of disadvantaged client groups without stigmatising families by assigning blame. Policy guidelines on the use of respite need to clearly acknowledge all these principles.

The context of the study
The study on which this article reports was carried out jointly by one social services department and the Department of Applied Social Studies and Social Research at the University of Oxford.

The county, Blankshire, had already set up a number of excellent respite care schemes for children with severe learning difficulties, and for elderly clients, within its six divisions, as well as a youth resources team, based in Small Town, which used respite care as a means of avoiding reception into care and creating a "bridge to independence" for adolescents. The study was thus a type of "action research", attempting to understand the current situation and make recommendations for change by examining how other respite schemes might be translated into a more flexible supportive service for children and families. A special feature of the study was the decision to elicit the opinions and attitudes of social workers and carers, so that any changes would be based upon the opinion of those actually delivering the services. It was heartening to realise that the Children Act 1989 reflected existing policy and would simply facilitate its extension in the future, rather than imposing on practice an alien set of ideals.

Given the constraints of time and resources, it was decided that the study should focus on a demographically representative sample from two of the county's six divisions and should cover different levels of social work practice and responsibility, as a means of ensuring that the study was reasonably representative and reliable. Therefore, three types of workers were distinguished:

- line managers (from principal social workers upwards);
- field social workers (from basic grade level to senior grades);
- direct carers: residential social workers, family aides and day carers.

Methodology

The study was designed as a survey project to find out about present and future uses of respite care. The context of respite care was examined by identifying what current respite services and resources were available in the county, by which client groups they were used and the extent of social workers' experience of using or implementing such schemes.

In addition, the study sought to explore social workers' definitions of respite care in theory, its similarities to or differences from other services, perceived difficulties in the current use of respite care (to guide against mistakes in future proposals), and how respite could be used within the framework of the Children Act 1989.

The results of the interview survey were either pre-coded or subsequently loosely coded by content analysis of responses, and a "key word" count to open-ended questions. Analysis on this small size sample was carried out manually.

Analysis of data

The findings fall into three headings of:

- the "current uses" of respite and its use in child care practice;
- the "conceptualisation of respite" in relation to aspects of social work practice and policy, and its relative significance or insignificance for practitioners;

- proposals for 'how to put respite into practice' and the difficulties and problems of such a venture.

Separating the discussion of findings into these sections is, however, somewhat artificial, since much of the information overlaps and the findings from each area tend to reinforce each other.

Current uses of respite care and its specific use in child care practice

All respondents were familiar with the term "respite care" and had come across it in a variety of contexts and client groups, including the elderly and child clients. Additionally, three-quarters of respondents had some experience of using or supervising someone using respite care.

For child clients respite was used for children with severe learning difficulties, relief for foster carers, for families under stress, and for adolescents and older children beyond control. Flexible respite care for children with learning difficulties or physical disability was used imaginatively and was a central feature of casework planning. Sometimes, respite alone could not solve all the problems of a family and was integrated with other help. Parents were always involved in the decision-making and drew up their own timetable of needs.

Respite was also offered to foster carers; sometimes two sets of fostering placements would be used to try to prevent breakdown of a difficult placement.

The most innovative uses of respite care in the study were those that provided a service to child clients whose families were under stress. A children's centre, which had respite provision as a specific criterion for voluntary admission, under section 2 of the 1980 Act, was used as a means of giving lone-parent families some relief and avoiding breakdown and long-term care. Weekend breaks over eight-week periods were used in conjunction with attendance and therapeutic intervention at a nearby family centre. These periods allowed both the parents and social workers to reassess the situation.

A number of practitioners said that the concept and use of respite care was initially regarded with suspicion by some families, particularly those whose children were received into care, but after agreements had been drawn up, and once the programme had begun, families saw the service as beneficial and supportive. A special feature to note was the emphasis on the role of residential workers in providing community support for families after discharge from care.

There was considerable potential for the use of respite for adolescents. The youth resources team in Small Town successfully used a boarding-out scheme in supportive lodgings for both adolescents in care and those at the point of being received into care. They also used respite care as a "bridge to independence" for adolescents who had spent long periods of their childhood in residential institutions. By applying a community-support strategy based on minimal intervention, this team provided respite accommodation for adolescents on both a crisis and planned basis.

Finally, residential homes or supportive lodgings offered respite care to the small number of children of varying ages in the county who were considered to be beyond parental care and control.

It was heartening to find that, while recognising the constraints of resources and services for families and children, three-quarters of the practitioner-respondents were aware of current alternative types of provision and how these might be used positively. It was clear that the extent of support for existing respite care would be instrumental in the development of any additional services. Many of the existing schemes would fit happily into the voluntary provision in the Children Act.

The concept of respite care in relation to social work practice and policy

In the light of the positive use of current services, it was not surprising that, when the views of social workers were elicited on the place of respite care within child care policy and practice, the importance of respite care as a key child care service provision was stressed by all respondents, with 70 per cent considering it to be "very important" and 30 per cent to be "important".

Significantly, all respondents thought that respite care could be an advantageous means of preventing long-term family breakdown and the drift of children into long-term placements. Although birth families might benefit most, the use of respite to prevent breakdown in foster homes also had potential.

Advantages of respite care

Respondents' views on the main advantages of using respite care can be summarised under four headings:

- the philosophy of social work methods and practice;
- user needs;
- the politics of "image" and economic motives.

The philosophy of social work methods and practice

In relation to philosophy and practice, respondents stressed the need to adopt a model which emphasised the prevention of family breakdown in the long term. Many respondents were against the current practice of emergency intervention or the "sticking plaster" approach, where a response was only made after a major crisis had occurred and which, to their regret, was practised all too often, resulting in the demoralisation of clients and workers alike.

Respite care offered the chance of positive intervention at an earlier stage. It was not only seen as a method of avoiding the use of long-term care, but also the means of emphasising community support networks that could be provided by social services in conjunction with other services. Moreover, some social workers were already aware that the use of respite care anticipated changes in perspective and legislation towards a user-led service. Such changes were generally welcomed: they would allow a more flexible service for families with difficulties, encompassing a variety of informal shared care arrangements based on a "partnership" model. A number of respondents thought that respite care could be used in conjunction with direct work with children, family therapy, assessment of family problems, and to give families "a break" in terms of both space and time that more privileged families might take for granted.

Two key practice issues were explored with workers – the optimal time periods for respite care, and the setting in which it should be provided. The majority thought that respite care could range from a weekend, a week, to a few hours or short periods of time over several months – responses which indicated a flexibility in fitting the service to clients' needs. Workers could also see a use for both residential and family-based care with family centres and other day care forming an additional viable resource. There was also a place for extended family offering placements and for various forms of peripatetic care.

It should, however, be emphasised that workers were viewing respite care within the framework of existing legislation. The services they talked about were generally seen as informal, being outside the current care system and akin to those offered to families whose children had severe disabilities. It was not, therefore, surprising that there was some confusion about how respite care might fit into the more formal arrangements for children being looked after by the local authority away from home. Current policy and practice tend to reinforce the idea of a strong divide between living with birth families in the community and being looked after by the local authority away from home, "in care". The intention of the Act is to break down that barrier, in response to research findings that families would benefit from a more flexible service (DHSS, 1985). Our findings indicated that some workers would need help to change the way they viewed use of accommodation under the Children Act.

The need to re-frame practice was also reflected in the division of opinion as to whether respite care should be used in crisis cases.

Over two-thirds were adamant that emergency provision through use of place-of-safety orders (emergency protection under the Children Act 1989) would not be appropriate. A clear-cut separation was indicated between planned shared care and emergency protection. Respite care was not considered to be useful for cases of sexual abuse, physical abuse and school refusal. In addition 40 per cent of respondents thought that it was not suitable for families with financial problems.

These findings tend to suggest that practitioners are sympathetic to using respite provision for families experiencing child care difficulties of an emotional/behavioural kind, but not in extreme or crisis-oriented cases where the child's welfare is at risk. Although this reflects the formal division in the Children Act between protection and voluntary services, it tends to run against the twin principles of avoiding the use of compulsory orders wherever possible, and of preserving links with families even in compulsory care cases. It indicates the need for a shift in emphasis so that "crisis intervention" can be used in a positive sense as an integral part of longer-term work. The emergency type respite policy and facilities recently developed in the United States for child protection cases are worth scrutiny here and could provide some useful guidelines (see Franz, 1980; Tovey, 1983 and Subramanian, 1985).

User needs

The views of social workers on the use of respite in a more general preventive context were more encouraging. The provision of a service to families whose children are "in need" is integral to the Children Act 1989 and therefore it was important to explore with workers where respite care might best be targeted. Respondents thought that respite care could be very useful in cases of parental illness and where family relationships were impaired.

There was also a consensus on the suitability of respite care for a wide range of children, with some exceptions in the cases of young children, where separation from birth families was seen as disruptive and potentially damaging or, in the case of adolescents, where respite care was unlikely to bring to an end the problems that had persisted for many years.

Benefits for children were seen to be the provision of a stimulating and varied environment outside the home, breathing space away from family conflicts, creating a gradual "bridge to independence", and allowing them to mix with another peer group. One family aide suggested that respite could be especially useful during the school holidays for families living in conditions of multiple socio-economic deprivation, and holidays at seaside resorts or adventure centres could be creatively developed for children, which recalled, with a sense of *déjà vu,* the imaginative preventive strategies of some children's departments following the implementation of the 1963 Children and Young Persons Act. Such a philosophy of the positive "promotion of welfare" is also integral to the intention of the Children Act 1989.

It was, however, the spirit of partnership with families which permeated the social workers' assessment of the needs of consumers. One respondent summed up the benefits as follows:

Respite gives everyone time to make a closer assessment of parenting abilities and allows the parents further choices, rather than us pursuing care proceedings. It is an intermediate measure that retains a working-together approach, and it also helps to establish a better working relationship with families in terms of trust and allows parents to retain responsibility.

The 'better working relationship' was clearly based on a philosophy that considered problems in family life as "normal" and not "pathological". Respite would provide a "safety valve" mechanism for potentially explosive situations, with parents continuing to maintain their responsibilities on a shared-care basis.

This important finding indicates that child care practitioners already accept the principle that families experiencing difficulties have needs to which social services can respond positively. Additionally, separation of parents and children in all circumstances does not have to be seen as finite and a sign of failure by families and workers alike. There remains some confusion over the incorporation of respite care into the formal services that authorities can offer under the Children Act 1989. Workers will need guidance on how the Act will allow them to apply their existing ideas in a more flexible framework, particularly in breaking down the barrier between the current concept of being "in and out" of care.

The politics of image handling
Another set of advantages could be described as "the politics of image-handling". This is the use of respite as a means of overcoming the somewhat tarnished image which local authority social service departments have acquired in recent times. The rationale behind this is to develop user-led services for children and families to ensure a positive image of social services in the public eye. Given the philosophy of the Children Act 1989, there is no doubt that the approach envisaged by the social workers surveyed in the study is exactly that which the legislation is striving to develop.

Economic motives
The final set of advantages mentioned by respondents can be termed "economic motives". Respite care was seen as cheaper by many than either long-term residential or foster care placements. Others, however, warned that a proper and comprehensive respite care service would demand proper funding and not be a cheap option.

Constraints on providing respite care

The financial constraints on providing a good respite care service were listed among the first of its four potential shortcomings which can be summarised as follows:

- inadequate resources and facilities;
- inter-agency tension;
- casework management; and
- family structure and dynamics.

Many respondents thought that respite provision was bound to fail unless adequate resources, in terms of money and facilities, recruitment and payment of foster carers, additional social work personnel and staff training, were provided. This would demand extra financial input or a well-thought-out diversification of funds already available. Respite might be difficult to justify statistically and this might raise questions for those planning budgets. Finally, there was the resource problem of both recruiting and supporting appropriate foster families who could work with parents.

The second set of disadvantages were couched in terms of inter-agency tensions between field and residential social workers. There was often a lack of consultation and joint planning between them when decisions were made about short-term care. Additionally, the growing market of specialist field workers might try to capture respite care as their own, thus excluding other workers.

Thirdly, there were problems of case-load management with the main source of concern being that, unless joint planning occurred between all parties involved through regular reviews, workers would soon lose sight of the main casework objective. Practitioners wanted to avoid situations open to challenge by clients, exemplified as follows: 'Respite is less clear-cut and tidy, and the boundaries are blurred' and 'It becomes muddy because we don't know where the responsibility lies'. Social workers were also worried that the legal status of the child would be unclear under the new legislation. Workers were concerned that they might set up families "to fail" by making false promises of partnership which could not be delivered. Hopefully, the guidance and regulations accompanying the Children Act 1989 will help to clarify the division of responsibility, but the concerns of the study social workers suggest that there will be no substitute for good practice.

The fourth set of potential disadvantages were based on social workers' perceptions of family structure and dynamics. Some astute claims were made: some families might give up trying to survive, seeing respite as an easy option; others might use respite as a threat to children, and might even create jealousies among other siblings who did not receive respite.

Another tension was the possible conflict between birth parents and foster carers. Additionally, there were concerns about shuttling children back and forth from placement to placement, and the fact that respite care too strongly emphasised the needs of parents and not those of children. Of course this can be countered with a claim that if problems are resolved for parents, then often children will benefit as a direct consequence of this. However, it is important that children do not perceive respite as a form of punishment, or that families relieved of pressure at home begin to take respite for granted.

The practitioners in the study bring an important message. For respite care to be successful, it is vital to integrate the new legislation properly with operational policies, resource allocation and practice-based skills in working with children and families. The findings also indicate that practitioners may need help in changing the emphasis of their work away from rigid divisions between voluntary and compulsory cases to a philosophy which embraces the use of intervention along a non-hierarchical continuum, which may be broken into at *any* stage and in which birth families play an important part at *every* stage.

How to put respite care into practice

The major aim of the study was to see how easily respite care could be grafted on to existing family-based and residential child care services. The majority of respondents said that special arrangements would have to be made to introduce respite care as a family placement or to develop its use in residential care.

Another issue was how the provision of respite care should be organised. There was a distinct preference for specialisation among respondents which may well reflect a bias in the study authority towards specialist teams in the area of fostering and adoption, child protection and juvenile justice. But the findings may also indicate a general trend away from genericism in all branches of the child care service.

When it came to looking at decision-making around the use of respite care, social workers had two main preferences: for joint but informal discussions and planning procedures, and for a "decentralised" decision-making structure which involved individual workers in the process from start to finish. These views were also reflected in their opinions that respite provision in child care on a residential basis should be set up at divisional level, and that voluntary and statutory agencies should work together to provide this kind of provision.

Another issue explored with workers was the question of whether clients should pay for services rendered to them. Around two-thirds of respondents thought that birth parents should 'sometimes' have to pay for respite care services, but the remainder thought they should never have to pay. These findings suggest that the majority of social workers were in favour of a type of means test in calculation of services based on 'ability to pay', while a minority thought that all state welfare provision should be free of charge. Of the former group, many said that having to pay for services provided an incentive for parents to maintain their sense of responsibility towards a child. Others were more cautious, claiming that if the provision of respite was conditional on making some payment, then poor families would be deterred from using it, thus leaving more affluent families to soak up the available resource provision. Clearly, this question is bound up with discussions of the changing role of the welfare state and the provision of social services within it.

Line managers believed that implementing a respite care service would demand a shift in attitudes: 'You need to get staff to think differently if you are going to pursue good preventive practice', and, 'Because child abuse is prioritised over everything, preventive work gets pushed further and further back'. It was suggested that staff needed to 'accept failure without at the same time absorbing kids into the system'. It is very much hoped that the Children Act 1989 will help social workers re-frame their attitudes in the way that the line managers in this study thought would be necessary.

Comprehensive respite provision would also mean adequate preparation in terms of training support workers to live with less cut-and-dried decisions, costing, delegation of responsibilities, setting up specialist facilities, recognising the importance of regular reviews and family meetings, and deciding how residential and fieldwork staff work together to provide a range of services from welfare advice and family therapy to direct work. In preparation for these changes, managers believed that the agency would need to set up a survey of needs in local communities, undertake costing exercises and investigate resource implications, assess the viability of recruiting respite carers, ask the consumers what services they required, establish staff training and procedural guidelines, communicate with other agencies (particularly voluntary bodies) and examine schemes operating elsewhere.

Most social workers thought that special arrangements would have to be made when considering either family or residential placements as a respite care facility. Carers would need better training and pay. There would also have to be a monitoring and registration system, the use of written agreements, link social workers to liaise between birth and foster carers and a pool of emergency respite carers. It would be necessary to bridge the gap between childminders, family aides and foster carers, so that the respite provision could move towards employing "one day" or "weekend only" foster carers. Such a move would clarify roles and demarcate responsibilities.

New arrangements for the use of residential placements could include special in-service training, upgrading and additional staffing in residential homes, discussion about what type of children to place in what type of home, the need to move from a controlling to a facilitating relationship in residential homes, the need for mutual agreements between workers and parents, and additional therapeutic input.

Whatever the pros and cons of a respite care service, respondents were almost unanimously in favour of some respite care provision as a central feature of child care policy and practice in the county. Respondents also believed that respite care should be implemented on a national basis in all social services departments.

Conclusion

In an earlier paper, Webb (1990) set out three models of respite care provision for the child care service: crisis-driven, contingency-driven and fiscally-driven.

This paper has explored the use of respite care from a practice standpoint and has concluded that practice supports theory. Respite care can have many successful permutations but is likely to work best in the context of the Children Act 1989 as a contingency-based service, which embraces shared care, therapeutic intervention and support in the community from a variety of professionals.

What was striking about our findings was the development of imaginative respite care practice within the framework of current legislation. We cannot believe our study authority is unique but it is hard to gain an overall picture, given the lack of information about current initiatives. Even though our study social workers were constantly frustrated by overarching restrictions, there is little doubt that their initiatives led the way for change within their authority and set standards by which others had to measure themselves.

Clearly, this study should be seen in the context of changes to be brought in under the Children Act 1989 to develop a flexible service aimed at preventing long-term family breakdown. The line managers and practitioners in the study were overwhelmingly in support of the development of a respite care service to support this aim. The provision of accommodation under section 20 of the Children Act 1989 will provide the framework to implement such a policy.

The need and willingness to perform a proactive facilitating role, rather than one based solely on negative emergency intervention or statutory proceedings, suggests that social workers are indeed able to work in partnership with parents and children. The social workers surveyed saw temporary respite care as a provision whereby parents might be included in a decision-making process through the use of written agreements. This attitude gives hope for positive implementation of this radical aspect of the Children Act.

There remains the problem which the legislation cannot address: adequate resources. Social workers in the study clearly recognised the effects which limited resources had on curtailing good practice.

Finally, while there are dangers of being over-prescriptive in legislation, there are equal dangers in not spelling out the positive possibilities. The specific terms "respite care" and "shared care" which appeared as central concepts in the Child Care Law – Review (DHSS, 1986) were dropped in the Children Act, thereby allowing any local authority social services department the opportunity to omit important practice options, although the statutory guidance and regulations will hopefully retain the options in their detail.

Respite care as a theoretical option for a wide range of families was first identified within the research findings of the "pink book" *Social Work Decisions in Child Care* (DHSS, 1985). What our small study has shown is that it is not merely theory, but a potential service rooted in current practice. Practitioners also have the will to adopt a wider definition of prevention and, in spite of obstacles, have thought about how changes might be executed. Respite care will be an important part of the services designed to promote the welfare of children in need, enhance parental responsibility and prevent family breakdown. The next step is to translate the philosophy of the Act into reality. In one county at least, a start has been made.

References

Aldgate J, Pratt R and Duggan M, 'Using care away from home to prevent family breakdown,' *Adoption & Fostering*, 13:2, pp 32–37, 1989.

Department of health, *Social Work Decisions in Child Care*, HMSO, 1985.

Department of Health, *The Law on Child Care and Family Services*, HMSO, 1986.

Franz J, 'Being there: a 24-hour emergency crisis care center', *Children Today*, 9:1, pp 7–10, 1989.

Subramanian K, 'Reducing child abuse through respite center intervention', *Child Welfare*, 64:5, pp 501–09, 1985.

Tovey R, 'The family living model: five-day treatment in a rural environment', *Child Welfare*, 62:5, pp 445–49, 1983.

Webb S A, 'Preventing reception into care: literature review of respite care', *Adoption & Fostering,* 14:2, pp 21–26, 1990.

9 Short-term family based care for children in need

Marie Bradley and Jane Aldgate

Marie Bradley is a Research Officer at Oxford University and Jane Aldgate is Professor of Social Care at the Open University, Milton Keynes.

This paper was published in Adoption & Fostering, 18:4, 1994.

The Children Act 1989 starts from the premise that children are almost always best cared for at home. It advises that a comprehensive and accessible range of services should be made available to families in need to 'safeguard and promote the welfare of such children . . . and to promote their upbringing by their families' (DoH, 1989).

Bringing up children is sometimes a weighty responsibility. All parents need support and most, though not all, will find this in their families and from their friends. Support is indispensable for the continuity and integrity of family life. The Children Act emphasises the responsibility of the local authority towards *children in need,* children whose lives and opportunities may be restricted by their family circumstances so that they are unlikely to achieve what is possible for them, in health or development.

Short-term placements

In the accompanying Guidance and Regulations Vol 3, short-term placements are described as a service which may be used to 'take the "heat off" at intervals and prevent family breakdown' (HMSO, 1991 p 39). Short-term family-based breaks can offer a vital breathing space and the chance to strengthen and build on family coping strategies.

In a study for the Department of Health, together with David Hawley we looked at the use of short-term breaks for children in need. We considered the experiences of the key participants – children, parents and carers – and evaluated the outcome, both in its immediate consequences for children and parents and in its long-term effectiveness in preventing family breakdown. In this article, we look at the short-term carers themselves and ask:

- who they are;
- what motivates and sustains them in their work; and
- whether they are different from full-time carers.

We found a group of skilled and highly effective professional people who were deeply involved in and committed to their work.

Who are the carers?

Of the carers we talked to, half had experience of long-term placements as well as short-term arrangements, though only a few were currently doing both. The carers were mostly aged between 25 and 50 years old, which corresponded closely to the age of user-parents. The group included married, separated, divorced and single carers, and one single male carer. Three-quarters of the carer families had their own children living at home, and of the others about half had children who were now living independently.

Over a third of the carers worked outside the home, usually on a part-time basis. Where carers had a partner, it was generally the partner who was the main wage-earner, and these families are in the middle income bracket (£15,000 pa and upwards). Single carers tended to be less well off, with an income of less than £10,000 per year. Carer families were mostly home-owners, though one-fifth lived in local authority rented accommodation.

In many arrangements, carer and user families lived fairly close by, within 15 minutes' journey of one another. Despite the relative differences in their lifestyles, the common experiences of living in the same community seemed to strengthen the links between user and carer families. In general, homes were not uncomfortably close so that children had additional difficulty separating from home, but were near enough for easy travelling between the homes and for continuity of links with schools, nurseries, childminders and sometimes health services.

In terms of their ethnic backgrounds, the majority of carer families we talked to were white; four were African/Caribbean, and two were

Asian. This was, in fact, very similar to the range of ethnic origins in user families, with the exception of three families of mixed-race origin in the user family group. However, both carer and user study populations are under-representative of the minority ethnic groups in the areas in which they live, which raises questions about understanding and awareness of cultural diversity in the community, about access to information, and about advertising and the selection of carers.

Linking carer and user families

While carer families seemed sensitive to the racial, ethnic, religious and cultural dimensions of families using short-term care, often specific matching was not possible, since short-term carers with similar characteristics were not always available. In practice, though choice was inevitably limited for all user-families, there were no children who could not be placed with a carer family which was responsive to and understanding of their particular needs.

The selection and training of carers

While the personal resources of the carers, and to some extent the experiences of their own lives, contribute much to the making of "successful" short-term arrangements, the preparation of the carers through the selection process and through training and subsequent support cannot be underestimated. Selection will in the first place be restricted to those who know that there is a need for short-term carers, and this will in turn be affected by where and to whom this information is available. The short-term care schemes with which we worked recruited carers through both specific advertising for "part-time" care and through responses to advertising for mainstream carers. The scheme leaders confirmed that many people who responded were previously unaware of the need for short-term carers, or were uncertain of their potential as carers. The scheme leaders noted that carers from minority ethnic groups were few and far between and they are giving careful thought to how best to reach and recruit them. Most carers felt they had been well prepared for their task.

Formal preparation consisted typically of six to eight initial training sessions which included:

- basic child development and management of children;
- the difficulties and the needs of the children and parents with whom the carers would be working and the skills needed for this work;
- the role of the agency and the roles of staff within the agency and interagency work;
- the making and working of arrangements, and the practical aspects of the arrangements.

The carers felt that the most important elements of the training were the opportunity to learn about the children and their families, and the training received on coping with the emotional and behavioural difficulties of the children. The opportunity to talk to other carers and to a range of other professional workers was also valued. Those carers who felt that additional training would be helpful felt it was in these areas, and also in practical matters like first aid and the bureaucratic complexities of working with the agency!

The carers' support systems
In the long term, perhaps support is the most vital element in sustaining carers in their work. We talked to carers about both the informal and the formal aspects of their support system.

Carers were unanimous in acknowledging that the "background" support of their own family and their friends was indispensable. Carers also mentioned the mutual support that carers give each other, through their common understanding and experience of the carer's task. The knowledge that their concerns are fundamentally understood gives considerable credibility to the advice and support received from fellow carers. Interestingly, many carer-links were informally organised and maybe this is to some extent essential to their success. For new carers, the advice and guidance of experienced carers was an important strand in the support network. This was sometimes formalised in a "buddy" system between experienced and beginning carers. Regular support groups, sometimes combined with a training event, helped to build the support network between carers. In this context it may be worth considering the formal recognition and payment of experienced carers in training and support roles.

On the agency level, carers wanted – and mostly got – regular contact and 'good working relationships' with their family placement social worker. For the carers, good working relationships with social workers meant:

- reasonable accessibility either in person or by telephone, particularly at difficult times;
- that the social worker listened to the carer and thought about what the carer said; and
- that the social worker gave thoughtful and appropriate advice.

Honesty and reliability were the most esteemed qualities of the social worker, along with the sense of working in a professional partnership. In these working relationships, decisions made and actions taken were likely to enhance the work and the confidence of the carer.

The carer as professional worker
The carers felt that their work was valued by their social work colleagues although the sense of the carers' professional standing was, in some respects, ambiguous. Conditions of employment and levels of pay were obviously very different from other professionals, though most carers did not *expect* an equal footing in these respects. Carers were more clearly confident of their "professional" selves when involved in discussing, planning, reviewing and evaluating arrangements. Our discussions with parents and with social workers confirmed this perception.

Becoming a carer
We asked carers how they reached the decision to become short-term carers. Two reasons predominated: first, that it gives the possibility of combining the carer's role with other family or employment commit-ments and, secondly, that carers felt a particular commitment to support services for families. Over half the carers spoke of having gone through a period of disruption at some time in their own family lives, which they now felt contributed to their understanding of user-family difficulties. Some carers mentioned that they thought their own experience of family disruption, particularly if they were single parents, might make them

ineligible as foster cares and there was a strong feeling among carers that this concern may hold back other potential carers.

Over two-thirds of the short-term carers had extensive previous experience of working with children in the community, especially in childminding, and they were fairly comfortable and familiar with working with parents, which they regarded as a central and vital part of their task. Some aspects, then, of the carers' personal and professional experiences seemed to make them particularly sensitive to the needs and the difficulties of user-families.

Working with families

Short-term carers undoubtedly have a capacity for working *with* families but they nevertheless clearly saw the main focus of their work as the provision of care and support for the *child*.

Short-term breaks give time and space in which parents can think, relax and recharge in order to address immediate and longstanding family difficulties. Carers put considerable thought into creating this opportunity for parents. Parents in many of the arrangements commented on the friendliness and supportiveness of the carers, their generosity and their nonjudgemental approach – which seemed to restore their self-esteem and confidence as parents.

In the arrangements where carer and parents shared a sense of mutual acceptance and regard, the child seemed more able to enjoy and benefit from what the carer-home offered. Only three arrangements were ended prematurely, though five of the arrangements needed some renegotiation as a consequence of difficulties between the child and the carer-home, and three where parent and carer were in conflict. Ambivalence between parent and carer was the most striking feature of all these relationships – and consequent conflict in the child's relationship with the carer.

While carers saw the breaks as giving parents a breathing space, respite is important for the children too, and the carer expressed concern that the experience should add to the quality of children's lives. Carers want children to feel looked after in a friendly and kindly, but unobtrusive way; to have some individual attention; and, where necessary, to experience some relief from responsibility. Many carers commented that eldest children, in particular those living in families under stress, tended to have a "parental" or prematurely adult approach to life. The carers felt that these children benefited from feeling that someone else was helping with the adult responsibilities in their family, though this took some time to achieve.

Carers were frequently asked to help children with other aspects of stress-related behaviour – most often bedwetting, sleep problems or the moderation of aggressive behaviour. The children consistently told us that what *they* enjoyed most about their breaks was the kindness and attention of the carers and the opportunity simply to "play", suggesting that carers were accurate in their perception of the needs of children and in meeting them. The material benefits of the carer-homes were much less frequently mentioned.

Two-thirds of the carers felt that the arrangements lasted long enough to meet the specific needs of children and parents as given in the plan for the arrangements, and that they gave enough respite from the ongoing difficulties to allow parents to think about longer-term coping. Where carers were uncertain about the adequacy of the arrangements, this was not generally about the usefulness of the breaks but about the possibility of change in the family's circumstances. Carers felt that some families needed longer arrangements, or perhaps an "open-ended", or "as necessary" arrangement.

In general, very specific matching was not possible since the availability of respite carers did not allow it. In practice, the effect of this was to limit choice for the user-family, though great discrepancies rarely arose. This may, of course, be attributable to the demographic similarities between the user and carer families and lifestyles.

Understanding of user-families' circumstances
The research team asked carers about their beliefs and attitudes towards user-families, and it seems that carers understood the difficulties of the user-families to be significantly determined by their life circumstances:
- four-fifths of the carers thought that poverty was a major problem;
- two-thirds thought poor housing was a significant problem;
- two-thirds thought poor physical and mental health was a problem, as a consequence of poor living circumstances.

Though a third of carers considered that user-parents sometimes failed to act responsibly, over four-fifths thought they generally managed well in difficult circumstances. A typical comment was: 'There but for the grace of God go I.' These compassionate and pragmatic attitudes may in part be shaped by some of the carers' own life experiences, but seemed also to be amplified by the quality of the information given in training sessions and support groups, and the experience of working in partnership that had been possible between the carers, users and social workers.

Satisfaction with their work
Carers felt arrangements were successful if in practice the breaks "took the heat off" children and parents, if they were enjoyable for children, and if the time enabled parents to build longer-term coping strategies which they could begin to put into practice. Successful arrangements were clearly associated with thoughtful planning – where all participants felt they had been fully involved in the processes of consultation, exchange of information and discussion. Well over two-thirds of the carers felt they made an informed and significant contribution to the planning of the respite arrangements and that the arrangements were made in the context of a working, though not necessarily equal, partnership between agency, user and carer. The carers estimated that all but a few of the user-parents were constructively and *centrally* involved in developing the plan, though only a tenth saw the children for whom the plans were made being similarly involved. This concurred with the views of both users and social workers.

Two-thirds of the carers attended reviews on a regular basis and all carers were aware of their purpose. Of those who were not able to attend, the most frequently cited reasons were practical, the greatest difficulty being time. In general, carers felt well informed about the content and outcome of reviews.

The carers felt that short-term caring for children is often more difficult than longer-term or permanent arrangements, and that the principle difference between the two is the greater emphasis in short-term care on direct work with the whole family. Carers found this work both demanding and rewarding. Over two-thirds reported that working with parents is a significant aspect of their work. The greatest difficulties

in working closely with parents were experienced as:
- the level of dependency which could develop;
- the expression of hostility and ambivalence towards the carer family; and on occasions
- the way in which parents behaved towards their own children.

We learned from the user-parents that they felt considerable anxiety about sharing the care of their children. They also felt a good deal of ambivalence towards, and rather sad envy of, the carers who could offer this. These feelings and worries were not often voiced but when they were they tended to be expressed indirectly to carers.

For the carers, the reward of working with the children lay in building a relationship with them. Many observed the obvious enjoyment of the children during the breaks and remarked on the apparent benefits for the child's general development.

Carers and parents seldom met formally, apart from reviews, though nearly all met informally when parents brought and collected children from their visits. This was seen as a valuable time to catch up on news and share concerns. It also seems to confirm for the child the fact that the adults are working together, which is essential if the child is to benefit from the arrangements. On the whole this contact was valued highly by the carers, though sometimes it could be particularly difficult and stressful.

Conclusion

A picture emerges of short-term care as intensive, complex and demanding work which is perhaps underestimated from the wider professional perspective. Social workers, other than those directly involved, may view it as a low-key or interim option – on the way to or from something else, rather than of value in its own right. The skill and expertise of the carers and the outcome of their work is convincing testimony to the value of community based, supportive work with families in need.

References

Aldgate J, Pratt R and Duggan M, 'Using care away from home to prevent family breakdown', *Adoption and Fostering*, 13:2, pp 32–37, 1989.

Aldgate J, 'Respite Care for Children – an old remedy in a new package', in Marsh P and Triseliotis J (eds), *Prevention and Reunification in Child Care*, BAAF/Batsford, 1993.

Department of Health, *The Children Act 1989*, HMSO, 1989.

Department of Health, *An Introduction to the Children Act*, HMSO, 1989.

Department of Health, *The Children Act 1989, Guidance and Regulations, Volume 3 Family Placements*, HMSO, 1991.

Gibbons J (ed), *The Children Act and Family Support: Principles into practice*, HMSO, 1992.

NCVCCO, *The Children Act and Children's Needs: Make it the answer – not the problem*, In Need Implementation Group, 1991.

Sellick C, *Supporting Short-term Carers*, Avebury, 1994.

10 The tangled web of short-term foster care: unravelling the strands

Judith Stone is now a Standards and Development Officer for Durham Social Services, developing policies, strategic plans, and services to achieve good outcomes for children looked after and children in need, within social services and across multi-agency boundaries. She was awarded the degree of M.Phil in Social Policy in relation to the research study described in this article. She is a member of BAAF's Publications Advisory Group.

This paper was published in Adoption & Fostering, 15:3, 1991.

It might be said that, until now, short-term foster care has been the Cinderella of fostering, carrying out basic tasks but largely unproblematic, insignificant and nowhere near as noticeable or interesting as those two ugly sisters, long-term fostering (with its disturbing breakdowns) and the specialist fostering of teenagers (with its intractable emotional and behavioural problems). Consequently, short-term foster care has received little attention in research and writing on fostering. That is until recently, when one or two important studies have noted the importance of this area of child care provision (Berridge and Cleaver, 1987; Rowe *et al*, 1989) and the surprising lack of interest in it. As they suggest, there are some urgent reasons why this particular Cinderella should now be invited to the ball.

Why short-term fostering deserves attention
First, it has become a very significant area of child care work, not only in terms of the numbers of placements made (Triseliotis, 1990, estimates that approximately 40 to 50 per cent of children entering care experience short-term foster care) and the fact that short-term admissions now take up a large proportion of social workers' time (Rowe *et al*, 1989; Dartington Social Research Unit, 1984), but also because it is likely to

be a child's first experience of care. Research (Rowe and Lambert, 1973; Millham *et al*, 1986) has shown that these first few weeks in care are crucial to the development of a child's "career" in care.

Second, since the Review of Child Care Law (1985) there has been growing interest in the positive use of short-term care as a service for families in the prevention of long-term family breakdown, to provide them with relief in much the same way that respite care is now provided for the families of children with serious disabilities. Theoretically, the possibilities for using short-term foster care in this way will be much greater following the implementation of the Children Act 1989, which introduces, under Part III, the provision of 'accommodation as a service to families of children in need'.

Third, it is becoming clear that short-term foster care is no longer as unproblematic as it may have appeared. Berridge and Cleaver (1987) drew attention to the fact that a number of these placements are indeed "too successful", i.e. they go on much longer than expected. Rowe *et al* (1989) also found that approximately 15 per cent of foster placements in their study lasted longer than planned, and noted the worrying finding that there was 'a preponderance of younger children' among them.

The Newcastle study
Being aware of the problems and significance of short-term fostering led me to undertake, in 1988–89, a small-scale survey of short-term foster placements in Newcastle upon Tyne (Stone, 1990). The study investigated 183 placements of children with short-term foster carers over a twelve-month period. Detailed information on the placements, the children and their families, and the social work intervention was obtained by means of a questionnaire, with the aim of investigating differences between the children who need only a short placement and those who experience longer stays in "short-term" care.

The findings have been useful in helping to understand the current role of short-term fostering and how it may be effectively used to meet the needs of a range of different children. Fostering has developed over the years to meet the needs of successive child care policies (Packman, 1981). My study has shown that "short-term foster care" now embraces a whole range of different tasks, and has indeed become a tangled web. Disentangling the strands is important in planning flexible provision for children's needs under the Children Act.

Where short-term fostering works

The study confirmed that traditional end-of-year figures for children in care have placed a disproportionate emphasis on older children in long-term care who have been the focus of much of the research in this area. They have not adequately reflected the large number of short-term foster placements made each year lasting three months or less. Seventy per cent of all placements ended within three months. The substantial majority were of pre-school children and babies (63 per cent of the sample), and five to nine-year-olds (20 per cent of the sample) who returned home very quickly. Ninety-five per cent of the placements resulting in a return home ended in less than three months. Only a very small minority of the shorter placements of younger children were complicated by difficult emotional and behavioural problems.

In approximately four-fifths of the placements the children were in voluntary care, and these children accounted for 87 per cent of placements which lasted three months or less. Two-thirds of the children in voluntary care went home at the end of the placement. Children such as these will presumably form the bulk of children who are going to require "accommodation" under Part III of the Children Act 1989.

The study findings have provided important information about these children, their families and their location which is of particular value in planning these accommodation services. One important question is whether existing short-term foster homes are going to provide appropriate care for children under this part of the Act, or whether innovative services need to be devised, and special training provided.

Evidence of drift

However, if a short-term foster placement has not ended within three months, then it has a very high chance of lasting well over a year and in some cases much longer. This is consistent with the findings of those studies which have contributed to our knowledge of the "Leaving Care Curve" (Dartington Research Unit, 1984; Vernon and Fruin, 1986;

Thorpe, 1987). Only around 15 per cent of placements ended between three and twelve months, and a large proportion of these were pre-school children who were expressly being sought adoptive homes, whose placements last for anything up to nine months. The study confirmed the finding of Rowe *et al* (1989), that a significant minority of very young children remain in the limbo of short-term foster care for long periods, often for a large part of their formative years. Twenty-five of the 41 placements which had already lasted over six months and nine of the 12 placements that had already lasted over a year were of pre-school children. Many of these placements were still ongoing when the data was analysed and might in the end last considerably longer. Providing temporary care for these children, and meeting their emotional needs in the framework of uncertainty, is clearly a very skilled task for foster carers to perform.

Teenagers
The study also showed that short-term fostering is a form of child care provision which is used much less often for teenagers, and hardly at all for teenage boys. Of the total sample of 183 placements, only seven were of boys aged ten years and over, and only one of these was in fact more than ten years old. Where it is used for older teenagers (15 years and over) the placements have a tendency to break down quickly and prematurely. Typically they move on to another form of public care provision, and rarely return home. Where it is used for younger teenagers (ten–14-year-olds) the need is again unlikely to be for a genuinely short placement, possibly because only a third of this age group return home. If the placement is successful it is likely to continue for a considerable time. Millham *et al* (1986) also found that adolescents have a greater chance of remaining in care a long time even when they are admitted voluntarily. As residential homes currently provide a large number of short placements for teenagers in care and residential provision is being cut back, we need to be purposely expanding fostering provision for these teenagers to meet their needs more appropriately (Bullock, 1990).

Short-term fostering ill defined
In one local authority at least, and it is unlikely that Newcastle upon Tyne is unrepresentative in this, it is clear that short-term fostering has become an umbrella term for a whole range of fostering activities that have not been up to now clearly differentiated. This being the case we can see why it is so difficult to adequately define short-term fostering. In terms of defining length, it rapidly becomes like the proverbial piece of string. To quote again from Triseliotis (1990), who attempts a classification of types of foster care, short-term is defined as 'usually ranging from a few days to about three months' but with the proviso that it sometimes overlaps with intermediate fostering which is defined as 'lasting for an average of two years but longer periods are not ruled out'. The detail from my research study may well help here, because it has identified a clear distinction between the shorter and the longer temporary placements over a number of variables, and suggests it is possible to identify the type of temporary placement a child is likely to need at the time of placement. Significantly, the important variables in this are not characteristics of the children and their families, but relate to the circumstances surrounding the child's admission to care (particularly their legal status and whether or not they are on the Child Protection Register), and the need for placement, coupled with aspects of social work involvement, the reason and purpose of the placement, and the plan for the child. Also important was the birth mother's commitment to her child's return home. Statistical tests (chi-square) showed the prevalence of these variables to be significantly different in the longer and the shorter placements ($p = 0.05$, or 0.01 or less). These findings are consistent with those of the Dartington study over a two-year period of 450 children who entered care (Dartington Social Research Unit, 1984).

Legal status
The legal status of the child has in the past been linked to the length of a child's stay in care, voluntary routes being associated with shorter stays, and compulsory routes with longer stays (DHSS, 1985). The findings from Newcastle clearly suggest that this is not in itself entirely indicative of a child's placement needs, showing particularly that a significant number of young children in voluntary care experienced long

stays in short-term foster homes. Two-thirds of the children whose placements had already lasted over a year were in voluntary care at placement. This highlights some of the potential difficulties of providing "accommodation" on a voluntary basis: it cannot be assumed that all voluntary stays will be relatively short; nor can it be assumed that there will not be children in compulsory care who would benefit from relief care in a short-term foster home.

Reason for placement

The reason for the placement was significantly related to its length. In half of the placements the reason for the placement could be broadly described as "service to families" (following the categories used in a recent NCB study – Vernon and Fruin, 1986), and it is important to note that the overwhelming majority of these placements (90 per cent) ended within three months. A third of the placements were made when intervention was required to rescue a child from a harmful or potentially harmful situation, and only a half of these ended within three months. Overall the findings indicate that the children in short-term foster care are largely the victims of their family circumstances, and they suffer separation on the whole through no fault of their own; in no placement, even those of the teenagers, was the child's behaviour given as the main reason for the placement. The families of these children in short-term foster care were, however, beset with problems of all kinds. Surrounded as they were by problems of low income, housing difficulties, poor health and, with little support from extended family, often experiencing relationship difficulties of all kinds, it is hardly surprising that the care of

Table 1

Age of child at placement and length of placement

Age in years	0–4	5–9	10–14	15–17
3 months or less	69%	83%	48%	82%
4–6months	10%		10%	
7–12months	13%	14%	33%	18%
Over one year	8%	3%	10%	
	(n = 115)	(n = 36)	(n = 21)	(n = 11)

Table 2

Birth families' problems and length of placement

% of placements where family was experiencing problems with	0–3 months	4–6 months	7–12 months
Care of this child	58%	75%	90%
Care of other child	53%	50%	68%
Relationship with child	42%	50%	63%
Marital/relationship	87%	75%	79%
Extended family	80%	63%	90%
Housing	34%	63%	37%
Income	63%	63%	79%
Health	49%	25%	26%
Drugs/alcohol	20%	38%	5%
Other	38%	38%	53%

the children became too much for these parents, over half (54 per cent) of whom were single mothers. Rightly or wrongly, taking children into short-term foster care is largely being used as a solution for family problems. This inevitably begs the question of 'the appropriateness of care as a solution to the difficulties of families' (Fisher *et al*, 1986). It is reminiscent of the finding of the Report of the Inquiry into Child Abuse in Cleveland (HMSO, 1988) that the children had become "double victims".

It is, therefore, very important that accommodation is offered to the families of children in need as part of a range of services; services which could reduce the need for children to experience separation from their families. The Dartington study (1984) of factors affecting children's length of stay in care asks:

> . . . *if so many children are able to leave care quickly, the question might be raised as to whether any of them might have been kept out of care in the first place and whether or not there are differences in policies surrounding the admission of children to care in different local authorities and field social work teams.*

Further research needed

My research indeed showed that the different area teams in Newcastle upon Tyne used short-term foster care for different purposes and had very different levels of demand for this resource, even where they were serving very similar catchment areas. Further research is needed to show what factors, including the provision of other services, could work to diminish the need for short-term foster placements for young children.

However, while in the future it may be possible to reduce the need for short-term foster care, social workers in Newcastle upon Tyne considered it to be a very necessary service. It was in most cases specifically the resource they were seeking for the child and they would not have preferred an alternative solution, even if one were available. Many of the placements were categorised as emergencies, where removal of the child seemed the only viable option.

In conclusion, some clear patterns in the use of short-term foster care provision have emerged, strands which have become enmeshed together over time as child care policy has led to changes in practice and altered the way in which short-term foster care is used. It may now be possible to untangle the threads and, with the impetus of the Children Act 1989, provide a more flexible range of services more closely related to the needs of children and families.

A model for short-term foster care

I would like to suggest a model for short-term foster care, based on four different types of service provision. The first service would provide genuine short-term foster placements of up to three months for children aged nine years and under. This is all that is required in the majority of cases (70 per cent of all the placements in the study) but needs to be planned for these children in a way that supports and rebuilds families, and takes account of children's need for continuity of relationships with parents, siblings, wider family and community in order to reduce the stress of separation (Millham *et al*, 1986). It is particularly important to take into account the culture and creed of minority ethnic groups. However, one of the factors raised by the research in Newcastle upon Tyne was that this area fails to reflect the ethnic mix that is found in many other large cities and other parts of the country. It is significant that only a handful of the children in these 183 placements came from minority ethnic groups. This is clearly a dimension of short-term fostering that requires further study. The Children Act rightly draws attention to the importance of attending to the particular needs of children of different cultural heritage and my research should not be seen as implying that this is something to be ignored in planning short-term foster care provision.

The service would be seen largely as preventive, aiming to reduce the likelihood of long-term family breakdown. Under the philosophy of the Children Act 1989 it should be seen as a *positive* service, and not as indicative of failure, and these children will not need to be in care. In practice it will be important to remember that evidence suggests that separation can in itself lead to further disintegration rather than the strengthening of family relationships (Fisher *et al*, 1986). Certainly, Schaffer and Schaffer (1968) found that the need to receive children into care was an indicator of weak family relationships and they discouraged the use of public care for short periods because it exacerbated rather than relieved this problem. My study confirmed the findings of many others, that children who need short-term foster care are living in situations of difficulty, stress and conflict, and if nothing is done to solve the deeper problems, then the children are likely to experience further difficulties at a later date (Wolkind and Rutter, 1973). Many of the school-age children in my study, needing more protracted stays in care, had experienced their first reception into care when they were much younger.

The second service would make provision for children aged nine years and under requiring temporary foster care, but for whom an early return home is very unlikely, perhaps because of abuse, neglect or rejection, or because of conflicts and difficulties in making decisions about their future. These children are more likely to have emotional and behavioural problems, and are less likely to return home at the end of their stay in short-term care. While being aware of the difficulties of children in an emotional limbo, and that children and foster carers may become bonded and attached, it is important to recognise that there is a need for these intermediate length placements for children of this age group, provided they do not become simply an alternative to more careful planning. The role of the foster carers in these situations needs to be particularly flexible and skilled. It may be that many of these placements form a bridge to a permanent substitute family.

The third service would be part of a package providing care for teenagers. The study highlighted differences in the way short-term foster care is used for children of ten years and over, and that there is a need for the development of a special service for children of this age. As seen above, a much smaller proportion of children in this age group return home and few genuinely need a short placement. However, there is a need for placements that can be provided in an emergency, yet can be flexible in terms of length, and are provided by foster carers specifically trained to cope with the needs of teenagers.

The fourth service would be a pre-adoptive service for babies and pre-school children, where the clear objective of the placement is to seek an adoptive home for the child. Some of these children may have medical problems or disabilities.

Using a framework such as this could be of great value in defining more explicitly and accurately at the outset the aim and purpose of a child's short-term foster placement. This is important because early definitions of a child's or a family's "need" have been shown to affect subsequent developments, and may become "self-fulfilling prophecies" (Dartington Social Research Unit, 1984). This framework helps to make these definitions explicit, enabling aims and objectives to be communicated to children and birth parents, and misunderstandings and disagreements to be cleared up at the start. The framework will also help in the adequate preparation and training of foster carers, as their tasks are defined more clearly, and in planning and locating fostering resources.

Note
It continues to be the case that around half of all placements last for less than three months, and this article stressed the importance of short-term fostering in providing a range of family placements to meet the various needs of children entering the looked after system. It contains important messages:

- *for the recruitment and selection of carers, if the "Quality Protects" aim of increasing placement choice is to be achieved;*

- *about the need for planning to return children quickly to their families if they are not to linger in the looked after system.*

A full report of the research study and more comprehensive examination of the use of short-term foster care as a family support service are provided by the author in "Making Positive Moves: Developing short-term fostering services" (BAAF, 1995).

References

Berridge D and Cleaver H, *Foster Home Breakdown*, Blackwell, 1987.

Bullock R, 'The implications of recent child care research findings for foster care', *Adoption & Fostering*, 14:3, pp 43–5, 1990.

Dartington Social Research Unit, 'Predicting children's length of stay in care and the relevance of family links', *Research Reports*, 1984.

Department of Health and Social Security, *Social Work Decisions in Child Care*, HMSO, 1985.

Department of Health and Social Security, *Review of Child Care Law*, HMSO, 1985.

Fisher M, Marsh P and Phillips D with Sainsbury E, *In and Out of Care*, Batsford/BAAF, 1986.

HMSO, *Report of the Inquiry into Child Abuse in Cleveland in 1987*, HMSO, Cm. 412, 1988.

HMSO *The Children Act*, 1989.

Millham S, Bullock R, Hosie K and Haak M, *Lost in Care: The problems of maintaining links between children in care and their families*, Gower, 1986.

Packman J, *The Child's Generation*, (2nd edition), Blackwell/Robertson, 1981.

Rowe J and Lambert L, *Children Who Wait*, ABAA, 1973.

Rowe J, Hundleby M and Garnett L, *Child Care Now*, BAAF, 1989.

Schaffer H R and Schaffer E B, *Child Care and the Family*, Occasional Papers on Social Administration No 25, Bell, 1968.

Stone J, *Children in Care: The role of short-term fostering*, City of Newcastle upon Tyne Social Services, 1990.

Stone J, *Making Positive Moves: Developing Short-term fostering services*, BAAF, 1995.

Thorpe D, 'Career patterns in child care: implications for service', *British Journal of Social Work*, 18:2, 1987.

Triseliotis J, 'Foster care outcomes: a review of key research findings', *Adoption & Fostering*, pp 5–17, 13:3, 1989.

Triseliotis J, *Foster Care Outcomes*, Highlights No 96, National Children's Bureau, 1990.

Vernon J and Fruin D, *In Care: A study of social work decision-making*, National Children's Bureau, 1986.

Wolkind S and Rutter M, 'Children who have been in care – an epidemiological study', *Journal of Child Psychology and Psychiatry*, 14, pp 97–105, 1973.

Section IV
Foster siblings

Although the phrases "foster *family*" and "birth *family*" have been in common use for many years, nearly always the focus was on the adults and the placed child. Other children in the household or family were largely invisible in the literature. This appears to have been true for most practice too, with both birth sibling and foster sibling relationships seldom attended to, if at all (Kosonen, 1994). Yet from the earliest research into foster care it has been consistently shown that the risk of breakdown was heightened if a child was placed in a home where another of similar age was already present (Trasler, 1960; Wedge and Mantle, 1991). It is evident that the experience of a fostered child will be greatly affected by the response of other children in the home. Similarly, a positive response from their own children will encourage foster carers to persist, whereas unhappiness or resentment may at the very least evoke doubts about whether it is worthwhile.

However, in the 1990s more attention has been given to the relationship among birth siblings, whether living together or apart (Kosonen, 1998). In addition a small flurry of studies has examined the foster sibling relationship, primarily from the point of view of foster carers' children rather than that of the placed child.

A long-standing issue has concerned dilemmas about whether birth siblings separated from their parents should be placed apart or not. In general the presumption has been that it is better for children to stay together. In the short run, they can give each other comfort, understanding and continuity in their shared experience of being "in care" or accommodated. In the longer term, siblings can be vital support figures when parents and others are not willing or able to take on that role. Yet sometimes separation of siblings has been advocated and carried out. **Maclean (1991)** stated that most social workers supported keeping children together, but her survey of foster and residential care revealed a complex pattern in practice. In the English authority studied, only one-third of the children were placed with all their siblings. About a quarter had been deliberately placed separately. Among the reasons for this were:

- the relationship was thought to be seriously detrimental to one or both (e.g. one abuses the other);
- one or both wished to live separately;
- the types of placement needed were incompatible;
- there was a large age gap.

Admissions to care at different times and lack of available placements for sibling pairs or groups at the time of admission were other factors. More children in foster care were living with all their siblings than in residential care, though this may have been in part due to age differences.

Children's own views about their birth sibling relationships are not well represented in the literature (though see Kosonen, 1998; Mullender, forthcoming). Curiously, rather more is known from a child's perspective about foster sibling relationships. This mainly takes the viewpoint to foster carers' children. Interest was reinforced by a video, interestingly titled 'Children who foster' to emphasise the central and active rather than marginal and passive role of children in the foster family (Natural Children's Support Group, 1990).

Part (1993) reported on the views of 75 children from 43 foster families who had responded to a questionnaire she circulated. Most were positive about their family being a foster family, although a few were against and several more uncertain. They saw two main types of benefit for themselves: direct amusement and social awareness. Many enjoyed the company of playmates or of looking after younger children. Some older ones also recognised the value of being challenged by contact with less fortunate and more troubled individuals. The disadvantages were coping with difficult behaviour, the fostered child appearing to have more attention, less privacy, and the need to share possessions or a bedroom. Thus having a foster child join the home was often intrusive and sometimes disturbing, but this was usually more than compensated for by immediate or longer-term satisfactions.

Pugh (1996) provided further insights gained from interviews with nine foster carers' children, as well as four adult carers. There was general agreement that one consequence for 'children who foster' is that they become more aware of social problems. This was often confusing and distressing, but could lead to greater maturity and responsibility. Some were also upset when fostered children left. This raised questions of whether it is harmful or fair to subject younger children to these stresses. More positively, Pugh discussed the valuable contribution that foster carers' children can make to placements in several ways:
- providing a role model for the fostered child;
- acting as a bridge between the child and their parents;
- giving support to their parents.

Pugh concluded that careful consideration should be given to involving the children of prospective and approved foster carers at each stage and that their own support needs must be identified and responded to.

Ames (1996) examined the views of 23 foster siblings about placements of children with severe learning difficulties. Most made significant contributions to the care of the fostered child and were happy about their level of involvement, but one-quarter (mainly females) did report serious dissatisfactions. Resentment usually resulted when they experienced care responsibilities as excessive or the presence of the fostered child too intrusive. More agency contact was wanted by those who were unhappy about the arrangement and also by some satisfied young adults who would have liked more training in specific skills to enhance their own caring role. Others were not particularly bothered about being involved with planning and discussions.

All these papers emphasise the importance of adults recognising the importance of children to each other. Besides siblings, peers are another important source of help and sometimes of trouble. McAuley (1996) found that foster children in Northern Ireland greatly missed friends they were separated from. Studies of older children emphasise the significance of age-mates in young people's lives (Cleaver, 1996; Marsh, 1997/8).

11 Meeting the needs of sibling groups in care

Kirstie Maclean

Kirstie Maclean has been working in social work, mainly child care, since 1972. At the time this article was written she was Assistant Principal Officer (Adoption and Fostering) for Bradford Social Services Department. She subsequently worked as a Children Act Development Officer and a Principal Training Officer. She has been an Inspector for the Social Work Services Inspectorate at the Scottish Office since 1996.

This paper was published in Adoption & Fostering, 15:1, 1991.

There would probably be very little disagreement among social workers with the statement that sibling groups in care should be placed together unless there are strong and well-tested indications to the contrary. This assertion is strengthened by the Children Act 1989 which states that the local authority will:

> *... so far as is reasonably practicable and consistent with (the child's) welfare, secure that ... where the authority are also providing accommodation for a sibling of his, they are accommodated together.*

However, there is very little research evidence of how often we succeed in this aim, what the barriers are to its achievement or even more basic information as to the numbers and proportion of children in care who are part of a sibling group. In this article I intend to outline a small piece of research I undertook in my own local authority, Bradford; to compare the results with the limited research evidence which is available; and to outline some of the steps which I consider need to be taken if sibling groups are to be successfully placed together.

In Bradford we have a very comprehensive central index of children in care. Monthly reports are produced giving details of numbers, categories and trends, which are extremely useful in planning placement resources. Nevertheless, there is a major flaw in the index: all the children are treated as isolated individuals and no record is kept of their relationship to other children in care. As a section (the Children's Care Services section which provides residential, foster and adoptive placements), we were concerned that both the number and size of sibling groups in care appeared to be rising. We had made considerable efforts over the previous two years to expand and improve our resources for sibling groups but were not sure, except by subjective observation, as to how far we were succeeding in meeting their needs. We consequently decided to conduct a census on 16 June 1989 of all the sibling groups placed in our resources. Due to insufficient time, this exercise had its limitations – the major one was that I excluded traditional long-term and "de facto" (i.e. relative and friend) foster placements as these are not recruited and managed by our section. In the case of traditional long-term foster placements, they are no longer, as a matter of policy, recruited at all and they are, therefore, a dwindling resource.

The children surveyed were those placed in residential care, those with emergency carers (short-term placements, mainly for children aged 11+), those with link carers (short to medium term placements mainly for children aged ten and under), those with community carers (medium to long term placements for children aged 11+), and those in adoptive placements where the adoption order had not yet been made. Where any of these children had a sibling or siblings outside our resources (e.g. long-term fostering, home on trial, independent living) those children were included. Children who had been adopted out of care were also included where they had a sibling still in care. The number of children found to be part of a sibling group was 281 (approximately 270 actually in care).

Findings of the census

One-hundred-and-five children (37 per cent) were found to be placed with all their siblings: 78 children as part of a pair; six children as part of a trio; one foursome and one fivesome. Ninety-eight of these children were in foster or adoptive homes. One-hundred-and-seventy-six children (63 per cent) were found to be part of a sibling group that was split. However, this did not necessarily mean that all the siblings were placed separately. Sixty-three children (22 per cent) were placed with one or more siblings, of which 52 were placed in foster or adoptive homes.

One's first thought, when hearing that a sibling group is split, is to assume that placements are not available to keep them together. In fact, looking more closely at the circumstances of the 176 children where this occurred, the reasons were considerably more complex and on the whole more positive. The reasons can be broadly summarised as follows:

Children coming into care serially rather than simultaneously (36)
In a number of these cases the younger child or children had not even been born when their sibling(s) came into care – in fact, it is probably incorrect to even consider these children as siblings. It is obviously not feasible to make long-term plans for children on the basis that their siblings may come into care at a later date, particularly if they have not even been conceived!

Children where a positive choice has been made to split siblings (75)
I have used the term "positive choice" to cover a number of situations, some in reality more positive than others. Basically it means that the reason for the split being made was not the lack of a placement which could keep the sibling group together. A sample of the reasons are:
- It would be positively damaging to keep the children together, given their very pressing individual needs;
- To separate a teenage abuser from younger abused siblings;
- It proved possible to send some of the children home on trial;
- A child strongly requested to be separated from his or her siblings;
- The children had previously lived together but the eldest sibling had moved into independent accommodation;
- There was a very large age gap between siblings – the younger one needed adoption, whereas the older was preparing for independence.

Children where part of the sibling group had disrupted (25)
While in terms of keeping children together, this was not a positive outcome, all the children who remained in their original placement were well settled and some of the children whose placements had disrupted have subsequently settled well in their new placements.

Children who came into care simultaneously but where placements were not available together (30)
While none of these placements were "ideal", a number were not inappropriate, e.g. a sibling group of six placed in two trios, and a sibling group of four placed in two pairs. Two-thirds of these children were placed with at least one sibling and there were plans to reunite a few more over the subsequent few weeks.

Children who were split where the reasons were not known (10)
All of these children had been in care for many years, and it was not possible, without considerable additional work, to discover the reasons for the split.

While splitting may not be an ideal outcome, of the 176 children who were split, it was a positive choice in 75 cases (42 per cent) and probably unavoidable in 61 cases (35 per cent) where the children were either received into care at different times or where disruptions had occurred. Lack of an appropriate placement was the reason for splitting a maximum of 40 children (23 per cent) and even then 24 (14 per cent) were placed with one or more siblings. Only between ten and 16 children, four to six per cent of the total of 281 children who were part of a sibling group, were placed on their own, separated from their siblings through lack of an appropriate resource.

Comparison with research findings
The scarce research findings on the placement of sibling groups are conveniently summarised by Roy Parker in his chapter on Children's Residential Care in Volume 2 of the "Wagner Report". I am not aware of any subsequent relevant research and so I have drawn liberally and gratefully from his chapter.

Roy Parker outlines a number of caveats when comparing this research data and I discovered others when writing this article. The following should be borne in mind before jumping to firm conclusions that like is being compared with like.

Definition of sibling group

Parker points out that most researchers do not define what they mean by a sibling group. Do they, for instance, include half siblings and step-siblings? We fell into this trap ourselves as we did not define what we meant by a sibling group before we undertook our census. Retro-spectively our definition would be, 'Children who share at least one biological parent and who have lived in the same household as each other or who would have lived together had they not been received into care before their sibling(s) was/were born'.

The age of the children

Age is not mentioned in Parker's chapter and yet it is very likely to be a significant factor, both in terms of the proportion of children in care who are part of a sibling group and the likelihood of them being placed together. It was only possible, given the data available, to make rough and ready estimates of the proportions in Bradford, but it is likely that approximately 70–75 per cent of children aged ten and under in care have siblings in care, whereas only about 30–40 per cent of children aged 11+ are likely to have siblings in care. Our finding was that younger children were considerably more likely to be placed with their siblings than older children; 69 per cent of children aged ten and under with siblings in care were placed with one or more siblings, but only 46 per cent of children aged 11+ were placed with one or more siblings.

The length of time children have been in care and their progress over time

Some of the research studies took a cohort of children received into care over a relatively short period of time and followed their progress over the next one to two years. (The evidence as to whether the passage of time is more likely to lead to children being split or reunited is conflict-ing.) Others looked at children *in situ* on a certain date, regardless of length of time in care (as we did in Bradford) and others talked to young adults retrospectively about their experiences. It is probably dubious to make strict comparisons between these three groups.

Table 1

Bradford compared with the research

| | *Children placed with siblings* | | | |
| | *Parker's estimates* | | *Bradford figures* | |
Placement	One or more	Complete	One or more	Complete
Residential care	30–40%	N/K	51%	18%
Foster or adoptive care*	30–50%	23%	67%	44%

* I have included adoptive placements which are not mentioned in the research as we no longer place children aged below ten in long-term foster care.

Complete sibling group or part sibling group?

Most of the research talks of children placed 'with some or all of their siblings'. If, as research demonstrates, children suffer feelings of loss and isolation when separated from their siblings, then placement with some as opposed to all of their siblings, may only be a second best solution. The only study which differentiated found that while 53 per cent of children in foster care, who had siblings in care, were placed with at least one sibling, only 23 per cent were placed as a complete sibling group.

Age of data

Most of the research looked at by Parker took place between 1981 and 1985 and some dated back as far as the 1960s. Consequently, it is not possible to claim that Bradford is doing better or worse than local authorities nationally now – only that we are doing better or worse than local authorities were some years ago. It could be that placement philosophy and practice nationally have changed over the intervening period and that more siblings are now kept together. Alternatively, if the number or size of sibling groups coming into care has increased, it may mean that more are separated.

Size of sibling group

Parker mentions this as a significant factor, especially when considering whether residential care is better able to meet the needs of sibling groups than foster care, and regrets that it is not mentioned in the research studies. There were 17 large (4+) sibling groups in our Bradford census. Of these 11 have come into care in the last two years and in a further four, admitted serially, some of the children have come into care in the last two years. This would seem to indicate the possibility of a trend towards the admission of large sibling groups. Only two of these 17 groups are placed totally together. Of the other 70 children, 41 are placed with at least one sibling. The rate of placement with one or more siblings for large sibling groups (63 per cent) is marginally higher than the rate for all sibling groups (59 per cent), but, probably not surprisingly, the rate of complete large sibling groups kept together (11 per cent) is considerably lower than the rate for all sibling groups (37 per cent). We hope, in Bradford, that we will never again have to face the situation which occurred last year when a sibling group of 17 were made Wards of Court. Luckily 14 of them were sent home on trial immediately!

Bradford compared with the research

Bearing in mind the above caveats, the following comparisons can be made. It would appear that we can be cautiously optimistic that our strategies for keeping sibling groups together are proving successful. These have included the alteration of an assessment centre into a community home for large sibling groups (often including placement with parents), the expansion of fee-paid fostering to foster carers for younger children, the provision of larger houses/vehicles for adopters of large sibling groups, and the use of residential workers and foster carers to provide peripatetic support to homes/carers with large sibling groups.

The figures for residential care need to be viewed very cautiously, as only a small number of children (39) are involved and therefore the admission or discharge of a large sibling group could significantly alter the percentages. Nevertheless, the worst figure of all which Roy Parker came up with was that only 12 per cent of children placed in residential care in Yorkshire and Humberside, who had siblings in care, were placed with one or more of the siblings.

Parker set out with the hypothesis that residential care was more likely to be used to keep sibling groups together than foster care, but found that this was disproved in that both seemed equally fairly poor at keeping sibling groups together. Bradford not only tends to disprove the hypothesis but to reverse it, i.e. foster care seems considerably more likely than residential care to be used to keep sibling groups together. Parker wondered whether residential care was more likely to be used to keep large sibling groups together, but again our evidence tends to disprove this. In the 12 cases where three or more children were placed together, nine were in foster or adoptive care (1×5, 1×4, 7×3) but only three in residential care (1×4 and 2×3). Parker points out that in order to keep large sibling groups together a high vacancy level needs to be maintained in at least some homes. The same thing applies equally in fostering and adoption. In Bradford we are currently operating on extremely low vacancy levels. This has led to a situation where almost half of our link carers who are able to take sibling groups have children in placement from more than one family, thus blocking a potential resource for a sibling group. If we could maintain a higher vacancy level, then it should be entirely possible to place a higher percentage of children with their siblings. (NB Since this article was written, our number of children in care has risen and our number of vacancies is even lower. It would be interesting to undertake a census again to see if our ability to place siblings together has reduced in consequence.)

Observations and conclusions

A prerequisite for considering whether we are meeting the needs of sibling groups is detailed information and data. How many children in care are part of a sibling group? What size are these sibling groups? Are the numbers or size increasing? Are they coming into care serially or simultaneously? How many are placed together? If they are not placed together, is this due to lack of appropriate placements? Research is needed urgently, both at a national and local level, and it is vital that local authorities begin to record sibling relationships as part of their central records so that placement resources can be accurately planned.

However, information is only the start. If, as seems likely, many sibling groups are split for lack of appropriate placements, their needs and the resource implications will need to be argued strongly with policy-makers and politicians. It is likely that specialist residential homes, fostering fees, material support in the form of larger houses, vehicles, washing machines, etc., practical support in the form of peripatetic workers/carers, home helps, respite care, etc., and higher vacancy levels, will be needed if the aim that, 'sibling groups in care should be placed together unless there are well tested indications to the contrary' is to be achieved. It is undoubtedly more expensive to keep sibling groups together than to split them, but the alternative cost is the emotional loss and damage that these children will suffer through separation in care. It also seems likely that splitting siblings must reduce the chances of rehabilitation. Are we prepared to continue countenancing that cost?

Note

While it is now ten years since the small research project described in this article was undertaken, the plea in the final paragraphs for further research and recording of information concerning siblings who are looked after, and for more resources to be provided to keep sibling groups together are still highly relevant. For most of us, our sibling relationships are the longest relationships we will have in our lives. It is very important that looked after children are not deprived of this source of continuity and support.

References

Berridge D and Cleaver H, *Foster Home Breakdown*, Blackwell, 1987.

DHSS, *Inspection of Community Homes*, 1985.

Maclean K, 'Towards a fee-paid fostering service', *Adoption & Fostering*, 13:3, pp 25–28, 1989.

Sinclair I (ed), *Residential Care – The research reviewed*, commissioned by the Wagner Review of Residential Care, HMSO, 1988.

The Children Act 1989, section 23 (7).

12 Fostering as seen by the carers' children

Diana Part

Diana Part has worked with children and their families over many years. Social work in adult and child and adolescent psychiatry was followed by time as a reviewing officer in Tayside region. Here she worked alongside families whose children or young people were living away from home and the carers of those children. Time as Assistant Principal Officer in Child Protection and later in Foster Care led to her present post as Programme Director for the B.A. in Social Work at Northern College Dundee, and, in a voluntary capacity, as Chair of Family Mediation, Tayside.

This paper was published in Adoption & Fostering, 17:1, 1993.

There is little in social work or foster care literature that looks at the part the carers' birth children can and do play in families that foster. They live with the fostered children, frequently share their bedrooms with them, can become close and grieve when they leave, or can dislike and resent them.

The evidence so far
The only reference given to the children of the foster carers in the practical handbook, *Foster Care: A guide to practice* (1976) was that they 'can sometimes be included in the discussions'.

Prosser investigated Wilkes' 1974 American study which examined 'the impact of fostering on the foster family'. This study found that minor upsets in the family's own children were common following the introduction of foster children to their home. Although these were generally transitory, unless such behaviour was understood and adjustments made in family functioning, the children could develop or display more maladaptive behaviour. Resentful feelings could be generated if the foster child's stay was longer than anticipated. Wilkes also found that hesitancy and discrepancies in the treatment of the fostered and the birth children's behaviour could lead to trouble. The children as well as the adults of the family needed to understand what was likely to happen when a foster child came.

Brown looked at support groups for foster families and how foster parents talked about the impact of foster children on their own children. She found that new carers wanted to hear and discuss more about the effects on families. The meetings she attended were all orientated to the foster children and not towards the families' birth children. This demonstrated the practice found in much of the literature that the foster carers' children were only discussed in regard to the fostered children, and the children themselves were not seen as a separate and important part of the dynamic.

The more recent HMSO publication, *Patterns and Outcomes in Child Placement* (1991), did call for more attention to be given to the needs and feelings of birth children. It referred to Thoburn's follow-up studies of older child adoptions and to an unpublished pilot study by Von Arnim (1988) which looked at the effect on children aged between eight and 12 years whose parents fostered adolescents. Both studies showed that children gained a great deal but also paid a price, especially at certain stages of their development. Both felt that the birth children's problems could cause a fostered child's placement to fail.

The video *Children who Foster* was made by and for children who foster. This followed recognition in one social services department, after a letter from two of the children of their carers, that the children of carers have an important role to play. It was realised that they need to know a certain amount about the children who are living with them, both to help and protect themselves and the children, particularly if the latter have or might have been abused.

The video showed a group of perceptive young people, aware both of their own feelings of displacement and of the needs of the children who came to their homes. There was an absence of the judgemental attitudes that mid-teenagers can display, but a feeling of being overwhelmed by the problems the children brought with them.

In my recent study, children of foster carers in a Scottish region were asked by questionnaire what they felt about being part of a foster family.

This was part of a larger piece of research by postal questionnaire in which all temporary carers in the region were asked to participate. A separate section was enclosed as a loose sheet for each of the children of the carers to complete if they wished.

They were asked their age, if they were a girl or a boy, if they liked their family being a foster family and what were the best and worst things about having a foster child or children in their home. They were invited to write a letter or draw a picture if they wished. Seventy-five children from 43 foster families replied, a response rate of 78 per cent of families with children living at home. The children ranged in age from three to 24 years.

The children who responded

Eighty per cent (60) of the children liked fostering. Only five per cent (four) were clear that they did not like their family being a foster family, and 15 per cent (11) were uncertain or said they 'sometimes' liked it. So a fifth were not certain that fostering was a good thing.

A problem for some of the parents was access visits being held in their homes. This did not appear to affect their children – most of the children who were unsure about fostering did not have birth parents coming to their home for access visits. Five children did, but it did not seem to impinge on them in the same way as it affected their parents. None of the children, whether they liked fostering or not, mentioned birth parents in their homes as one of the worst things about fostering.

Many replies about the worst aspects of fostering showed that although the majority liked fostering, it was often difficult and upsetting for them.

The best about fostering

The children were asked what 'The best things about having a foster child or children in our home are'. This enabled them to choose what they felt was the best about fostering for them and not have to select from a list. Their replies fell into three main categories:

- companionship;
- looking after babies and young children;
- the challenge of helping.

Companionship

For 43 per cent of the children the best thing about having a foster child in their home was the company:

> *There is someone to play games with and read to, and I can be the teacher when we play schoolies.* (Girl, aged 7)

> *They are always funny, and they make me laugh. I like having lots of brothers and sisters because they keep me company.* (Girl, only child, aged 13)

> *It is like having a younger brother or sister. I like being with younger children. I feel sorry for them and I want to help them as much as I can.* (Girl, aged 14)

These replies were mainly from children in families which fostered young children. Few recorded company as the best thing about fostering if they were fostering teenagers.

Looking after babies and young children

A quarter (24 per cent) of the children chose 'looking after babies and young children' as the best thing about fostering for them:

> *Being able to give them the things that they appreciate because they have never had them before, which other kids their age would take for granted.* (Girl, aged 17)

> *The best thing is when we get babies because I like playing with them.* (Boy, aged 12)

The challenge

Fifteen per cent of the children said that the best thing about fostering was the challenge and the need to help. These tended to be from the older boys:

> *You realise how lucky you are to live in a caring family, and you get to show the kids another side to life.* (Boy, aged 20)

> *It's good to know that you are giving a child who has had problems at home or with their family a good home and a caring family.* (Girl, aged 17)

I believe I am more socially aware than children who do not foster. Partially through the experiences of fostering I believe I have matured and become more responsible. (Boy, aged 15)

There were several other responses which could not be categorised: a 14-year-old girl wrote that 'everything' was good about fostering (while her brother was not happy as he had to share a room with the fostered child). A 15-year-old girl who 'sometimes' liked her family being a foster family said that the best thing for her was that it 'keeps Mum at home but still working and earning'.

Fifteen per cent of the children did not record anything for the "best things", but did write about the bad times. It is interesting to speculate whether some children, knowing that their parents could read their replies when they were handed back, were conscious of their parents' opinions and feelings and wrote accordingly. One mother wrote on her children's behalf that although neither of them had recorded any "best things" they both enjoyed having children in the home.

The worst about fostering
The worst things about being a foster family fell into three main categories:
- difficult and annoying behaviour, and stealing;
- the attention given to the foster children;
- the lack of privacy.

Difficult behaviour
For a quarter (24 per cent) of the children the worst thing about having foster children in the house was their difficult behaviour:

When they're narky, when they're selfish, when they moan a lot. (Girl, aged 11)

She constantly stole from us when we felt we were trying so hard to get her to like us and for us to like and accept her. (Male, aged 21)

They always talk and are loud all of the time. I can't have a decent conversation with any of them because they are all under ten . . . they annoy me when I'm in a hurry to go out. (Girl, aged 15)

Attention given to the foster child
Closely following, and related to the difficult behaviour, was the attention received by the foster children, which 20 per cent felt to be the worst aspect:

I think that the foster child gets too much pocket money. I don't have as many designer clothes as them. I don't like their friends coming to the house as I don't always get mine in. (Boy, aged 10)

Foster child gets too much attention mostly when they are bad. Also they get away with things that I would never be allowed to do. They get things too easy from the social workers. I don't get someone to come and take me out for tea, or ten-pin bowling paid for by the social worker. (Girl, aged 15)

Some of the children are a real pressure to look after, e.g. disruptive, badly behaved. Sometimes, partly due to fostering I believe my young-est brother does not get the same amount of attention as myself and my other brother received at his age due to having the foster child. (Boy, aged 15)

Lack of privacy and sharing
Twenty-three per cent of the young people regretted the lack of privacy and having to share with the fostered children:

You don't have the same privacy. (Girl, aged 19)

Privacy trying to keep them out of my room and leave my things alone. (Boy, aged 15)

Associated with the lack of privacy was the difficulty of sharing a room, and sharing the foster child with their parents:

The only thing I would like is to have my own room and I know my sister would like this as well. (Girl, aged 15)

Sometimes I would like to get out by myself with my mum because the others go out with their mums/social workers. (Girl, aged 13)

Sometimes I wish that it was just our own family together again with no-one else. (Girl, aged 12)

Five per cent of the children said that the foster children crying was the worst thing about fostering for them:

They cry all the time. (Girl, aged 8)

Five per cent of the children said that the foster children leaving was the worst for them:

When they go away it makes me upset. (Girl, aged 14)

When we are fostering someone that I like they have to go to somebody else. (Girl, aged 10)

Three per cent of the young people said that:

The babysitting is sometimes a pain in the neck and also the constant chatter and noise when watching something on TV, etc. But that's part of being in a foster family and the pros balance with the cons. (Girl, aged 17)

Seventeen per cent of the children said there was nothing that was the worst thing for them.

It was apparent that some found it difficult when the foster child seemed to get a great deal of attention. This was mainly with reference to fostered teenagers and their behaviour both in the home and outside. Some of the replies which spoke of practical issues may have veiled less tangible feelings of resentment and displacement which are not so easy to put into words. Only a couple of children stated that they wanted more of their parents' time. One was a child who had been fostered and then adopted by a family who continued fostering. There was a thread of wistfulness that life was never as it had been before fostering.

One of the positives that was apparent was the altruism and understanding that some of the children showed. This confirmed the feelings presented in the *Children who Foster* video. The sample examined in this study, while not without some angry and resentful youngsters unsympathetic to the difficulties of the fostered young people, also showed a high level of understanding and tolerance.

The young people who did not like fostering
There were four young people, two girls and two boys, who stated that they did not like their families being foster families. The parents were asked what they felt the effect of fostering on their children had been. One said the effect had been good, two said they thought it had sometimes been bad, and one felt fostering had had a bad effect on their teenage daughter and their other children.

Case A
The first, a teenage girl, had brothers and sisters who "mostly" enjoyed fostering. A harrowing few months following a placement breakdown had led all of them to comment:
> *She stole constantly from us . . .*

> *She sometimes called me names and it made me cry.*

> *It put a strain on the whole family which resulted in us being angry and easily annoyed with each other. What I could do in my own home was limited by the presence of the foster child and also my private possessions were at risk. I could not trust her. . .*

However, all but the one girl also gave positive comments about the experience:
> *The challenge of trying to integrate a person into family life who isn't used to coping within a family situation . . .*

> *It gives you a sense of being able to help people worse off than you.*

> *Playing board games with her was good.*

This placement had turned into a nightmare for all concerned; the father said that he couldn't wait to get the fostered teenager out and commented elsewhere in the questionnaire, 'I found the experience physically, emotionally and almost spiritually draining'. Three of five children of that family recorded that they liked being part of a foster family, however. This demonstrates how children's experiences can be different from that of their parents. In stressful situations children can still have positive experiences, perhaps by being sheltered by their parents.

171

Case B

The second child who did not like being part of a foster family was an 11-year-old girl in a family that fostered teenagers. Her older sister 'sometimes' liked fostering. The girls were able to see beyond the immediate circumstances:

It is good to learn that other kids don't get loved or cared for in the same way as we do.

I get extra pocket money for putting up with them.

There were aspects of being a foster family they were not happy with involving their parents, the foster children, and social workers, including:

I don't usually get on with them which isn't much fun having someone in your home that you don't like.

I don't like when my mum and dad argue about them.

Some of the children don't deserve to have kind, loving families because they just kick them in the teeth when they try to help.

The social workers stay so long that by the time they leave our tea is overcooked. If they came on time maybe they wouldn't leave so late.

Case C

The third person disagreed with his sister who liked 'everything' about fostering, whereas he, a 17-year-old, did 'not really' like fostering. He recorded no best things but 'sharing a room', which he felt was the worst facet of fostering, may well explain much of the difference in attitude between the siblings.

Case D

The final young person who did not like fostering was a 16-year-old boy. The preceding families all fostered teenagers. His family fostered babies and young children. His 14-year-old sister liked being part of a foster family and commented:

You get satisfaction when you see the child/children happy and see how you have given them a good start in life.

However, her brother did 'not really' like fostering as it gave 'a lot of extra work for Mum'.

Conclusions

The overall impression is that most children and young people enjoy, or at most tolerate, being part of a foster family. It can give them a greater appreciation of their own family, and an awareness of the difficulties that some of their peers have to live with. Several commented on the greater maturity they thought they had because of the experiences the family had with fostering. They can undoubtedly gain a great deal.

Fostering is not without difficulties for the birth children of the foster families, however, and they can pay a price. Some of the children had to share bedrooms and missed their privacy. Possessions were tampered with, if not broken or stolen.

The conclusion seems to be that fostering is difficult, that fostered children can be annoying and intrusive, and that the nuclear family is never the same again. Despite this, almost all the children of the foster carers said that they enjoyed being part of a family that fostered. Their views are important and should be heeded – to help families continue through and after the difficult times.

Note

The Children Act (Scotland) 1995 introduced new terminology which was not in use when this paper was written and is therefore not reflected here. Whether "fostered" or "accommodated" and having "access" or "contact" with the families of the children and young people, however, the issues remain the same. Living and sharing lives with other people's children is often hard, marks out the carers' children as different from their peers and changes the dynamics in their family. Social workers are still seen as being late, disrupting their routine and making it too easy for the accommodated young people while not considering the family of the carers. Plus ça change . . .

References

Brown J, 'Foster parent support group in a rural area', in Triseliotis J (ed), *Groupwork in Adoption and Foster Care*, BAAF/Batsford, 1988.

Department of Health, *Patterns and Outcomes in Child Placement*, HMSO, 1991.

Natural Children's Support Group, *Children who Foster*, (video) Vera Publications, Leeds, 1990.

Prosser H, *Perspectives on Foster Care*, NFER Publishing Company, 1978.

Social Work Services Group, *Foster Care – A guide to practice*, HMSO, 1976.

13 Seen but not heard? Addressing the needs of children who foster

Gill Pugh

Gill Pugh is a Team Leader in the After Care section at Barnardo's (Barkingside). She previously worked as a homefinder with Cambridgeshire Social Services.

This paper was published by Adoption & Fostering, 19:1, 1996.

As a homefinder in a local authority social services department, I had long suspected that the biological children of foster carers held the power to make or break a placement. Yet all too often it seemed that only lip-service was paid to recognising the role of this group of young people.

In 1994, as part of an Advanced Certificate in Social Work course at the University of East Anglia, I took the opportunity to undertake a small research project into the role and needs of these "children who foster". In sharing the findings of this study, I hope to lift the curtain on the impact of being part of a family who fosters; to show the skills which many young people are quietly contributing to the fostering process, and to explore the strains upon them, which often go unnoticed.

I drew on my experience as a homefinder over the past eight years, recruiting, training, supporting and reviewing mainly time-limited foster carers. But for the study I also conducted interviews with nine foster carers' children and four adult foster carers from different families across Cambridgeshire, whom I selected to reflect a range of ages, gender and ethnic backgrounds. All had experienced at least three different time-limited fostering placements. Some families additionally had experience of long-term fostering or adoption. Due to limits on my time I was not attempting to achieve a representative sample, but hoped to reflect a variety of views across the spectrum of families who foster. I also sought the views of social workers from one Area Team in relation to children on their caseloads who were then or previously had been in foster care.

In all the interviews I sought views on the preparation for fostering of children in prospective foster families; young people's likes and dislikes about fostering; what both parents and children felt were the gains and losses for carers' children from fostering, and what role the host children actually played in relation to fostered children. I also asked about support available to carers' children, and explored how this might be improved.

Findings
Recruitment and preparation of new foster families

> *Our homefinder did ask the children what they'd like . . . They wouldn't understand what it's all about until you have actually got a child here . . . All Keith knew was he was going to have someone his age to play on the computer with him.* (Foster mother)

This somewhat superficial approach to "involving" children in the preparation process seems fairly typical of many families' experiences. One family in the sample had been shown the *Children who Foster* video. However, the foster mother felt that for her junior-school-age children 'it was a bit over their heads'.

Two of the foster carers and one of the young people felt that it was 'down to parents to pass on the information in a controlled way', and all the parents saw themselves as having a significant share of the responsibility for educating their own children about fostering. However, they acknowledged the difficulties in conveying a realistic picture, not least because in the initial stages they were still learning themselves. One adult daughter said:

> *I felt I had enough knowledge from what I'd been told by mum and dad . . . . I think that [a course] would be giving kids too much responsibility. I don't think that's fair.* (P, aged 22)

But other young people wished they had been given more information, both at the preparation stage and afterwards, as long as it was 'aimed at young people' and 'nothing too heavy':

> *You can knock people out with too much information.* (Son, aged 20)

The value of meeting other young people was raised by one foster mother:

It would have been nice for them to have met some other children who foster, so they could say what it's like, do you get ones who are a pain in the neck?, etc.

Preparation courses or sessions specifically for foster carers' children appear to be the exception rather than the rule in this country, although the NFCA's training programme 'Choosing to Foster' does go some way towards redressing the balance.

In Cambridgeshire some homefinders have introduced a children's session into their 'Prepare to Care' course for new and prospective foster carers, and have accepted older teenagers as participants in the adults' course. Both were felt to have been helpful by the participants, though this has yet to become standard practice.

Young people's likes and dislikes about fostering
The findings from my study showed many similarities with a study by Diana Part of 75 children from 43 foster families in one Scottish region (1993). Eighty per cent of the children who responded to Part's question-naire indicated that they 'liked fostering', but a fifth either did not or were not certain that fostering was a good thing.

The aspects of fostering which the children and young people I interviewed said they most liked and disliked fell into broadly the same categories as those identified by Part. They most enjoyed:
- companionship;
- looking after babies/young children;
- feeling good about being able to help others and 'make a difference'.

Their chief dislikes could be summarised as:
- sharing – especially bedrooms, possessions and parental attention;
- coping with difficult behaviour, including the tensions of living with sexually abused children;
- coping with social workers/the agency, by whom they want to be noticed and feel valued.

Gains and losses

During my interviews I was also able to explore the perspectives of carers (two of whom were parents of children I interviewed). When asked how they felt their children had benefited or suffered from being part of a fostering family, one foster mother with 15 years' fostering experience replied starkly:

> I don't think they have benefited. They had to learn at a very early age that there was an awful world out there and kids got abused.

Loss of innocence

This was mentioned in different ways by almost all the interviewees adults and children. Undoubtedly children who foster are exposed very much more than most of their peers to areas of life which many parents would like to protect their children from: violence, sexual abuse, drug abuse, suicide, etc. There is remarkably little research into the effects of sharing day-to-day family life with a child who has undergone these kind of profoundly disturbing experiences.

Most foster carers, however, saw a positive aspect to this, for instance remarking that 'They're more worldly wise.' They pointed out the gains they felt their children experienced from comparing their own family life with others less fortunate: 'They realise they're not as hard done by as they thought they were!'

Interestingly, nearly all the young people, especially the older ones, saw one of the most striking effects upon them of fostering as 'becoming more open-minded'. Mostly this was seen as a gain: 'It's made us much more caring', 'I don't stereotype people so much . . .' and so on. But one 18-year-old went on to say:

> Some of the things you hear would absolutely shock my friends; you just wouldn't be able to say it in front of them. To begin with I used to be quite easy to shock but now, it's quite sick really, you hear things and joke about it. It's not funny but it's a way of coping.

Emotional maturity

All the young people I spoke to displayed a striking concern for others and awareness of complex emotional issues beyond their years. Two teenage daughters said fostering had 'given me more sense of responsibility' . . . 'it makes you appreciate your family more'. However, I also heard the anxieties of young people coping with high exposure to pain and loss; trying to be tolerant and understanding in the face of considerable provocation and stress; finding it hard to accept differing expectations of behaviour and discipline within the family, and feeling guilty for their negative feelings.

The following comments come from teenage girls (the eldest siblings in their families):

. . . makes me feel guilty . . . confused . . . you're not sure whether you're supposed to be treating them like a normal brother or sister or wrapping them up in cotton wool, treating them differently . . . (D, aged 20)

It makes me feel quite sad. Some of the things you hear are horrendous. No child should ever have to go through things like that. That's quite a weight to carry around really. (P, aged 22)

These comments reflect the way in which fostering impacts differently according to age, gender and cultural factors. Older siblings, and especially girls, were more likely to feel confused about whether they were peers or parent figures, whereas younger children were more egocentric and less able, or less willing, to put things in a wider perspective.

From this sort of evidence one has to question whether children who foster are at risk of growing up prematurely, or having certain aspects of their development distorted. Indeed, could they be suffering emotional harm?

Security v insecurity
Research by Kaplan (1988) into the psychological impact on children who foster suggested that mothers may presume greater maturity in their children than actually exists. Most of the children in her US study rejected their parents' explanations of children coming into foster care through "sickness" or temporary difficulty and believed that such children were unloved or had been "bad". This led to high levels of "separation anxiety", particularly in the younger children who foster,

who feared they might themselves be abandoned if they were naughty.

My own hypotheses were that children who foster were likely to be affected to some extent by problems with attachment and loss, especially with the repeated comings and goings of short-term foster care. It was beyond the scope of this study to investigate this area in any depth, but the following comments illustrated this:

P did think she was moving on when she was about three. She thought it was normal that you came and stayed a while and then you left . . . We told her off one day and she thought that was it. We had to explain that she was stuck with us! (Foster carer)

A family who fostered a child from two to eleven said, before he was rehabilitated back home, that 'It was like a bereavement.'

Family relationships

Satir (1967) describes the family as a 'mobile': whenever a member leaves or a new one joins it produces a shift in relationships, power and alignments among the whole family. Nowhere is this more striking than in the foster family. Foster carers' birth children experience not only a succession of new members with very differing histories which they bring with them, but often have to cope with changes in respect of their status as eldest or youngest child.

Caring for a large sibling group has a particularly dramatic impact on the existing family dynamics; one family interviewed had adopted a sibling group of five children! Fortunately the birth children in this case felt that the impact on their own family relationships had generally been very positive:

You depend on each other so much more. We're so much closer as a family than we would have been otherwise. (C, aged 14)

Parent–child relationships in foster families were influenced by factors previously mentioned: on the one hand, children sometimes felt they were deprived of parental attention but on the other hand, they tended to become more self-reliant, and were often protective – almost parental – towards their parents in the face of pressures from outside. A grown-up daughter admitted:

*Many days I thought what about me? I'm here as well. What can I do
to get some attention?*

Yet the same girl told me earlier:
I was there for mum if she needed a shoulder to cry on now and then!
(P, aged 22)

Despite the mixed feelings of carers about the effects of fostering upon
their own children, I found them broadly optimistic overall (they were,
after all, still fostering) and most tended to refute any suggestion that
stresses impacting on their children had led to the disruption of placements. This response did not entirely correspond to the opinions
expressed by social workers concerning the cases they were dealing with.

The social workers' views

Although this was only a snapshot of opinions, I was impressed by the
level of attention and commitment shown to the carers' children by the
workers I questioned, whose primary focus was the child being looked
after. Two social workers were jointly involved with a family fostering
an attachment disordered ten-year-old. The foster family had two children of the same sex and close in age to the foster child. The workers
made a point of having periodic meetings with the carers' children alone
(with the carers' approval) in order to recognise the stresses upon them
and offer appropriate support. They also focused on the foster child's
impact upon his foster brothers as a therapeutic tool towards helping the
foster child to modify his social behaviour. In this way, although one
might have felt that the initial matching of child to foster family went
against research wisdom, the presence of the carers' own children was
seen to be of significant benefit to the foster child.

Several instances were cited by other social workers of placements
which they felt had either disrupted or been severely stressed due to factors
associated with the carers' own children. One such example involved a
six-year-old boy who was placed with considerably older girls, but his
learning difficulties and disturbed behaviour were said to have contributed
to many problems between the children, including rivalry, aggression and
sexualised behaviour. Eventually the carers felt their own family was

suffering unduly and terminated the placement prematurely.

On a more positive note, a number of examples were quoted of carers' children playing a helpful role towards foster children, for instance: 'Teenage boys have been welcoming and protective of a younger female foster child.'

Although only a small sample, these findings do tend to confirm impressions from my own caseload and from the families interviewed that the older sons and daughters of foster carers are generally less threatened by the presence of incoming children than younger ones. They are perhaps more likely to see themselves as contributing to the caring process, rather than having expectations of the fostered children as potential companions – expectations which are often disappointed.

How does the contribution of children who foster enhance the fostering experience?

A role model

Most foster carers saw significant benefits in their own children model-ling the behaviour which was expected of the foster child. This was generally more effective than trying to explain house rules and expecta-tions to a newcomer. A foster mother explained how this worked:

> *They've got the example of my children and can follow them; if I tell [the foster children] off and I also tell mine off for a similar thing, it relieves it . . . they're not the centrepoint of that emphasis . . .*

The same foster mother also pointed out that sometimes another child could deal with a problem more effectively than an adult:

> *To see the horror on another child's face when C makes his nose bleed, it goes home much more than if I'd said something to him . . . They can say 'we don't do that here' and he'd take that from them much better than he would from me!*

A bridge between foster child and foster carers

The twenty-year-old son of experienced carers said:

> *A lot of the time kids tend to come to me first. If they've done some-thing wrong or they want to ask a question, they'll come to me first to find out what the reaction's likely to be: 'What's [your mum and dad]*

going to say? . . . Why haven't they shouted at me yet? . . . I can tell them how they work.

This young person needed considerable skills to respond appropriately in these situations; such young people have great potential to influence the relationship between foster children and their carers. As he astutely described:

It's a way [for the foster child] to get through to mum and dad without actually having to talk to them face to face.

Catherine Macaskill (1991), in her book on caring for sexually abused children, points out that even very young carers' children may become the first recipients of a disclosure and there may be pressure upon them to keep such intimacies secret. This may be another example of children being seen by other children as a less threatening means of "testing the waters".

Once again this issue demonstrates the power of young people who foster to make a real difference to the lives of the children who come into their families. It also demonstrates the crucial importance of preparing them properly for that role, so they can be of maximum benefit to others with least damage to themselves.

Support to their parents
The unusual maturity of many children who foster led to many instances of young people acting in a supportive way towards their parents. This entailed both emotional and practical help such as babysitting.

The need for support for children who foster
"Support" encompasses many elements. It is partly about feeling valued and this has implications for ensuring that all levels of the agency understand the importance of the role played by children who foster.

Among both adults and young people in my study, some felt it was primarily the parents' role to inform, educate and support their own children (especially younger children), while others believed there would be something gained from involving the professionals and/or other carers outside the family.

It was universally agreed that children would gain mutual support from meeting other children who foster, either informally or in a group setting. This was a typical comment from a young person:

I can talk to friends but you have to be so careful about mentioning too much and they don't really understand unless they've done it or been there. (C, aged 14)

Although few agencies in Britain seem to have developed support groups for children who foster, there appears to be widespread consensus about their potential benefits. These children can feel isolated and gain reassurance that others face similar problems. Shared solutions can emerge from shared difficulties. Groups can provide a safe outlet for venting frustrations when young people feel reluctant to "bother" parents with their worries, guilty about hostile feelings towards foster children or resentful about getting reduced parental attention. Groups can combine functions of mutual support with educational and social activities.

Several carers felt that the role of the family's homefinder or link-worker could be usefully extended to include individual time spent with their own children (and this has been borne out in my own practice).

Importantly, many young people who foster expressed a desire to be kept informed by parents and social workers, and for their voices to be heard by those with power. They argued that being given full information would help them to understand the child who is joining their family and protect them from the pain of experiencing unexpected disclosures from the child him or herself.

Some agencies are now including the views of carers' children in their annual foster carer review in order to highlight the impact of placements upon all members. This may also serve to check that responsibilities placed upon carers children in respect of fostering tasks are realistic and acceptable.

What price do we pay for ignoring the needs of children who foster?

The last decade has seen a marked trend away from residential care for children being looked after and towards foster family care. Changes in the tasks now required of foster carers have major implications for their selection, training and support. The 1994 Audit Commission on Foster Care stated emphatically that, more than anything else (including payment levels), the lack of good training and support for foster carers adversely affects their recruitment, retention and quality.

In their research on fostering breakdowns, Berridge and Cleaver (1987) found that increased experience in fostering was associated with significantly lower breakdown rates. Placements which disrupt prematurely often result in children being moved on to another placement at short notice, leaving little opportunity for proper assessment of needs, good matching or preparation of either the foster child or the new foster family. Carers who suffer a disrupted placement often feel so hurt or disillusioned that they give up fostering altogether and the costs in emotional damage of placement instability to the fostered child are incalculable.

Particularly in the present climate of economic stringency, it therefore makes very good sense to increase the effort put into retention of carers. It follows from an awareness of the crucial role played by foster carers' own children that the need for support and preparation of the whole family, not just the parents, must be addressed.

In summary, agencies must address:
- ways of involving prospective carers' children fully in the fostering assessment and preparation;
- the importance of careful matching, considering the needs of the *whole* family when making placements (and paying heed to the key research findings on placement-related factors and outcomes);
- giving carers' children access to support for themselves;
- ways of showing recognition and appreciation of the role of carers' children;
- the empowerment of carers' children through representation of their needs and interests in fostering policy and practice at all levels.

Listening to and responding to the needs of children who foster is not always easy. It may require changes in attitude, policies or practice. But to ignore them is to neglect a key element in achieving successful outcomes for children in foster care.

References

Berridge D and Cleaver H, *Foster Home Breakdown*, Blackwell, 1987.

Kaplan C, 'The biological children of foster parents in the foster family', *Child and Adolescent Social Work*, 5:4, 1988.

Macaskill C, *Adopting or Fostering a Sexually Abused Child*, BAAF/Batsford, 1991.

Natural Children's Support Group, *Children Who Foster* video, Vera Publications, 1990.

Part D, 'Fostering as seen by the carers' children', *Adoption & Fostering*, 17:1, pp 26–31, 1993.

Verity P, ' "Seen But Not Heard": The Audit Commission Report', *Foster Care*, 79, 1994.

14 Fostering children and young people with learning disabilities:
the perspectives of birth children and carers

Janet Ames

Janet Ames undertook the research reported here while working at the National Children's Bureau. She is currently an Associate in the Cheshire Public Health Research and Resource Unit at Chester College and an independent researcher. She has continuing research interests in the construction and experience of disability in childhood, including the perspectives of disabled and non-disabled siblings. She is a non-executive director of an NHS Trust providing community and mental health services.

This paper was published in Adoption & Fostering, 20:4, 1997.

In a recent contribution to this journal, Gill Pugh (1996) discussed the experiences of a group of birth children in foster families. Presented here are some findings from another small-scale study of fostering which tapped the experiences of both birth children *and* adult carers in foster families looking after a different group: children and young people who had serious learning disabilities. The rationale for including birth children in the research was, as for Pugh, the growing recognition that foster carers' own children are very much involved in and affected by fostering. Indeed, birth children themselves have been influential in gaining acknowledgement of their role (Natural Children's Support Group, 1990).

A specific concern in this article is to juxtapose the viewpoints of birth children and adult carers. To set the discussion in context, I begin with an account of the work of the fostering agency in the study and outline the methods of data collection. Secondly, some key findings on the experiences of the particular group of birth children in this research are summarised. Finally, the support offered by the fostering agency following a placement is explained and the somewhat different views expressed by birth children and adult carers on this aspect of the agency's work are analysed.

The fostering agency

This study of the perceptions and experiences of adult carers and birth children in foster families was part of a research programme commissioned by Barnardo's. All the foster families included in the research programme were working with a fostering service managed by Barnardo's in the North-West of England. This "professional fostering service" was established in 1979 to identify and manage suitable foster placements for young people with severe learning disabilities. At the start of the research programme, in November 1990, 66 young people (49 young men and 17 young women) were in placements supported by the fostering service (see Table 1). All the young people had learning disabilities; a significant proportion of them also had physical disabilities of varying degrees of severity. Most of the foster placements managed by the fostering service were long term and most could appropriately be described as quasi-adoptive.

The abilities and level of independence of the young people in placement varied quite considerably but all required high levels of support and personal assistance. This is illustrated by two pen pictures.

Twelve-year-old C was mobile, had serious visual impairment, and needed someone to watch over him *all* the time. He attended school in the day. Two or three evenings a week it could take all evening to settle him in bed. When left, he would start spinning round the room and screaming. He woke the foster carers in the night perhaps once a week.

E, aged 13, required personal assistance with meeting every need: lifting, washing, toileting and entertainment. Apart from the normal caring routine, her foster carers undertook a daily routine of physiotherapy exercises with her. The only bathroom in the house was upstairs, as was E's bedroom. Carrying her up and downstairs was physically strenuous. She was sometimes cheerful and smiling but also had lengthy outbursts of screaming. During the school week, she generally slept through the night. However, there had been extended periods when she

Table 1

Young people in placement at November 1990

Age in years	Numbers in placement
0–4	5
5–9	9
10–14	24
15+	28
Total	66

only catnapped at night. E had no speech and could not explain what was upsetting her. When upset she would bite her hands, which was distressing for all concerned.

The households where C and E lived each comprised two adult foster carers and several birth children. This was typical of most young people placed by the fostering service; in total 54 of the 66 young people were placed with foster carers whose own children were living permanently at home.

Barnardo's has a clearly stated equal opportunities policy but it is important to note that, at the time the research was undertaken, all the foster families recruited by the fostering service were white and that only one of the young people in placement was of minority ethnic origin.

The study

The views of 23 birth children were obtained. All but four took part in one of several group discussions about fostering. These took place away from their home, at a church centre or on premises belonging to Barnardo's. In addition, two young people were interviewed at home when their parents were not present. Two others joined in interviews held with their parents and offered some comments on their own experiences. These 23 young people (nine male and 14 female) ranged in age from eight to nearly 20 years. They included six pairs of siblings. In other words, 17 foster families were represented. The sample of birth children was self selected but, in terms of the level of personal assistance and support required, the young people in placement with their families were a cross-section of all the placements made by the agency.

The data on the experiences of adult foster carers which are drawn upon in this article were obtained from 16 semi-structured interviews conducted in the adult foster carers' own homes. They were looking after either one or two young people placed by the fostering service.

Experiences of the birth children

Many of the findings in this study echo those cited by Pugh (1996) and by Part in an earlier study (1993). An important feature of the relationships with the foster children reported by the birth children were their shared activities (Ames Reed, 1994). For younger children these were typically the games they played with the young person their family fostered: '. . . we have pretend boxing fights'; '. . . we do exercises together, play, lots of things'. Some of the older teenagers explained how they involved the young person living with them in their social life outside the home, for instance, going out for a meal with friends.

Several older birth children also described their involvement in helping support the young person placed in their household. Their contributions ranged from staying in the same room as the fostered child while an adult carer was elsewhere preparing a meal, to taking full responsibility when adult carers were absent from the home. In some households daughters appeared to undertake more caring tasks than sons; yet in others, sons reported helping out on a regular basis.

Most of those interviewed suggested that they were happy with their current level of involvement with fostering and many of their accounts reflected a concern to safeguard the welfare of the young person living with them. Several of the young adults said that if their parents discontinued fostering, they would still wish to remain in contact with the young person currently placed with them and/or to contribute in some way to their care.

Nevertheless, as Pugh found, birth children expressed a range of opinions and some voiced resentment about the effects of fostering on both their parents and themselves. The findings of the research overall suggested that the greater the pressures experienced by the adult carers, the more worried they were about having enough time and energy for their own children, and the more likely the birth children were to show irritation about having to wait their turn for attention.

Around three-quarters of those consulted talked about the young person living with them in a very affectionate way – even when acknowledging the changes which fostering had meant for them – but nearly a quarter stated that they found being part of a foster family difficult. Irritation was clearly uppermost in the mind of the young person who wrote the following (amended slightly to protect identities) about the change and upset in her life:

First I thought it would be fun. Now some days I wish we hadn't begun, although I love them very much. But they can be a pain in the bum.

Although the sample was small, an apparently significant division was that of gender. All five of those who offered predominantly negative accounts of fostering were girls or young women.

A number of factors appeared to play a part in dissatisfaction with fostering. With one exception, the girls or young women unhappy about fostering were close in age to the young person placed in their household. Furthermore, it seemed that fostering had had a particularly significant impact on the lives of all of these young women. For example, they had to share their personal space following the placement; to take on considerable and apparently unwelcome responsibilities and/or to experience frequent tension in their home. This group of girls and young women were not able, unlike some others, to avoid the disruption which they felt fostering had brought to their lives. This was *either* because they judged that the adult carers relied on their help, *or* because they were too young to gain much independence from family life.

This was a small-scale study of the experiences of foster families offering support to a group of young people with disabilities. Further research would be needed to test the more general applicability of the findings and, more specifically, to assess the relative significance of gender, as compared with other variables, in shaping attitudes to fostering. Nevertheless, evidence of variation in the reactions of birth children to fostering prompted questions about how this group of birth children viewed the involvement of the fostering agency. This issue is explored next, with special reference to the support offered by the fostering agency following a placement.

The involvement of the fostering agency: post-placement support
The fostering service sought a long-term commitment from families looking after a young person, while at the same time guaranteeing these families continuing support. Every young person placed by the fostering service was allocated to one of the project's social workers. In the early stages of a placement, the social worker would visit the foster family, normally at home, at least once a week. Once the young person was established in the household, then the pattern was for a social worker to visit once a month. She or he would make the appointment with the adult carer or carers. On such routine visits the social worker might incidentally meet the birth children, but this was rarely planned.

The Barnardo's Psychology Service also worked with the young person in placement, and with the foster family, with the objective of enabling the young people to reach their full potential.

The foster carers recruited by the fostering service received a professional fee in return for the work they undertook. They were also entitled to four weeks' respite care annually. A training programme was organised for the foster carers, for which any travelling expenses were reimbursed.

At the time of the study, the Children Act 1989 was being implemented and procedures were introduced to ensure that all members of a household, including the children, would be involved in the annual review of a foster placement (HMSO, 1989). None of the birth children who took part in this research reported having participated in such a review, though apparently some were about to do so.

The discussion here includes the views of both birth children and adult carers regarding the general support offered by the fostering service's social work staff. In their accounts, adult foster carers generally emphasised the ready availability of the project social work staff and welcomed the emotional support which they offered. Two foster carers endorsed the post-placement support in very similar terms:

There's always somebody there at the end of the phone.

They've been great . . . they've been sympathetic to me when I've
needed it . . . given me propping up when I've needed it. At one time
when I was having a very rough time, the social worker was on call
almost 24 hours a day . . . On the other hand I ring when something
good happens, like when I had had 15 nights without a soiled bed.

In some contrast, this routine post-placement support was often largely
invisible and irrelevant to the birth children in foster families. Only one
older adolescent commented that she felt party to all that went on:

I get told everything . . . have every opportunity to find out from the
social worker all that is going on.

Nevertheless, the "role plays" acted out by younger children in the group
interviews suggested that Barnardo's social workers were perceived as
influential figures, while the children of the family were portrayed as
somewhat marginal to any decision-making. So, how did the birth
children in the study react to the support provided by the agency?

Those birth children who evidently accepted being part of a foster
family appeared unconcerned about whether or not they had contact
with the social workers from the fostering agency. Certainly, none of
them argued that they needed social work support. One adolescent
expressed his view with some vigour:

The Barnardo's social worker asked us a few questions before [the
child in placement] arrived. This was so they had asked us; it wasn't
very in-depth. [The social worker] talked to us casually, as part of the
family . . . I can't remember any private chat . . . you can be too young
for that sort of thing [at 12 years]. If we had wanted to talk to the
social worker, we probably could have . . . but it didn't occur to us . . .
[Now] I sometimes see the social worker when I come in from school.
We have a brief chat, ask how each other is. But the social worker
doesn't come to talk to us especially. What would I possibly want to
tell the social worker anyway? . . . If [child in placement] were my
brother, I wouldn't run and talk to a social worker if he did something
that bothered me . . . He is part of the family and any problems are
dealt with in the family.

Some of the young adults among the birth children, however, differed in their assessments. They suggested that they would welcome the opportunity to become more closely involved with the fostering process. Their argument was that if they were included in some of the training activities run for adult carers, particularly those in practical skills such as Makaton signing, their contribution to making a success of the placement would be enhanced: 'We should be able to do more things . . . we need to be involved.'

A third viewpoint was expressed by young people who were unhappy about being part of a foster family. Some were openly critical about the lack of involvement they had with the fostering agency and felt that they should have been better informed and more fully consulted about the impact of fostering on them:

> *The children in the family need to know more. They live with the foster brother or sister as well as their parents do.*

> *They need to tell the other children in the family more about the person and talk to them to find out what they feel about the child.*

Thus dissatisfaction about lack of involvement could relate to a wish to be better informed in order to help the foster child more, *or* a concern to have more account taken of the impact of the placement on the birth children themselves.

Conclusion

The young people in this study were making important contributions to the foster placements through shared social activities and sometimes taking on personal assistance tasks. In most cases, this was seen as enjoyable and satisfying, although a minority resented what they saw as loss of attention and privacy or excessive responsibility.

There was clear variation among the birth children in their views about the role of the fostering agency. The findings considered here suggest two distinct dimensions affecting those who wanted more discussion with support workers. One reflects the degree of contentment about being part of a foster family: those relaxed about fostering saw less need for involvement with the agency, while those apparently unhappy about fostering sought greater involvement. The second dimension cuts across the first to some extent and seems to reflect maturity. Thus some of those who were happy and involved with the fostering placement sought greater contact with the agency, so as to develop skills that would enable them to contribute more fully to the care and well-being of the young person living in their household.

A further contrast was apparent between the satisfaction expressed by adult foster carers with the general post-placement support offered by the fostering agency, and the more varied range of viewpoints expressed by the birth children in foster families. The apparently un-critical stance of the adult carers might be explained by their status as, in effect, paid staff of the fostering service, though this possibility is countered by more critical comments which a few adult carers made on other aspects of the work of the fostering agency. Relevant examples include annoyance about delays in the provision of much-needed aids and adaptations, and in the organisation of respite care. The interviews with this particular group of birth children, then, suggest that birth children's expectations of post-placement support may well differ from those of the adult carers.

While this study, like Pugh's, involved only a small number of birth children, it can hopefully contribute to building up a broader picture. Pugh's conclusions included proposals that the staff of adoption and fostering agencies should consider:

> ways of involving prospective carers' children in the fostering assessment and preparation; the importance of careful matching, considering the needs of the whole family . . .

Certainly the combined findings of the two studies add weight to the argument that greater knowledge and understanding of the experiences of birth children could assist fostering agency staff to develop more adequate and appropriate support to those "children who foster".

Acknowledgements
My warm thanks go to the birth children and adult carers who took part in this study. I am very grateful also to the staff of Barnardo's Divisional

Fostering Service North-West for their assistance with all stages of the research programme.

Note

On re-reading this article for the anthology, I am struck by the omission of any reflection on the experiences and perceptions of the disabled children and young people. My current research on the experience of disability in childhood aims to encompass the viewpoints of both disabled and non-disabled children and young people.

References

Ames Reed J, 'We live here too: birth children's perspectives on fostering someone with learning disabilities', *Children & Society*, 8:2, 1994.

DoH, *Children Act 1989: Guidance and Regulations, Volume 3, Family Placements*, para 3.45, 1991.

Natural Children's Support Group, *Children Who Foster*, Vera Publications, 1990.

Part D, 'Fostering as seen by the carers' children', *Adoption & Fostering*, 17:1, pp 26–31, 1993.

Pugh G, 'Seen but not heard? Addressing the needs of children who foster', *Adoption & Fostering*, 20:1, pp 35–31, 1996.

Section V
External relationships

As noted in the Introduction, a key feature in understanding foster care is the relationship between members of the foster family and the child's external network, particularly the birth family and the social work agency. Policy and practice all favour openness and co-operation, but the different roles, perspectives and interests of the main parties mean that achieving genuine partnership is not easy.

In this section we consider both the informal relationships, particularly with birth parents, and contacts with formal agencies, especially social workers. It is important to recognise that these interconnect. Social workers can have a considerable impact on the relationship between foster and birth families, while this in turn can colour attitudes to social workers. **Oppenheim (1992)** proposed that it was helpful to see foster children as part of a network with different subsytems, requiring careful attention to communication processes. At times of crisis, as when a child is accommodated, it is desirable to identify the significant members of the network so they can form *action sets*, working together to agreed plans. This includes professionals as well as birth family members, friends and foster families.

Boushel (1994) also recommended a wide vision of how the welfare of children in foster care can be best protected. She had in mind particularly children who have been abused or are at risk of abuse, but the principles apply more generally. Boushel identified three concentric contexts that can cherish and protect children, or alternatively harm them:
* the immediate family;

- the extended family and community;
- the state and society.

At each level, four factors have a special influence on the ways children are treated and brought up:
- how children are valued;
- how women and carers are valued;
- the social interconnectedness of the informal network;
- the quality of professional safety nets.

Thorough assessment of these elements of the protective environment can identify strengths to be built on and weaknesses to be remedied. This framework can be used not only to prevent abuse in foster care but also to enhance the rights and opportunities of all fostered children.

Most foster carers are sympathetic towards most birth parents, as shown by the study of **Bradley and Aldgate** in Section III, for example. Nevertheless there are inevitably potential tensions when two individuals or couples with different backgrounds, aspirations and life-styles seek to share care of a child. Also practical difficulties are present on both sides when it comes to arranging times and places for contact which fit in with other routines and commitments. On top of this, some birth parents have serious difficulties in relation to alcohol, drugs or aggression. Thus to achieve satisfactory working together requires considerable skill and goodwill, as well as careful clarification of expectations and responsibilities.

Foster carers' views about contact with birth families are explored in the paper by **Waterhouse (1992)**. She observed that attitudes were often marked by ambivalence, with both strong positive and negative views expressed by the same person. Most carers were child focused in their approach and did not see themselves as collaborating with parents. Carers favoured contact when there was a good parent–child relationship, the parents were easy to get on with, and social workers were available and informative. Difficulties arose when parents were seen to be unreliable about access, had difficult behaviour or personalities and had abused or neglected the child. A more recent Scottish survey has similarly found that many carers do not regard work with parents as a central part of their role and half found it sometimes or always difficult to relate to children's parents (Triseliotis *et al*, 1998). In both studies, only a minority welcomed contact with parents in the foster home itself. Many preferred children to see their parents in the birth family home or in a neutral setting like a social work office. If children see the two main adults in their lives only in separate places, this hardly conveys an impression of partnership. Butler and Charles (1999) also described how foster carers' images of themselves as offering a good model of family life affects their relationships with children and birth parents. If a young person's expectations do not fit in with the carers' self image, disappointment or conflicts arise; while if birth parents are too different in values and life-styles then foster carers tend to revert to a more exclusive view of their role (see Introduction). Waterhouse concluded that the relationship with birth families needs to be a central consideration in selection and training of foster carers.

A different perspective on contact was provided by information from over 300 social work practitioners and managers in England and Wales **(Cleaver, 1997/8).** This revealed some of the difficulties in promoting contact, especially when birth parents have irregular life-styles or combative attitudes. Foster carers, children and parents may all have different views about the desirable frequency, nature and location of contact. Children can change their minds. Ascertaining views and facilitating contact could be very time-consuming for social workers, especially when the extended family was taken into account. Sometimes foster carers were involved in supervising and monitoring contact. Fitting birth family contact in with foster family and children's activities was often problematic. Finally, Cleaver observed that contact was often regarded as an end in itself, when it could have more long-term purposes such as improving interactive skills. All these considerations combined to show the major resource implications, including time, skills, transport and premises, which are required to sustain let alone develop a foster child's family relations.

The role of social workers in relation to foster care is a complex one. As in much of their work, there are social care and social control aspects. They are there to provide information, advice and support, yet assessment, monitoring and review are also important functions (Triseliotis *et al*, 1995b). For a long time there have been laudable aspirations for foster carers and social workers to be more equal partners, but foster carers have few legal rights or powers. However good the personal relations, local authorities ultimately make the decisions and have a duty to ensure safe care and respond to any allegations of abuse. Thus, as with foster carer–birth parent relationships, good intentions and shared concerns for the child intermingle with inherent role tensions.

Many agencies have sought to resolve certain of these issues by separating the roles of (a) support or link worker for the foster family and (b) caseworker for the child and birth family. This can help keep distinct functions separate, but risks creating splits in attitude and communication. **Sellick (1994)** analysed these two roles and their implications. He observed that nearly all authorities employ specialist staff to recruit, assess, train and support foster carers. These staff usually also have an important role in co-ordinating services and developing services. Children's social workers are typically in separate locations and carry a more general workload, often including child protection. Reviewing a range of consumer studies on social work, Sellick noted that foster carers normally appreciate qualities in social workers that service users also tend to value. These consist of practical competencies – availability, reliability, efficiency – and interpersonal attributes – warmth, trustworthiness and good listening. In general, foster carers have expressed greater confidence in their link workers, who are after all primarily there to support them (Sellick, 1992; Triseliotis et al, 1998). Feedback on the foster child's social workers tends to be less fulsome, which again reflects their competing commitments. Nevertheless, foster carers do report satisfaction with the child's worker more often than not (see also **Ramsay, 1996** in Section II). Sellick argues that the "faultline" between the two types of workers needs to be bridged by greater proximity, different modes of supervision and improved training.

15 The importance of networks to partnership in child-centred foster care

Lesley Oppenheim

At the time of writing Lesley Oppenheim was Senior Lecturer in Social Work at Middlesex Polytechnic. She has extensive practice experience in this country and abroad. .

This paper was published in Adoption & Fostering, 16:2, 1992.

Essentially partnership implies *shared parenting.* Shared parenting immediately suggests there are several systems around the child in interaction with each other. These systems embrace a range of fostering styles, forms and functions, but also a variety of relationships, and if partnership as envisaged by the Children Act 1989 is to be realised, shifts in our conceptions of "parenting" will need to be made.

The complex web of relationships surrounding fostered children may be more helpfully conceived of as a *network* rather than a family system. Manor (1984) has suggested that, 'it seems more appropriate to regard the new unit as a network with a number of sub-systems rather than hope for a normalisation' of the child into a system that bears the semblance of a natural family but by definition cannot be one.

In this article, drawing on the work of Gerald Erickson (1984) I will explore the meaning of networks on different levels as they might apply to fostering. I will then attempt to illustrate the relevance of networks to partnership in child-centred fostering.

The definition of network

Systems theory, which underpins network practice, has enabled social workers to understand some of the interplay of relationships, in terms of mapping them and identifying change within systems and interactions between these systems. The Ecomap, for instance, is a systemic technique which records a child's network at a particular time.

While networks can be used in this mapping sense, they can also be engaged as a dynamic for change. Gerald Erickson (1984), in his paper on networks relating to mental illness, defines them as 'the social universe of the person . . . [which] provides the social and communicational matrix for enculturation and the social supports for coping with a variety of stresses'.

This definition is important in the fostering context in three ways: firstly, it stresses the importance of social identity which is gleaned not only from immediate family ties but also from wider sources such as religious, recreational and cultural activities. Secondly, it incorporates the notion of survival and coping strategies which take a range of meanings from the network itself. Thirdly, it stresses the significance of communications.

The significance of network communications for the fostered child
Generally we can expect the structure of a family's sub-systems (e.g. parenting, parent–child, sibling) to form an overlapping matrix which meets each member's needs. Both the symbolic and practical meanings of much interaction between the family members are normally largely assumed by them. However, for the fostered child this assumptive world alters dramatically. Firstly, the new range of sub-systems is neither identical to that of the family of origin, nor able to meet a child's needs in quite the same way. Secondly, the new matrix now contains sub-systems or networks on different levels. Therefore the interactional patterns themselves will differ in the new social matrix formed by these sub-systems. How then will communication take place within and between these new levels?

In human systems, *communication* is the actual currency of interaction and is vital to the system (Watzlawick, 1974). Further, and particularly significant from the child's point of view, there is no such thing as "noncommunication" – silence itself is a "message" which must be deciphered. As we know, children of all ages create their own explanations, especially in the absence of accurate messages.

Poor communication exchanges between child and family of origin, child and foster family, child and social worker, and so on, will lead, therefore, to some weakening of the new matrix. Triseliotis (1989), for instance, in his review of foster care outcomes indicates that lack of parental contact is quite strongly and consistently associated with negative outcomes from the child's point of view. This recognition of the importance of parental contact to children is now enshrined as principle 12 of the Children Act regulations and guidance (HMSO, 1989): 'Parents should be expected and enabled to *retain* their responsibilities and to *remain* as closely involved as is consistent with their child's welfare.' Partnership as shared parenting highlights both the significance of communication and the importance of exchanges of commonalities and differences between the two sets of carers (parent and foster carer).

From the child's perspective, the process will be affected by his or her structural position on the interface of his or her own family and that of the carer. By implication, the child being the common focus, there are complexities of communication for the members of both these systems. For example, the child may become torn between connectedness and separateness. If he or she has been used to one prime carer, it may be harder to connect with another alternative carer. Somehow the child must be enabled to receive the message, 'It's all right to have two carers, they both have care to offer you, and they offer it together, but sometimes in different ways.'

This kind of message contains two important subtexts: firstly, the parent's inclusion means *continuity* in some form; secondly, difference means some *adaptation to change* is required.

Placement with a family will introduce the child to patterns, rules and processes different from his or her own experience. The new situation may offer greater stability and security in the long run, but it will also necessitate change and adaptation by the child, the parent, the foster carer and the foster carer's family (Eastman, 1974). In order to absorb rather than amplify this change, some features of continuity are needed to offer stability. A key stabiliser may be the parent.

I recall from my own past practice an example which illustrates the importance of retaining this level of continuity. A crisis arose in a family (previously unknown to the agency) when escalating domestic violence led to the woman killing her partner in an extremely violent manner. The shock to the children aged three, seven and nine (who had witnessed this event) was somehow less than it was to the "systems" (particularly the welfare and police systems) which became engaged in the case. After considerable entanglement on my part with both social services, who had placed the children, and the prison where the mother awaited a much deferred trial, she was allowed to have a few visits from her children accompanied by myself. The communication the children received from these visits, though she did not explain why she had done it, nor even referred to the death, filled in some important gaps which they could not have begun to complete without this contact. They were able to demonstrate the real affection and respect they held for her, in stark contrast to everyone else's attitude. This also enabled me to recognise some of the commitment she had, in turn, to them.

Looking back on this case now, this most dramatic of changes for the family seems to have had within it an internal logic consistent with the children's understanding of their family life (continuity). They did not have to have it explained to them – they knew why she had done it. However, they had to have the experience of seeing her for themselves to commence the process of adapting to what had happened and the consequences (change). Until this point, their private trauma had made them inaccessible to me as their social worker. The visit, however, had addressed their first need – continuity. Though the children could not be with their mother, symbolically she was able to remain an intact parent for them. Only then could they begin to adapt to the changes in their lives.

What they needed were meaningful networks on different levels. Though these could not replicate, or be congruent with, the lost family of origin they could still be sufficiently effective to be helpful to them despite the tragic circumstances.

Levels of network
To delineate this dimension of *level,* we need to consider Erickson's differentiation between extended, available and effective networks (cited above). Extended networks are essentially *all* relationships that any one individual may have; available networks are those *potentially* present which can offer appropriate help and support, and effective networks are the *new* networks created, for example, by social workers to meet the needs of the focal person. These new groupings of people are called

action sets by Erickson (similar to Pincus and Minahan's earlier action systems, 1973). Action sets comprise helping networks which aim to meet different levels of need. While no single configuration is likely to overlap comprehensively with the original family network, in combination they can offer a coherent framework for the child.

To achieve coherence, this framework would probably cover the following needs, among others:

- *affective* – those offering affectional bonds and ties and meeting the emotional needs of the focal person: the child;
- *cognitive* – those providing stimulation and opportunities for learning;
- *material* – those providing basic material needs which may not necessarily be the same as on the affective level;
- *social* – sport, friendship and recreational companions; and
- *symbolic* – the parent and others significant for their symbolic importance to the identity of the individual such as religious and ethnic connections.

Extended personal networks

The extended family is a familiar term to social workers. However, the extended *network* is the sum total of *all* relationships – friends, neighbours, relatives and caregivers, instrumental ties (to employment, a GP, a health visitor, etc.) and acquaintances over time. Networks may shrink or expand, and may range from a large number for some individuals to relatively few for others. For the child the range will be partly a result of personal circumstances, and partly an aspect of his or her development.

Generally, the younger the child the narrower the range of relationships, though not necessarily the smaller the number of people involved. A negative aspect of expanding networks in fostering is sometimes seen with quite young children who may have had a bewildering number of fleeting connections with surrogate parents, other children, sets of grandparents and so on. The task may become, through life story work, to establish continuity, but within a less extended network.

On the other hand, a positive aspect of the enriching nature of a wide range of relationships may be seen in some extended families or large families, where lessening the range may be unhelpful.

At the point of entry into the systems, younger, dependent children are likely to have a high level of overlap (congruence) in terms of membership with their parents' network. Shrinkage in the network, for instance surrounding the mother, will therefore also mean a shrinkage in the "natural" network for the child. The task may become to expand networks for both mother and child.

With older children such as adolescents, less overlap might be expected between the family's network and that of the adolescent, since the latter will have individuals such as peers who are unique to his or her own expanded network (Jones, 1980).

Extended networks, therefore, are potential sources of important experience to the child, but will be culturally and developmentally variable. Connections to *kith* (friends, symbolic others) as well as to kin may be significant considerations in establishing active partnership relations within the helping networks around the child.

Available personal networks
Despite these possibilities, however, extended networks are insufficient in themselves to provide the kind of supportive net intended. Who of these individuals are actually *available* for the support system? Availability is 'a measure of the members regularly interacting with the focal person'. The concept presumes that usually 'a normative image of cohesiveness and helpful ties between people' (Erickson, 1984) already exists. Initially, the available network for a child would normally include his prime carer at the time, on symbolic, material, social and affective levels. But what happens to available networks under stress?

Our present knowledge of networks is inadequate for us to identify in any great detail what the characteristics of these available networks' might be in different population groups. For instance, social isolation is often put forward as a key feature in those families with whom social workers come into contact. How far these parents are truly isolated socially, as opposed to isolated from formal resources, is often unclear and untested.

Although at first sight it might seem obvious that the reason why the child needs help is because of some lack in the available network, several studies have implied that this may not necessarily be the case, since the sources beyond the immediate family may not have been considered (Rowe *et al*, 1989; Ahmad, 1990). Once we cast the net wider, we may find that members of the family at large, or cultural institutions such as the Church are potential resources for helping children. This has been the experience, for instance, of the Thomas Coram Foundation, in their imaginative drive to recruit black adoptive families (Kaniuk, 1991).

What seems important here is not to assume that social isolation is a given in a particular case. Prime carers, however, may well need our support in recognising symbolic or social sources as being "available".

In the case of young children, we might think in terms of significant others who already had a connection with the child. With older children, they could be directly consulted on this point. Certainly in planning longer-term placements, we might want to identify a potentially significant other, apart from the parent, as a means of continuity to a child – along the lines of the much needed friend who advocates on the child's behalf.

Effective personal networks

A crisis in the parenting system which might lead to the need for fostering is frequently associated with crises in other parts of the available network. For example, a marital break-up might cut off the opportunity, at least initially, for one partner to make use of in-laws who normally would be part of the available network. This may lead to an apparent shrinkage in the levels of network. It will certainly leave the child in a position caught between those who are familiar and those from whom he or she has now become estranged. This kind of loss is unfortunately an all too frequent theme for children in care, and may include the deprivation of relationships on all levels of need.

Social networks must meet the varying needs of the child over time. It is therefore important for social workers to transform these networks into effective means of actively minimising these losses. This is where action sets may be particularly helpful.

Action sets and partnership

Erickson's typology draws on the natural networks established by individuals in their everyday social interactions. In our role as social workers in partnership, understanding this typology is not enough. In order to meet a child's needs, networks may have to be purposefully arranged. Such arrangements or "action sets" are 'a special kind of *instrumentally* activated personal network'.

Action sets should serve the purpose of balancing change with continuity. The *change* in children's social connectedness once they are in the care system can be reduced through the inclusion of significant others in the child's life, that is through appropriate attention to *continuity*. Initially, at least, the key significant individual in these action sets around the child in most instances will be the mother or father. Their role as sole prime carer may be taken over by the foster carer. These action sets may well also include added professional members. Nevertheless, the parents' continued involvement on some level, as we have seen, is invariably crucially important to the child, and may be a source of reassurance.

The commitment to shared parenting should mean we offer a real opportunity to parents to participate and contribute to their child's well-being through such arrangements, even where they may feel (as we often do) that in some way they have "failed". The challenge lies in finding ways from the time when care or accommodation is offered, where rather than leaving the parent to somehow prove themselves, we actively engage them in specific tasks, as a participatory member of the new action set, alongside carer, child, worker. In other words, this continuity perspective can be incorporated into the child's welfare, and also go some way to reduce the stigma for children within the care system (DoH, 1989).

It may well be that circumstances do not allow the parent to participate on certain levels. For instance, they may be unable to offer material support, but able to continue in a symbolic sense (e.g. providing feedback, acknowledging key events in the child's life). They may have shown themselves unable to offer the appropriate affective climate for the child (e.g. in some cases of child abuse) yet could still retain some capacity to offer symbolic continuity, say by their attendance at reviews and case conferences. By identifying the *level* in the network in which they participate, we can pinpoint those areas where the parent can or cannot remain 'the most significant resource for the child' (Aldgate, 1991). This may also clarify tasks for future attention between worker, foster carer and parent. This differentiation of level in the various action sets is therefore necessary to provide an enriched experience for children, without depriving them of their significant links, either with their families or with their core communities. The worker's key tasks would be to establish, maintain and co-ordinate these action sets, whose membership and purposes may change over time.

Partnership in practice – an illustration

Were I now to be undertaking work with the children described earlier, new possibilities might present themselves in the light of the above.

- Backed by a more comprehensive legislative and procedural framework, my commitment to the mother and children retaining some form of contact would be stronger. Hopefully, my negotiations about this would be less constrained and hence easier to include the mother as part of the children's effective network.

- To do this, I might use the attachment between the children and their mother more explicitly. It would become easier for her actions to be reframed as a misguided but intelligible attempt to protect her children (a possibility which was largely overlooked at the time). Child-centredness should help me to shift the networks' focus to the children's needs in relation to their mother, especially the need for continuity. Even in a limited way she might be able to exercise some parental responsibility. I would consider on which level she might do so, so that she remained accessible to them in the affective and symbolic, if not the day-to-day physical sense.

- After the initial crisis, effective action sets could be formed on several levels: firstly, with the prison probation officer and the mother in which information about the mother's and children's network could be gathered. The probation officer could become an important link between the mother, social services and the children. This would also be particularly important to identify possibilities for long-term placement. The family's ethnicity would be an important consideration, around which further action sets might be formed, to help in the search for carers of the same race and, as near as possible, a similar culture.

- The second grouping of action sets would revolve around the children

211

and their new carers. These carers would need to be rather special! Despite the circumstances, they would need to be inclusive enough to accept the significance of the mother to the children, and their attachment to her. They would probably need to be involved in further action sets, obviously with the social worker, but possibly, if therapy were necessary, with others.

- Perhaps most significant of all, in relation to partnership, this placement would be, though not a supplement to the mother's care, not a total substitution for her either. In the light of the mother's inaccessibility, it would in some ways be an alternative. For continuity purposes, these carers would be offering affective, material and social support. Although attachment by the children to them would still be an aim of the placement, the symbolic attachment to their mother would continue too.

- Scanning the available networks for sources of continuity would be important. Members of the community network might emerge as potential sources of help. A family friend, minister, or cultural contact for instance, might be the appropriate "significant other" to retain links between the children and their mother. Informal contacts from their community of origin, in addition to more formal sources, would give the children another set of messages about identity, continuity and acceptance.

- A further action set between worker, the sibling group and their mother suggests that visits to the mother might still continue to be 'in the children's best interests'. Here the link with the prison would be important in sensitively weighing up the advisability of such visits, for instance to arrange appropriate interviewing space. It may also be that the children's need for direct contact would diminish over time. Nevertheless, reviews would incorporate considerations of this kind.

Conclusion

My intention here has been to focus on what Aldgate (1991) has described as 'vulnerable people' – firstly, the children and secondly, frequently their parents. Empowerment through partnership implies re-thinking our approaches to find ways of actively including them and also to managing continuity alongside change.

The foster care system cannot offer the same degree of overlap between its sub-systems as can the family of origin. Networking could be a useful means of transforming a complex web of interrelationships into arrangements (action sets) which can offer different levels of response to a range of needs. A major role for social work would be to set up and co-ordinate these action sets.

Even with a comprehensive policy framework in place, without support and resources, the best intentioned social workers may be hampered in setting about developing such strategies. I believe that would be an opportunity missed and certainly not in children's best interests.

References

Ahmad B, *Black Perspectives in Social Work*, NISW, 1990.

Aldgate J, 'Partnership with parents – fantasy or reality?', *Adoption & Fostering*, 15:2, pp 5–9, 1991.

Department of Health, *An Introduction to the Children Act 1989*, HMSO, 1989.

Department of Health, *The Care of Children: Principles and practice in regulations and guidance*, HMSO, 1989.

Eastman K, 'The foster family in a systems theory perspective', *Child Welfare*, 58:9, 1979.

Erickson G, 'A framework and themes for social network intervention', *Family Process*, 23 June 1984.

Jones R and Pritchard C (eds), *Social Work with Adolescents*, Routledge & Kegan Paul, 1980.

Kaniuk J, 'Lessons from the past – 40 years of family placement experience', *Adoption & Fostering*, 14:3, pp 38–42, 1990.

Kaniuk J, 'Strategies in recruiting black adopters', *Adoption & Fostering*, 15:1, 1991.

Manor O (ed), *Family Work in Action*, Tavistock, 1984.

Pincus A and Minahan A, *Social Work Practice: Model and methods*, Peacock, 1973, USA.

Rowe J, Hundleby M and Garnett L, *Child Care Now*, BAAF, 1989.

Triseliotis J, 'Foster care outcomes, a review of key research findings', *Adoption & Fostering*, 13:3, pp 5–17, 1989.

Watzlawick P, Weakland J and Fisch R, *Change: Principles of problem formation and problem resolution*, Norton, 1974, USA.

16 How foster carers view contact

Suzette Waterhouse

Suzette Waterhouse's research interests, besides that below for an M.Phil. degree, include "The Organisation of Fostering Services" (1997) and "Placement Choices for Children in Temporary Foster Care" (forthcoming), both for the National Foster Care Association (NFCA). She has worked with social services, child guidance, the NSPCC and guardian ad litem panels. Other published work relates to communicating with children in a court context and kinship care.

This paper was published in Adoption & Fostering, 16:2, 1992.

Findings of a study of short-term foster carers' attitudes to access and links

In 1989 I carried out an exploratory study, using qualitative research techniques, to examine the experiences, perceptions and attitudes of a group of short-term foster carers towards birth family contact. The study sample consisted of 17 short-term foster carers from two central counties (Southshire and Midshire) who were interviewed. A recent placement with contact was also discussed in detail, and the transcribed interviews were subject to content analysis. This article summarises the conclusions of this research a full account of which is available at Leicester University (Waterhouse, 1990).

The findings support existing research literature in emphasising that the attitudes of foster carers towards parental contact play a very significant part in a complicated process of inter-relationships that militate against the maintenance of links between children and their families. Millham (1989) highlighted this in stating that:

> . . . the problem of maintaining links [is] multidimensional, stemming from both the legal, social and economic powerlessness of parents, the change and turbulence of their households, the ideology and organisation of social services and their management of separation.

Foster care is just one factor in the planning process for children being looked after by local authorities, and foster carers are only one interest group among all those professionals and family members whose attitudes subtly interweave. While recognising that contact is a multi-dimensional problem this study examined in detail one particular interest group, namely the foster carers. While such an approach may not fully address the above inter-relationship nor the dynamic processes at work, it does provide a useful snapshot of foster carers' views and attitudes.

Some important findings emerged from the study that confirm previous research and provide a differing emphasis to the problem of substitute parenting and links. The findings have underlined how powerful foster carers' attitudes can be when considering the question of contact. The need to recognise this in practical terms is especially important within the context of the new demands placed on carers by the Children Act 1989.

Specific findings

Foster carers found parental contact most successful where:

- The child was obviously happy and content following contact and thus appeared to be benefitting from it.
- An easy rapport with the parents could be established.
- A neutral venue outside the foster home was used.
- The foster carer could see a role for contact, for example, as part of a clear rehabilitation plan.
- The reasons for entry to care related to the parents' failure to cope rather than abuse/neglect issues.
- A good rapport was established with the social worker who was easily available to offer support.
- The social worker provided good information to the foster carer regarding the child and his family.

Foster carers found parental contact most difficult where:

- Parents were haphazard in adhering to the access arrangements.
- The extended family became unexpectedly involved in the contact arrangements without the foster carer being prepared for this.
- The foster carers were given responsibility for supervising the contact.

- Conflict existed between parent and substitute carer over discipline.
- Certain parents were perceived as difficult personalities.
- The child was in care for reasons of abuse or neglect.

General findings
Ambivalence and uncertainty
The attitudes of foster carers towards contact appeared very complex and there was much ambivalence towards contact, often with both strongly positive and negative views being held by each individual foster carer. Ambivalence and uncertainty seemed more marked where the foster carer was inexperienced. Attitudes towards *parental contact with a foster child* might be quite different to the attitude of *the foster carers towards the birth parents* and this could be an area for further exploration. Approximately half of the sample of foster carers appeared on balance to hold negative views about parental contact, but such a figure masked the many positive comments made by these respondents about contact. A feature of several of the foster carers' experience was their *lack of contact with the parents* of the children they had fostered. Parental contact was generally seen as a complicating factor in placements and particularly strong attitudes were expressed against parents where children had entered foster care for reasons of abuse or neglect.

Traditional approach
The respondents demonstrated a traditional, child-focussed approach to their task and at the time of the study were a long way from the ethos of the Children Act, with its emphasis on parental partnership and responsi-bility. There appeared to be nothing in their selection, training and support which significantly challenged this traditional alignment, although the Children Act will hopefully change this. The Act demands a reappraisal of attitudes by all involved professionals, including foster carers, which should be reflected in the quality of support for foster carers if they are to be a part of this working partnership.

Partnership
Unfortunately the notion of partnership between foster carers and the social worker and their agency was not reflected in practice. Foster carers

perceived themselves as having low status and little information or influence; many respondents did not perceive themselves as part of an active team working together with social workers and parents to find a satisfactory outcome for a child. This was borne out in the way contact plans and decisions were made by the agencies, with little involvement and nurturing of the foster carers.

Lack of child care strategy

Respondent foster carers were aware of the lack of a coherent strategy in child care which has been identified by other research (see particularly Wilkinson, 1988). Child care plans were sometimes perceived to change with the social worker, his or her personal ideology, and whether the child or the parent was perceived by them to be the client. Inconsistencies within social work teams were apparent, although there appeared to be pockets of good practice and social work attitudes of which the foster carers approved. Against this background of apparent changing strategies and philosophies, the foster carers' consistently child-focussed approach was striking and perceived by some of the respondents as positively in the child's interests.

Simplistic view of access

Foster carers' attitudes towards contact had not been developed but left to emerge through their own motivation, perceptions and experience. Traditionally, fostering has an image of child rescue and exclusivity which is founded upon historical reality, and so the child-focussed substitute parenting model that many of the respondents held on to was not surprising. Little or no attempt appeared to have been made by agencies to ensure that foster carers had the training, skills, or knowledge of child care research to provide a framework for understanding and managing parental access. The foster carers tended to take a simplistic view of access: if they had a rapport with the parents and the child was happy, then access was a good thing. Negative feelings tended to emerge where this was not the case.

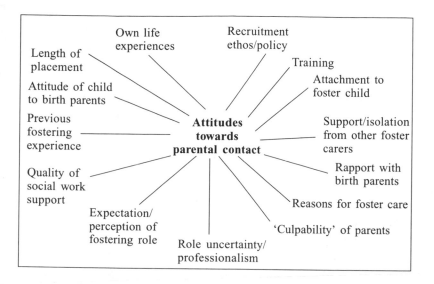

Venue for access

Foster carers had particular views about where they thought contact should take place which were often at variance to those of the social worker, and their experiences regarding venue subsequently affected their attitudes. The foster carers in the study felt that venues other than the foster home were more neutral and therefore more beneficial. Unsupported access in the foster home appeared much more difficult than social workers appeared to think, especially if it was set up prematurely and without a proper assessment of the situation, as was often the case. The extra demands regarding contact in the Children Act 1989 now place an additional strain on foster carers, who are now expected to work with any contact orders made by the court, as well as voluntary arrangements agreed by the local authority with the parents. They are likely to find themselves under great pressure for the foster home to be used as a venue for contact, with information to the parents about the child's whereabouts being routinely provided. These extra demands regarding contact may necessitate the setting up and regular use of visiting centres for children to meet with their parents, particularly in the early stages of children being looked after by local authorities. An additional problem for the case-study children was the rarity of home-based (as opposed to foster home-based) contact and many children thus lost their continuity with these connections. The benefits to children of home-based contact do not appear to be fully recognised.

Variables that influence foster carers' attitudes to parental contact

It has been seen that the *sense of rapport* or otherwise that foster carers establish with birth parents during a placement, and the attitude of parents themselves are particularly important in shaping carers' attitudes. *The reason the child entered foster care* appeared to be a potent factor affecting attitudes, often overlooked by social workers in their support for foster placements. This is tied in with issues concerning culpability of the parents, attitudes towards abuse and neglect, and towards non-coping mothers.

"Professionalism" remains a potentially important factor that this research was unable to address as none of the foster carers were recruited into any formal "professional" scheme. Professionalism remains a way forward for fostering. It has distinct advantages regarding the resolution of role uncertainty, partnership and motivation. Wilkinson (1988) and Berridge and Cleaver (1987) found that professional foster carers were less antagonistic towards birth parents than traditional foster carers, suggesting that such schemes can have unexpected spin-offs. Clearly there is scope for further exploration of this, as it would appear that professionalism affects expectations and perception of the fostering role.

Research by Cautley (1980) and Thorpe (1974) found that the length of placement was also important in affecting attitudes, and this is linked to the significance of the child's relationship with his or her family of origin and the attachment of the foster carer to the child.

The results of this study also suggested that the foster carers' *own life experiences* could be important, as could a carer's previous fostering experience.

Study respondents had little recollection of their assessment/selection process addressing issues of parental contact. Indeed, even in 1990, poster recruitment campaigns in both Southshire and Midshire stressed the child-focused nature of fostering and gave no indication of the child as part of the wider family. Clearly, the message given by local authorities at the recruitment stage is fundamental to expectations and any shift in orientation of the ethos of the service needs to be in evidence at this stage if it is to be effective.

Implications of the Children Act

The findings of this study need to be linked in with the changes which have occurred with the implementation of the Children Act. The legislative changes concerning access are an attempt to ensure that research knowledge is put into practice in terms of links planning. The Children Act provides a coherent framework for vital issues, including contact, to be addressed and places considerable emphasis on social services departments facilitating openness and participation in child care planning *vis à vis* the birth parents. The movement towards a working partnership between parents and agency should avoid the marginalisation of parents in child care planning; birth parents and foster carers have in this respect not been in a dissimilar position regarding power, status, influence and hence marginalisation. However, the notion of partnership with parents makes the role of substitute parenting more complex and difficult, and is likely to necessitate a considerable shift by agency, worker and new recruits from the perception of fostering as the foster parenting of a child towards fostering being about caring for and involving the whole family.

It is an important research fact that family links are central to all social work with children. The Children Act now ensures that the full weight of the law is available to help achieve this and that courts can intervene in the management of cases as necessary. Links need to take up a central position in the chosen child care strategy, whether it is to sustain family roles, change family roles, or to terminate them. Because visiting is so very hard, good and clear local authority policy guidelines are critical to ensure consistent practice and a platform for moving forward.

However, the weight of both legislation and local policy will not in themselves result in this shift. It has been seen that there is a complicated tripartite interweaving of attitudes of foster carers, birth parents and social workers regarding contact which can help or hinder contact and which policy or law can only marginally address, and it is these attitudes that play a crucial role. As demonstrated by this research, those foster carers who are in the frontline and thus in touch with the trauma of the child on reception into care experience feelings and thoughts which may not assist contact, and it is known that parents in this situation also find it especially difficult to visit. Foster carers, social workers and birth parents need to understand the significance of visiting because grass-roots support for any policy is essential if legislation is to have an impact. Great effort will be needed to effect such an upheaval in attitudes; contact is already a very familiar topic and it is easy to give lip service to its necessity, or adopt the "DATA" syndrome that practitioners are, "Doing All That Already".

The difficulty in changing attitudes in this context should not be underestimated even within the context of a clear legal mandate and a good policy framework; the concluding remarks of the DHSS document *Decisions in Child Care* (1985) still have continuing relevance:

> *The most urgent need appears to be a shift in attitudes and priorities, increased understanding, more sensitive perceptions of clients' feelings by social workers and of social workers' feelings by management.*

Following on from this, the Department of Health document *Patterns and Outcomes in Child Placement* (1991) states:

> *. . . the child's welfare has to be understood in the context of a web of relationships. It is not enough to offer a service. The way in which it is offered and the attitudes of the service providers are also crucial.*

Training and selection

The desired shifts in attitudes obviously have resource implications although one suspects that training for foster carers regarding the Children Act and its key principles is likely to be given little priority by departments. Agency ethos regarding recruitment and selection of foster carers needs to be carefully considered alongside not only their training but also that of social workers and birth parents in order that the issues can be fully appreciated. Foster carers will need more pre-service training about the changing nature of foster care and how they can support visiting with more emphasis on foster caring as opposed to substitute parenting.

Professor Peg Hess, speaking at a British Agencies for Adoption and Fostering conference on maintaining links in 1990, stated that many new foster carers in her Indiana project were willing to work in this way although there was a mixed response from more experienced foster carers, emphasising that the more entrenched people's attitudes, the more difficult it is to embrace changes. A further problem is that the continual shortage of foster carers may mean that agency placement units find it difficult to be selective, and the child-centred model of foster caring will remain an attractive and potent image of fostering to use in recruitment.

Recent developments in training have attempted to respond to these demands. A major training pack on 'Maintaining Links' was launched by Barnardo's in 1990 which emphasised the importance of links and is intended for use with not only agency workers but also foster carers. Other good practice material is also available to stimulate and challenge practice.

Even with more vigorous and energetic joint planning, there remain grey areas and gaps in knowledge and understanding about contact. It is not clear who are the parents who manage to sustain visiting and why they are successful. Indeed, Rowe (1984) stated that her data, gathered retrospectively, did not make it possible to discriminate between those parents who were or were not likely to visit. In addition, more information is needed as to whether systematic clear agreements really do ensure an improvement in visiting and, most important, affect outcomes. These issues, and the centrality of family contact in child care, will continue to be a focus of attention.

Note

Post-Children Act practice has reflected the belief of social workers that there are significant benefits for children in care of contact with their parents. The frequency of contact for children is considerable (Cleaver ongoing: Waterhouse and Brocklesby forthcoming; Berridge and Brodie, 1997), and contact is such an established norm for children entering care, it is now no longer a predictor of those children who are likely to return home (Bullock, Gooch and Little, 1998).

In the initial years after the Act's implementation, appropriate training and support regarding contact were undoubtedly available for many carers who were able to work with these changes. However, during the late 1990s a major crisis in fostering has become apparent which has highlighted the absence of choice of foster placement for children (NFCA, 1997; ADSS, 1997; Utting, 1997; Waterhouse and Brocklesby, forthcoming).

Our latest research has found a continuing high level of crisis-led and unplanned admissions to temporary foster placement, which, combined with overall carer shortages, have detrimental effects on both children and carers. It seems that carers are now adapting and managing inspite of the system rather than because of it. The over-riding of carers' agreed approval criteria to achieve a placement for a child, the movement of children between placements to remedy mismatches with carers and the use of carers for concurrent placements of different foster children concerned us greatly. Such practices raise significant welfare issues for children and place great strain on foster carers. Contact now seems just one of an increasing range of pressures that carers have to cope with. The research showed that:

- *Contact arrangements were more likely to be set up in haste where placements were unplanned leaving carers vulnerable.*
- *Contact could now be so frequent, especially for the under -fives, that it made considerable demands on carers and in some cases could dominate a child's care experience.*

It seems that the process of placement can now be very unchild-centred, even if the decision to admit to a placement is in a child's interests. In contrast, the carers themselves appeared very child focused in their task, and still had the same child-orientated motivation to foster as did the 1989 carers. Indeed, what seemed like a traditional, almost outdated stance at the time of the research interviews in 1989, now a decade on is arguably a crucial "safety net" for children.

References

Association of Directors of Social Services Children and Families Committee Report, *The Foster Care Market: A national perspective*, ADSS, 1997.

Barnardo's Video Training Pack, *Maintaining Contact: Partnership in practice*, Barnardo's, Ilford, Essex, 1990.

Berridge D and Brodie I, *Children's Homes Revisited*, Jessica Kingsley, 1997.

Berridge D and Cleaver H, *Foster Home Breakdown,* Blackwell, 1987.

Bullock R, Gooch D and Little M, *Children Going Home: The reunification of families*, Ashgate, 1998.

Cautley P W, *New Foster Parents: The first experience*, Human Sciences Press, 1980, USA.

Cleaver H, Personal communication to researcher regarding current study at Leicester University, ongoing.

Department of Health and Social Security, *Social Work Decisions in Child Care: Recent research findings and their implications,* HMSO, 1985.

Department of Health, *Patterns and Outcomes in Child Placement*, HMSO/ London, 1991.

Family Rights Group, *Using Written Agreements with Children and Families,* Practice Reader 2, Family Rights Group, 1989.

Hess P M and Proch K O, *Family Visiting in Out-of-home Care: A guide to practice*, Child Welfare League of America, 1988.

Millham S, Bullock R, Hosie K and Little M, *Access Disputes in Child Care*, Gower, 1989.

National Foster Care Association *Foster Care in Crisis*, NFCA, 1997.

Professor Pegg Hess, School of Social Work, Indiana University, USA, speaking at BAAF seminar on 'Maintaining Contact: Partnership in Practice', London, 26 June 1990.

Rowe J, Cain H, Hundleby M and Keane A, *Long Term Foster Care*, BAAF/ Batsford, 1984.

Thorpe R, 'The experiences of children and parents living apart', in Triseliotis J, *New Developments in Foster Care and Adoption*, Routledge & Kegan Paul, 1980.

Utting W, *People Like Us: The Report of the Review of the Safeguards for Children Living Away From Home*, DoH and the Welsh Office, 1997.

Waterhouse S and Brocklesby E, *Placement Choices for Children in Temporary Foster Care*, NFCA, forthcoming 1999.

Waterhouse S, 'Foster parents' view parental contact: A study of short term foster parents' attitudes to access and links', M.Phil. thesis, University of Leicester, 1990.

Wilkinson C, 'Prospect, process and outcome in foster care', PhD thesis, University of Edinburgh, 1988.

17 **Keeping safe:** strengthening the protective environment of children in foster care

Margaret Boushel

Margaret Boushel is a Lecturer in the School for Policy Studies, University of Bristol. Her previous experience includes social work practice, management and policy development. Her research interests are in the planning and provision of child and family support and protection services, and "race" and gender issues in child welfare.

This paper was published in Adoption & Fostering, 18:1, 1994.

Until recently, concerns about children in foster care have centred on the child's past experience of abuse rather than any current need for protection. The response to reports of sexual abuse by carers has been one of concern, confusion and defensiveness. The Children Act 1989 and related guidelines emphasise assessment and investigation as means of ensuring protection (DoH, 1991). Training strategies have stressed the need to help children avoid inappropriately sexualised behaviour (NFCA, 1988; 1993). Fostering organisations have been concerned with the possibility of false allegations of abuse (Moorat, 1991; NFCA, 1993). Such initiatives form a useful but partial response to the challenge of keeping children safe. A more comprehensive approach to the assessment and support of the 'child's protective environment' (Boushel, 1994) is needed to develop existing good practice in a spirit of partnership with foster carers, children and birth parents.

There are significant tensions underlying current responses. The 'belief that children are better cared for following placement than would otherwise be the case prevails among professionals as well as the community' (Nunno and Motz, 1988, p 523). A disclosure calls into question the ability of the state to provide a safe alternative to intra-familial abuse. Its implications can be devastating for the fostered child, and for all those concerned with the child, reinforcing a breach of trust and the inadequacy of the resources available to meet children's needs. Other concerns of principle may arise. While practice developments in foster care have been built on a strong commitment to working supportively with carers, British approaches to child protection seem overwhelmingly concerned with procedures, with detection, investigation and assessment, rather than with discretion, prevention and support (Lynch, 1992). There is a realistic fear that the introduction of such procedures to family placement settings may undermine existing supportive practices, including partnership with parents.

This problem of focus in child protection work raises important issues. Dominant British and North American definitions of abuse are almost exclusively concerned with abuse within the family, contributing to a climate which can leave both parents and foster carers feeling targetted rather than empowered. These definitions are criticised for taking inadequate account of the economic and social contexts of people's lives and of the abuse caused by discrimination (Violence Against Children Study Group, 1990; Marneffe, 1992; Jones, 1993). However, there *is* an alternative, supported by cross-national and cross-cultural research. A more comprehensive interpretation of abuse and protection as 'the range of structural, cultural, personal and interpersonal factors which combine to make the child's world a more or less safe and fulfilling place' (Boushel, 1994) allows us to consider how to assess and strengthen the child's wider "protective environment". It also encourages workers, carers, parents and agencies to work together to protect children, acknowledging each other's strengths and limitations. The rationale for this approach, and for the framework developed to aid its implementation, is provided elsewhere (Boushel, 1994).

This article examines the usefulness of such a framework in family placement work. The framework identifies four factors as particularly important in assessing a child's "protective environment":

- attitudes to children;
- attitudes to their carers;
- the social interconnectedness of child and carer; and
- the existence and quality of statutory and professional "safety nets".

In each of these areas the child's experience is mediated by the state, the community and the family.

This more comprehensive approach keeps the central focus on the child (or potential child) and the child's environment. It helps identify strengths as well as weaknesses, and it allows the impact of discrimination, disadvantage and cultural diversity to be acknowledged.

The framework may be of particular use in the selection and assessment of foster carers, giving all involved the opportunity to understand the strengths and limitations of the overall environment of potential carers, as well as the support offered from professional sources. It can

Figure 1

The child's protective environment

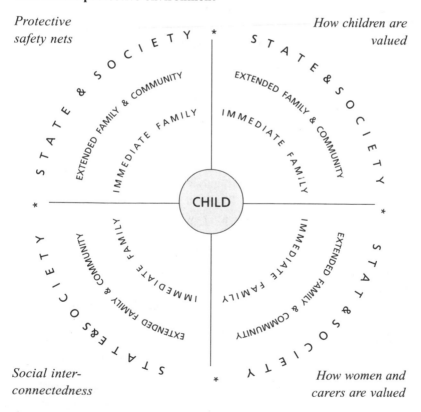

Protective safety nets

How children are valued

Social inter-connectedness

How women and carers are valued

also be used with birth families to indicate areas of strength and vulnerability which a placement would need to complement. It may be used at various other points in the "looking after" process, to assess progress, breakdowns or plans to return home or leave care. The focus on the wider "protective environment" helps identify where strengths and limitations in one area can be acknowledged or compensated for in another. The approach encourages the participation of all concerned, in keeping with the partnership principles of the Children Act 1989. For me, it also provides a useful reminder that service users and carers are, and must remain, the experts on the unique texture of their lives. Effective interventions depend, in great part, on the extent to which we can understand and take account of the systems, strengths and stressors which form these unique environments.

The following sections illustrate some of the issues which use of the framework may raise. In practice, strengths and limitations will be specific to particular situations and cannot be covered in detail here.

How children are valued

They call me bad names . . . I try to ignore them . . . Boys at school who can beat me up tease me and keep asking. It hurts my nerves so I go and hit them and it gets them crying. (Martin, aged 11, black child transracially fostered; Rowe *et al*, 1984)

'In cultures in which children are highly valued . . . maltreatment is less likely to occur' (Korbin, 1991, p 70). State and professional neglect has undervalued many children looked after away from home, by "last resort" approaches to accommodation, lack of attention to family contact, racial identity, health and educational needs (Ahmed, 1986; Milham *et al*, 1986; Colton and Jackson, 1993). Pre-placement circumstances and the impact of separation will affect children's self-esteem in a variety of ways. Once in placement, a child may be safe within the carer's home, but not within the extended family or a particular neighbourhood. In these arenas children may be vulnerable because of the attitudes of others or their own previous experience. For example, girls are more likely to be sexually abused and, as a result, re-abused (Finkelhor, 1986). Boys seem more likely to encounter racial abuse in single-sex schools and may be more often bullied and physically abused by carers and others (Rosenthal *et al*, 1990; Tizard and Phoenix, 1993). A particular child may have had little opportunity to acquire the knowledge and skills necessary to explore their sexuality or their use of personal power safely, leaving them vulnerable and, in some cases, a danger to others (NCH, 1992).

It is easy to be overwhelmed by the vulnerability of many children who are looked after away from home. Often, however, existing good practice suggests ways in which vulnerability may be limited or diminished. Issues such as confidentiality, the placement neighbourhood, school choice and carer and community attitudes to race and gender may be more or less relevant to an individual child's protection and will need to be taken into account in the assessment of carers and in placement finding. Children may need help to diminish their own vulnerability by increasing their opportunity and capacity to make choices and decisions. As Gardner says, 'One way in which children may survive stress is the discovery that they can learn from it – they can find creative solutions' (1987, p 23). The ability to provide help with cover stories and assertive, non-violent strategies for dealing with bullying and discrimination will help a child value themselves and be valued. Racial and gender identity and self-esteem, and a child's health and education may need to be monitored and strengthened (Parker *et al*, 1991). Information and advice on sexual orientation, family planning and drugs and alcohol use may be crucial, as may be support about ways of developing appropriate expectations and behaviour in relationships (NFCA, 1993). Some of these risks and opportunities may exist within the carers' family, others may be identifiable in the wider protective environment.

How women and carers are valued
Carers have a central role in developing and sustaining a child's "protective environment". This does not happen in isolation from the structural, social and interpersonal factors governing gender roles within families and within society. "Women's work" inside or outside the home is not highly valued, socially or financially in this society. The limited financial and other support available to foster carers reflects this (Smith, 1991) and has implications for the child's protective environment in a number of ways.

Professional, family and community recognition of the skills and challenges involved in fostering, and the availability of practical and emotional support to carers, affect the level of placement breakdown and stress-related abuse. More research is needed in this area, but foster carer "burnout" and social isolation have both been identified as significant "systems stressors" in US studies of abuse by carers (McFadden, 1984).

Women are less likely than men to sexually abuse children. A US study suggests that in foster care, too, male carers are more likely than female carers to physically and sexually abuse (Rosenthal *et al*, 1990). Systems for assessing the sexual interests and behaviour of carers are, as yet, crude and unreliable. In these circumstances, the burden of protection often falls on women. We need to be aware of how the link between gender and caring may affect a foster carer's perceptions and choices. Allegations of abuse by a family member are likely to have a major impact on her self-esteem and mean that she faces many of the same dilemmas as other non-abusing mothers. The access she has to emotional support and to adequate, non-discriminatory legal and practical resources will have a direct bearing on her ability and willingness to offer protection (Mama, 1989; Boushel and Lebacq, 1992; Hooper, 1992).

The protective environments of fostered children will be strengthened by a more open acknowledgement and assessment of the ways in which these gender-linked issues affect carers, and the practical and emotional dilemmas to which they give rise. Improved supports for non-abusing carers, opportunities for single-parent and part-time care, and encouragement to increase skills and confidence in areas outside fostering, will also help avoid "burnout" and diminish the impact of abuse that may occur within the carer's family.

Similar initiatives need to be taken to ensure that a parent to whom a child is returning has the support necessary to offer adequate protection. Carers and workers who understand the impact of the structural and social inequalities facing mothers and other carers will be better able to appreciate and support a child's birth family.

Social interconnectedness

When you tell them it sort of brands you out from certain things that they want to tell you, like secrets. Most people don't tell me any secrets. (Jamie and Jason; NFCA, Video and Tape Transcripts, 1988, p 11)

A child's interconnectedness with a rich social network provides potential confidantes, role models, opportunities to develop social skills, and intellectual and social stimulation. The move away from home may fracture important protective connections for children, even when they have not been able to prevent abuse. Little attention has yet been paid to the protective potential of these links. A child may be helped to retain contact with siblings or friends who protect in the school playground; relatives and neighbours whose "inside" knowledge helps develop strategies for self-protection within the family; youth leaders who have taken a special interest, etc. Similar networks may need to be developed in the new setting, as the quote above indicates.

In general, children seem more likely to disclose abuse to peers than to adults (Kelly, 1991). However, they may need considerable encouragement to develop and sustain protective peer group networks in stigmatising circumstances (Davis, 1989). The Children Act has been criticised for excessive regulation of the friendships and informal contacts of children who are "looked after". Inadequate resources for supportive after-care is a further criticism of current childcare provision.

The foster carers' social interconnectedness is equally important. The quality and extent of the foster carers' links with potential protective networks will affect the ease with which they can be developed to suit a child's individual circumstances. Social interconnectedness also provides carers with assistance with child care tasks and responsibilities, allows for the redistribution of caring, and encourages greater consensus and closer monitoring of children (Korbin, 1991). Social isolation has long been connected with an increased risk of intra-familial abuse. Perhaps the tendency to view such isolation as pathological (e.g. DoH, 1988) has prevented us from examining other circumstances and situations which may diminish social interconnectedness, such as inadequate financial and practical support, a child's disturbed behaviour and the response of relatives and friends. These and other factors may diminish carers' opportunities to maintain and develop their social networks and to include the children they look after in the social fabric of their lives.

These areas need careful assessment and adequate support if child and carer are to avoid the hazards of isolation.

Protective safety nets

I was told they had come for the children and would I put a few things in a suitcase for them. (Foster carer whose husband was accused of sexual abuse of own daughter; Moorat, 1991, p 10)

The fourth area to consider is the efficacy and protective potential of the legal, professional and resource framework within which child protection work is carried out. Its strengths and limitations at a local and national level need to be explored in relation to the individual situations of children, birth families and carers.

The child's past experience may have left her or him with strong fears about the implications of disclosing abuse – for example, further court appearances, fears of removal and self-blame. On the other hand, there is concern that some children see accusations of abuse as one of the few ways they have of exerting control over their lives. Foster carers fear false allegations, but they also fear the consequences for children who become involved with child protection investigations. When this framework was shared with foster carers at the 1993 International Foster Care Association Conference, *all* present expressed their reluctance to involve statutory agencies in disclosures of sexual abuse, because of the "secondary abuse" they foresaw for the children involved.

What children's and carers' perceptions may have in common is a fairly realistic appraisal of the events that can follow disclosure. It may lead to precipitous interventions, perhaps because of the breach of trust involved, or because the traumatic effect of removal from carers is underestimated. It may be assumed that carers will put their own needs before the child's, or agency responses may reflect defensive professional practice rather than the needs of an individual child. From the child and the non-abusing carer's point of view, an approach that validates and empowers them will need to take account of their perceptions of the abuse, and its consequences, and build on the strategies they themselves may have identified (Boushel and Lebacq, 1992).

The approach adopted here encourages workers to use the framework to help assess and improve the strength of carers' environments as one of the ways of ensuring that the child's environment is a protective one. Undertaking this task jointly with carers will help explore their willingness and ability to acknowledge the possibility of abuse, to discuss concerns and to identify areas of vulnerability. For carers it will indicate the willingness of workers and agencies to hear and respond to concerns in ways that build on the existing strengths within their own and the foster child's "protective environments". The rehearsal of "worst case" scenarios may be used to explore together the ways in which the carers and the agency might best respond. If problems in agencies' response strategies are identified, they need to be acknowledged and attempts made by both workers and carers to have them addressed at a policy level.

The child also needs to know that social workers and carers are aware that abuse can happen during a placement and that worries she or he may have about the safety and quality of her or his life will be listened to and responded to. The child will need an indication of the extent and limits of her or his own control and power in such situations, and the likely form that professional responses may take. Information about confidential telephone help-lines, the identification of trusted people who agree to offer support and advice, contact with other children in care, confidential medical advice (and encouragement to use it) all encourage children to identify and use the protective strategies they find most helpful.

Conclusion

The approach suggested here will not stop all abuse in foster care settings. Rather, it indicates the extent to which much broader social values and expectations underlay individual behaviour.

By focusing on the whole of the child's "protective environment", however, opportunities can be created for workers, carers, children and their birth families to work together to assess and strengthen the safety of the child's world. In doing so, it encourages all involved to acknowledge the supports that parents and carers need, as well as the initiatives that children themselves may be helped to take. A joint approach such as this has the potential to increase the child's feeling of interconnectedness, and to create a climate that acknowledges the risks to the child's current and future safety in a realistic, well-prepared and constructive way.

References

Ahmed S, Cheetham J and Small J, *Social Work with Black children and their Families*, BAAF/Batsford, 1986.

Boushel M, 'The protective environment of children: towards a framework for anti-oppressive cross-cultural and cross-national understanding', *British Journal of Social Work*, 24:2, pp 173–90, 1994.

Boushel M and Lebacq M, 'Towards empowerment in child protection work', *Children & Society*, 6:1, pp 12–24, 1992.

Colton M and Jackson S, 'Against all odds', *Community Care*, p 23, 8 April 1993.

Davis I P, 'Intervention with adolescents in foster family care and their families', in Aldgate J, Maluccio A and Reeves C (eds), *Adolescents in Foster Families*, BAAF/Batsford, 1989.

Department of Health, *Protecting Children: A guide for social workers undertaking a comprehensive assessment*, HMSO, 1988.

Department of Health, *Working Together Under the Children Act 1989*, HMSO, 1991.

Department of Health, *Child Protection: Messages from research*, HMSO, 1995.

Finkelhor D, *A Sourcebook on Child Sexual Abuse*, Sage, 1986, USA.

Gardner R, *Who Says? Choice and control in care*, National Children's Bureau, 1987.

Hooper C A, *Mothers Surviving Child Sexual Abuse*, Routledge, 1992.

Jones A, 'UK anti-racist child protection', *Race & Class*, 35:2, pp 75–85, 1993.

Kelly L, Regan L and Burton S, *Exploratory Study of Sexual abuse in a Sample of 1,244 Young People*, Child Abuse Studies Unit, Polytechnic of North London, 1991.

Korbin J, 'Cross-cultural perspectives and research directions for the 21st century', *Child Abuse & Neglect*, 15:1, pp 67–77, 1991.

Lynch M, 'Child protection: Have we lost our way?', *Adoption & Fostering*, 16:4, pp 15–22, 1992.

McFadden E J, *Preventing Abuse in Foster Care*, National Foster Care Education Project, Eastern Michigan University, 1984, USA.

Mama A, *The Hidden Struggle: Statutory and voluntary responses to violence against black women in the home*, London Race and Housing Research Unit, 1989.

Marneffe C, 'The confidential doctor centre – a new approach to child protection work', *Adoption & Fostering*, 16:4, pp 23–28, 1992.

Milham S, Bullock R, Hosie K and Haak M, *Lost in Care*, Gower, 1986.

Moorat D, 'Allegations against carers', *Foster Care*, 68, pp 10–11, 1991.

National Children's Home, *The Report of the Committee of Enquiry into Children and Young People who Sexually Abuse Other Children*, NCH, 1992.

National Foster Care Association, *The Challenge of Foster Care*, NFCA, 1988; 1993.

National Foster Care Association, *Child Abuse: Accusations against foster carers*, NFCA, 1993.

Nunno M and Motz J, 'The development of an effective response to the abuse of children in out-of-home care', *Child Abuse & Neglect*, 12, pp 521–28, 1988.

Parker R, Ward H, Jackson S, Aldgate J and Wedge P, *Assessing Outcomes in Child Care*, HMSO, 1991.

Rosenthal J, Motz J, Edmonson D and Groze V, 'A descriptive study of abuse and neglect in out-of-home-placement', *Child Abuse & Neglect*, 15, pp 249–60, 1991.

Rowe J, Cain H, Hundleby M and Keane A, *Long-term Foster Care*, BAAF/Batsford, 1984.

Smith B, 'Australian women and foster care', *Child Welfare*, 2, pp 175–84, 1991.

Tizard B and Phoenix A, *Black, White or Mixed Race? Race and racism in the lives of young people of mixed parentage*, Routledge, 1993.

UK Joint Working Party on Foster Care, *Consultation Document on National Standards in Foster Care*, NFCA, 1998.

Violence Against Children Study Group, *Taking Child Abuse Seriously*, Unwin Hyman, 1990.

18 The role of social workers in supporting and developing the work of foster carers

Clive Sellick

Clive Sellick is Lecturer in Social Work at the University of East Anglia, Norwich. He is a former social worker, Team Manager, Magistrate and Guardian ad litem. His publications include "Foster Care: Theory and Practice", with John Triseliotis and Robin Short (1995) and "What Works in Family Placement?", with June Thoburn (1996). As his School's Director of International Programmes, he has assisted in the development of child welfare services, including fostering, in Moldova, Romania and Russia.

This paper was published in Adoption & Fostering, 20:2, 1996.

> *She was approachable, always attentive. She gave you the confidence that she knew what she was doing.*

The notion of people working together as fellow participants in a service has underpinned social work activity for much of its existence. Working relationships exist between clients and social workers, student social workers and practice teachers, social workers and managers, social workers and foster carers, and foster carers and parents. These relationships form the basis of how people negotiate, what they achieve and whether or not they are satisfied with the outcome. Research and practice wisdom which describe these various relationships come up with remarkably similar findings and comments about what sustains them and what can be achieved because of them. This article will discuss both the content and potential of these working relationships by referring to the wider social work literature. It will concentrate on what makes the particular relationship between foster carers and social workers both satisfactory and effective. It will do so by extracting what we know from the published accounts of research and practice about the qualities and competences which social workers need to exhibit in this vital area of their working lives. In order to do so it starts by looking at how social services and social work departments in both the statutory and voluntary sectors organise their social work personnel.

Service arrangements

Most local authorities separate the tasks and responsibilities of family placement from family support and child protection social work in two key ways. Firstly, different social workers with different job titles are employed to undertake each of these. This role division is virtually universal throughout Britain. Although it has many operational benefits it also has shortcomings which will be discussed later in this article. Family placement social workers have various titles ranging from the rather dated "fostering officer" to the somewhat incomplete "home-finder", whose title includes recruitment and assessment tasks but implies that support and retention tasks are less important. In this article the term "link social worker" is preferred to describe this role since it sums up the whole range of the work with foster carers, children and their relatives, and with the social workers of the children and their families. It is also a term which is used widely in practice (see, for example, Ramsay describing foster care in Fife, *Adoption & Fostering*, 20:1, 1996). In addition to the specialist tasks of recruiting, assessing, training and supporting foster carers, link social workers play a significant role in co-ordinating services for foster carers by liaising and negotiating with their colleagues, managers and administrators. Children's social workers based in district, area, health care or other specialist teams are principally responsible for the design and implementation of care plans, for discharging other statutory duties and for working directly with children and their families, but they too have an important role to play with foster carers. This is particularly relevant in respect of short-term foster carers who regularly handle "real life" situations with distressed children, demanding families, and pressing practicalities that require ready access to children's social workers (Sellick, 1992, p 63).

Secondly, most local authorities house these two types of social workers in separate sections which are often geographically distant. Family Placement Units tend to be centralised although some departments post link workers out in district teams. A recent study conducted by the National Foster Care Association on behalf of the Department of Health indicates that the separation of tasks and locations of link and family social workers is widespread in local authorities across England (Waterhouse, 1997). Volume 3 of the Children Act Regulations does not require the establishment of such a distinct service but acknowledges its value, especially for foster carers themselves (DoH, 1991). Although this arrangement is generally based on experience rather than research, some descriptive studies indicate that foster carers themselves find it helpful (DoH, 1995b). The major study by Rowe *et al* (1989) of more than 10,000 placements in six English local authorities over two years investigated the possible links between placement outcomes and the organisation of fostering services. Although no clear link was found, there was evidence that there were advantages from having separate link social workers able to form good working relationships with foster carers (Hundleby, 1989). This study also reported that separate family placement units or the posting of link social workers in district teams led to effectiveness in recruiting foster carers and a greater expertise in their assessment. Respondents in the study by Waterhouse also report increased recruitment activity.

Independent non-profit making fostering agencies have no formal or statutory authority to employ staff to undertake the work of local authority children and family social workers. Their strength springs from the specialist and often pioneering nature of their family placement work. Both large-scale and long-established voluntary organisations such as Barnardo's, and small-scale and relatively recent ones such as Pro-Teen, have recruited and developed a workforce of foster carers who report very positively about their working relationships with their agency staff (Sellick, 1992; DoH, 1995a). Government proposals for the introduction of inadequately regulated fostering-for-profit agencies have been widely criticised by both local authority and independent agencies' staff (see, for example, Rickford, 1995). However, if such agencies invest in high quality support services to their foster carers they are likely to command the respect of these carers in much the same way as those who foster for the independent agencies or who highly regard the work of their local authority link social workers.

Components of an effective working relationship

In recent years a number of evaluative studies of child care social work have included descriptive accounts of the activities of social workers. Consumers of a social work service describe what they value from social workers. Clients and carers have by these descriptions allowed us to dissect the core features of an effective social work service delivered by social workers themselves. Two major categories have emerged which are summarised below by Howe (1987). He writes that in order to be effective social workers must succeed in two areas – personal relationships and the organisation of work:

They must create those personal conditions which establish a relationship of trust, caring and acceptance thereby increasing the client's amenability to therapeutic influence. It appears, therefore, that the quality of the relationship is important in social work practice. Social workers should be responsive.

They must employ careful and explicit procedures. The purpose of the worker's involvement must be understood by the worker and the client. Good practitioners make deliberate use of well-articulated theories and methods which organise, order and direct practice in a way that is recognised by both worker and client. Social workers should be "systematic".

These two major components are expressed in different terms but include remarkably similar features elsewhere in the literature. For example, in a more recent publication in which he describes the processes of counselling and psychotherapy, Howe (1993) refers both to the 'core conditions' of genuineness, empathy and warmth as well as the theoretical base and therapeutic techniques of the therapist. Elsewhere in a recently published reader on the theory and practice of foster care, Triseliotis *et al* (1995) also divide effective social work practice into two areas: the personal qualities and the professional competences which social workers display.

Two influential child care studies, Fisher *et al* (1986) and Farmer and Parker (1991), contain clear consumer descriptions of social work practice which build on our knowledge of social work qualities and competences.

The study by Fisher *et al* had a great impact upon child care practice, especially with regard to the notion of parental responsibility and the working relations between parents and social workers. An in-depth sample of 55 cases gave rise to 331 individual interviews with parents, children, field and residential social workers. These spanned the study's three phases of admission, in-care and discharge. Social workers were praised by parents when they were:

- open and honest and "put their cards on the table";
- consistently showed concern by staying in close touch with parents;
- exhibited a desire to involve parents in the decisions and activities of care;
- took parents seriously;
- acted purposefully and in a business-like manner, for example by using written agreements or by discussing various options with parents.

This applied even where they were at odds over what they each considered to be in the children's best interests.

Farmer and Parker (1991) studied case files in four local authorities in England covenng over 300 children who were returned home while they were still subject to care orders. The authors used the phrase 'purposeful social work' to describe what seemed to be a key ingredient in successful rehabilitation cases. This meant that social workers had to be clear about their responsibilities; they needed to be persistent and they needed to be flexible, adding that:

It was this clarity of purpose, plus the ability to use their authority, combined with steady, reliable visiting that seemed to mark out the most effective social work input.

A very helpful recent addition to the body of child care research sheds further light on the positive components of another working relationship in child welfare, that of parents and foster carers. Bradley and Aldgate (1994) studied the use of short-term breaks for children in need. The experiences of the key participants were considered. Among them parents commented on:

the friendliness and supportiveness of the carers, their generosity and their non-judgemental approach which seemed to restore their self-esteem and confidence as parents.

The relevance to social work practice with foster carers

By looking beyond the manner in which social workers and foster carers relate to one another we can then establish a list of descriptive terms from those who are both consumers and generally less powerful protagonists in a working relationship. In these cited examples parents talk about what makes for a good social worker and, elsewhere, a good foster carer. When we go on to focus on what carers say about social workers many of their descriptions echo those of parents. Triseliotis and his colleagues cite Freeman's (1991) prerequisite qualities for creating the conditions of a working relationship or partnership:

> ... *honesty, naturalness, reliability, keeping clients informed, understanding their feelings and the stress of parenthood, offering combined practical and moral support.*

They go on to suggest that if we substitute "foster carers" for "clients" and "caring" for "parenthood" these prerequisites are equally appropriate for social workers in their work with foster carers (Triseliotis *et al*, 1995).

Carer studies

The views of foster carers and adopters as consumers of a social work support service have been reported in many studies. Some of these are now quite dated and many are North American. Since these carers were saying what many contemporary British carers say today there is a sobering as well as a fascinating element about them. The findings will now be briefly summarised.

Kline and Overstreet (1972) refer to carers wanting 'knowledgeable assurance' from social workers rather than 'vague generalisations, evasion and indirection'. Hampson and Tavormina (1980), in a study of foster mothers, reported that their most frequent complaints related to the case management, poor communication or availability, and constant turnover of social workers. In a report based on interviews with government officials and agency managers in Canada, the USA, Denmark and the former West Germany, Southon (1986) wrote that 'successful fostering really does require a good rapport with the social worker'. Others talk of the need for social workers to praise and reassure foster carers (Littner, 1978; Cautley, 1980).

More recently two British publications reached similar conclusions. The first was an account of the service provided to adopters and permanent foster carers of children with special needs in a Scottish local authority (O'Hara, 1986). The second was a study of the support of short-term foster carers in four local authorities and two independent fostering agencies in England (Sellick, 1992).

O'Hara (1986) lists an interest and commitment to the carer, availability, reliability, trustworthiness, warmth, an ability to listen and competence over official matters. Sellick (1992) cites:

> . . . workers and managers who make themselves available on both a regular and emergency basis, especially outside of office hours, who consult and inform carers, who offer recognition to foster carers for their work and for the personal costs to their families by, for example, the provision of respite and specialist support, and who combine a working relationship with a personal touch are valued.

The words of the foster carer at the beginning of this paper are representative of carers from different statutory and independent fostering agencies when they describe the work of their link social workers (Sellick, 1992). For example, another carer in the same study said her link worker:

> . . . was always really on the ball. If I wasn't happy with things that she [the child's social worker] was doing, I'd have a word with her. She was straight in writing memos, speaking to her, trying to get things sorted out. Things like that which was a great help. It wasn't just me having to struggle. She was on our side, backing us up, making some of the running as well.

These foster carers, along with many others, identified a number of different qualities. For instance, foster carers regularly report that they value or seek social workers who are energetic, purposeful, reliable and flexible, in addition to being friendly on the one hand and knowledgeable on the other. Foster carers are in the thick of things without day-to-day colleagues, without the opportunity to offload on to them or a manager, and without service conditions like paid holidays and sickness benefits, so little wonder that the personal skills of social workers can matter so much to foster carers. Foster carers in the same way as clients, students and social workers value being understood, respected, listened to and having interest shown in them by the social worker, therapist, manager or whoever happens to be on the other side of the working relationship in which they are engaged. Once established, collaboration acts as a springboard to allow foster carers to get on with the job. However, it seems to be at this point that foster carers require more from social workers than social skills and sound personalities. Social worker competence is needed if the working relationship is to survive.

Foster care studies continually refer to the difference between the support provided to foster carers within a working relationship by link social workers and the social worker responsible for the child in the foster placement. However, a study of 72 foster carers in one Scottish local authority reported recently in this journal (Ramsay, 1996), noted that over two-thirds of the foster carers were satisfied with the support of their foster child's social worker either all or most of the time. The report of the second in a series of governmental inspections of six local authority fostering services stated that foster carers valued the support of their link workers and, because they respected their abilities, willingly accepted constructive criticism and the need to be accountable for their work as carers. In contrast most had developed low expectations of the children's social workers who were often described as irresponsible, unavailable, unreliable and poor at administration (DoH, 1995b). These accounts also contrast sharply with those of foster carers in two independent fostering agencies recently studied by the Social Services Inspectorate (DoH, 1995a). In these agencies foster carers considered they were encouraged to contribute to shared decision-making as team members, gained professional status and recognition, received a professional fee, and worked with specialist fostering social workers who were available around the clock to support them and the placement. These workers function as link workers within the independent agencies. The children's social workers as local authority employees are therefore even more organisationally distant from the independent agencies' staff and carers than they are from link workers in their own agencies.

The way forward

There are clearly many advantages for both local authority fostering agencies and foster carers in separating out responsibilities for family placement on the one hand and child and family social work on the other. Yet this virtually universal arrangement has, it seems, one major structural fault: the expressed dissatisfaction of foster carers with the service they receive from children's social workers. In contrast the overall satisfaction that foster carers experience from their working relationships with local authority link social workers and independent agency specialist and support social workers serves to expose this faultline even further.

Certain arrangements may reduce these differences. Placing link social workers in district or area teams (Hundleby, 1989), regular joint training sessions for foster carers and children's social workers (Triseliotis et al, 1995), and the participation of social workers in foster care social events (Sellick, 1992) are reported as assisting the development of collaborative working practices and mutual respect of foster carers and children's social workers. But real solutions depend upon major change which may be beyond the grasp of most local authorities at least in the short term. Many children's social workers are inexperienced and some move quickly to less stressful jobs only to be replaced by other newly qualified social workers. The professional training of social work students does not adequately cover the contemporary realities of foster care and the demands upon the largely volunteer workforce of foster carers and their families. Group care practice placements, for example, are still more likely to be sited in residential or day care establishments for children than in foster family settings.

Further leads may come from our knowledge of the stresses of social work and foster care practice, and the vital contribution of supportive supervision in developing and retaining social workers and foster carers alike. The range of supervision arrangements beyond the formal hierarchical one traditionally practised, as described by Sellick (1992 in Appendix B), may be further adapted. This could include peer or small group supervision involving link and children's social workers and foster carers together.

There are very few published practice accounts of these sorts of arrangements, although clearly opportunities are there to be taken. However, possibilities are not endless in a system which separates the activities, professional development and workplaces of link and children's social workers. Even the most effective and respected social worker for the child and family cannot be "there" for the foster carers in the same way as link workers. Children's social workers have divided loyalties, many are subject to the unpredictable demands of child abuse investigations and court appearances, and can spend much time arranging contact visits and departmental meetings. The different responsibilities of link social workers allow them to be more measured. There is no real excuse for unreliability, inefficiency, lack of openness or inconsistency in link or children's social workers but maybe all of us, including foster carers, should understand a little more that organisational constraints rather than individual failure are often responsible.

References

Bradley M and Aldgate J, 'Short-term family based care for children in need', *Adoption & Fostering*, 18:4, pp 24–9, 1994.

Cautley P, *New Foster Parents: The first experience*, Human Sciences Press, 1980, USA.

Department of Health, *The Children Act 1989: Guidance and Regulations*, Volume 3, HMSO, 1991.

Department of Health, Social Services Inspectorate, *Independent Fostering Agencies Study*, Health Publications Unit, 1995a.

Department of Health, Social Services Inspectorate, *Inspection of Local Authority Fostering Services*, HMSO, 1995b.

Farmer E and Parker R, *Trials and Tribulations*, HMSO, 1991.

Farmer E, 'Restoring children on court orders to their families: lessons for practice', *Adoption & Fostering*, 16:1, pp 7–15, 1992.

Fisher M, Marsh P, Phillips D and Sainsbury E, *In and Out of Care*, BAAF/ Batsford, 1986.

Freeman M, *Children, their Families and the Law: Working with the Children Act*, Macmillan, 1991.

Hampson R and Tavormina J, 'Feedback from the experts: a study of foster mothers', *Social Work*, pp 108–12, March 1980.

Howe D, *An Introduction to Social Work Theory*, Ashgate, 1987.

Howe D, *On Being a Client*, Sage Publications, 1993.

Hundleby M, 'The pros and cons of specialisation', *Adoption & Fostering*, 13:3, pp 22–9, 1989.

Kline D and Overstreet H, *Foster Care of Children: Nurture and treatment*, Columbia University Press, 1972, USA.

Littner N, 'The art of being a foster parent', *Child Welfare*, 57:1, pp 3–12, 1978.

O'Hara G, 'Developing post-placement services in Lothian', *Adoption & Fostering*, 10:4, pp 38–42, 1986.

Ramsay D, 'Recruiting and retaining foster carers: implications of a professional service in Fife', *Adoption & Fostering*, 20:1, pp 42–6, 1996.

Rickford F, 'Regulation or speculation', *Community Care*, pp 18–24, May 1995.

Rowe J, Hundleby M and Garnett L, *Child Care Now: A survey of placement patterns*, BAAF, 1989.

Sellick C, *Supporting Short-term Foster Carers*, Avebury, 1992.

Southon V, *Children in Care: Paying their new families*, HMSO, 1986.

Triseliotis J, Sellick C and Short R, *Foster Care: Theory and practice*, BAAF/ Batsford, 1995.

Waterhouse S, *The Organisation of Fostering Services*, HMSO, 1997.

19 **Contact:** The social workers' experience

Hedy Cleaver

Hedy Cleaver is a Senior Research Fellow in the School of Social Work, Leicester University.

This paper was published in Adoption & Fostering, 21:4, 1998.

Introduction

The implementation of the Children Act 1989 in England and Wales was intended to have a profound effect on social work policy and practice with regard to contact between children "looked after" and their families. Two aspects are particularly relevant. First, the incorporation of the principle of parental responsibility. This affected children "looked after" and living away from home because parents now retain responsibility for their child even when a care order applies (s 2 (5)). Second is the emphasis on contact when children are "looked after". Where children are accommodated local authorities must, whenever practical and consistent with the child's welfare, place children near home and promote contact with their families (see s 23 (7) and Schedule 2 (15)). When children are in care the authority is required to allow reasonable contact between children and their families (see s 34 (1)).

Research which predated the Act had revealed the problems families experienced in maintaining contact when a child was in care and the reasons why a change of practice was needed. In some cases formal restrictions were imposed. However, most barriers to contact were informal and non specific. They included actual or perceived hostility of the substitute carers, distance and inaccessibility of the placement (Millham *et al*, 1986). When families were eager to maintain contact, in many cases parents found themselves in a "Catch 22" situation: initial attempts to visit were discouraged because "best left to settle" was still a popular notion, while later efforts to re-establish contact were frowned on through fears that renewed contact would prove unsettling (Rowe *et al*, 1984).

Most children "looked after" were shown to benefit from keeping in touch with their family. For example, the maintenance of family links was related to children returning to live at "home" (see, for example, Fanshel and Shinn, 1978; Aldgate, 1980; Millham *et al*, 1986). But even when reunification was not the immediate plan, contact was associated with fewer fostering breakdowns (Berridge and Cleaver, 1987; Thoburn and Rowe, 1988; Wedge and Mantle, 1991) and enhanced children's sense of identity (DoH, 1996).

To explore the impact of the Children Act 1989 on contact the Department of Health funded a three-year study to look at the experiences of foster children and their families. The research has two parts: a retrospective survey of social work records for a particular year; and a prospective, qualitative study of 32 children, aged from five to 12 years.

A study like this, which wishes to work with children and families, depends on the co-operation and collaboration of local authorities and their staff. Six local authorities agreed to participate. All welcomed the research because they believed social work practice with regard to contact had fundamentally changed since the implementation of the Children Act.

The research is still only at the half-way point and it is anticipated that the results will be published in late 1998. However, interesting insights into current practice with regard to contact are beginning to emerge. This paper explores some of the problems social workers encounter and illustates examples of good practice.

Social workers' views on contact
In order to develop an acceptable and workable access procedure the research team needed to work in partnership with social workers. This meant that in addition to discussions with senior staff, meetings were held with social work teams responsible for children and families, disability and family placement. These sessions were used not only to explain the aims and methods of the study, but also acted as a forum for staff to talk about their experiences. In all 22 senior managers, 43 team leaders and 245 social workers were involved. Managers and social

workers were asked to focus on fostering arrangements made since the implementation of the Children Act 1989 and to consider contact with regard to all children looked after and living in foster homes. Notes were taken at these meetings and what follows is based on the wealth of material that social workers shared with us.

The importance of contact for foster children was universally accepted by social workers at all levels in the service, and the Children Act 1989 and the Guidance and Regulations (DoH, 1991) were thought to have influenced practice. In line with the Guidance and Regulations 6.9, contact was mainly conceived of in terms of personal meetings. Other means of keeping families in touch, such as letters, telephone calls, tape or video recordings, were rarely mentioned. In terms of direct contact, there was some confusion over what constitutes "reasonable" contact (Children Act 1989, s 34 (1)). Problems arose when court judges, social services and parents applied different interpretations. For example, when parents perceive daily visiting as "reasonable", social workers might consider this an unrealistic target.

The value of contact for children also became an issue when social workers feared that the stress of direct contact with the family might outweigh its expected benefits. For example, mentally ill parents whose behaviour was unpredictable caused social workers considerable anxiety. Difficulties also arose when parents undermined the role of foster carers.

Some social workers struggled to accommodate the wishes of separated parents, aware that regular separate visits stretched resources while splitting a single contact session meant halving the actual contact time for each visitor. When warring parents used their contact visits to invalidate each other, social workers found it difficult to see where the child's best interests lay. They expressed concerns that arrangements had more to do with satisfying the courts and/or the family than in meeting the needs of the child.

For children in care, contact visits with their family may place them in situations which are dangerous so that contact will need to be supervised. In some cases social workers themselves supervise visits. In others contact takes place in social services venues, such as family centres, where supervision is carried out by staff. Alternatively, parents may visit at the foster home when foster carers are responsible for the supervision. All approaches have implications for social services resources. On the other hand in circumstances where contact between children in care and their families does not pose a risk, or when children are accommodated, organising visits should be less of an issue for social services resources.

Hess and Proch (1993) note that contact visits may serve a number of purposes. They can help children to maintain relationships with people who are important to them. Visits may reassure children that they have not been abandoned and that their family is safe and well. Alternatively, contact can be used by social workers to assess parenting skills and motivation. Finally, contact visits may be used to help children and families develop better ways of interacting and communicating. Social workers involved in the current study talked of contact primarily in terms of keeping children in touch with their families. There was little mention of the different roles contact can have and no discussion of it being used therapeutically to improve poor parent–child relationships. If contact is to be used creatively, time is needed to plan objectives, prepare parents and children, debrief them afterwards and inform foster carers of what happened. If this is undertaken, regardless of whether contact is supervised or unsupervised it will have a considerable impact on social workers' time.

Five themes regularly came up in our discussions with both senior management and social work teams: the courts; balancing the wishes of children and families; supervision; timing; and venue.

The influence of the courts
The introduction of the Children Act 1989 has in some cases resulted in discussions about contact taking place in the courts. A number of social work teams believed that as a result there were occasions when decisions were dependent more on the arguments of lawyers than on the best interests of the child. Social workers felt that some courts undervalued their professional judgement while elevating the guardian ad litem to the position of expert. When this happens they fear that magistrates place too great an emphasis on contact and not enough on the child's safety. As examples, social workers cited a few instances where, because social services could not guarantee weekend contact, an Emergency

Protection Order requested on a Friday had been restricted to a single day. Working in close partnership with the guardian ad litem to resolve conflicts prior to going to court was advocated by many social workers as a way round this type of problem.

Social workers said they felt some courts held rather unrealistic expectations in terms of the amount of contact. To specify visiting on a daily basis was not uncommon. Managers feared that when social service personnel needed to be involved, this placed severe stress on staff resources which tended to be reflected in increased sickness rates.

Balancing the wishes of children and families

When the wishes of the child and family are not in accord social workers found striking the right balance could be difficult. For example, it was felt that because the families of many children "looked after" lead disorganised lives, a pattern of regular contact is difficult to sustain. But missed appointments leave children disappointed and anxious. One social worker told of her experience:

> This is a fragmented family. Dad's in prison for assault on Peter and drug dealing. Since Peter has been "looked after" we've had difficulty keeping track of mum. Peter and his mum are quite closely attached . . . but no regular pattern of visiting has been established. I think Peter is quite angry with his mum about this and obviously quite confused about what is happening. It's been difficult to ensure that contact is frequent enough to keep the strength of the bond that there is.

Another factor which sometimes influenced contact arrangements was the arrival of a new partner. Social workers thought there were occasions when the actions of the new partner influenced the parent's commitment and "sabotaged" existing arrangements. A new partner could also affect social workers' attitudes to contact, particularly when the newcomer was a Schedule 1 offender.

A strategy mentioned by many social workers to balance children's wishes for regular contact with parents' disorganised lives and fitful visiting, was to apply a combination of support and pressure. This might involve social workers writing to remind parents of forthcoming visits, ferrying parents to and from contact venues, arranging for parents to arrive 30 minutes before their children, supporting parents after a visit and making parents aware of their child's reaction when visits are missed.

But ensuring the wishes of children are met could incur a high resource cost. For example, to support contact between a lone mother and one of her seven children, two home care workers were needed to look after the other children. In addition, a taxi had to be organised and paid for to take the mother to and from the foster home. Any number of problems threatened to disrupt the arrangements – a breakdown in transport arrangements, an emergency demand on the home care worker or a child's sickness.

If maintaining contact with parents was sometimes difficult, adhering to the Guidance and Regulations on the wider family posed even greater problems: 'The contact arrangements should include those made in respect of relatives, siblings, grandparents and unmarried fathers . . .' (The Children Act 1989, Guidance and Regulations, Vol 3: 6.15, 1995). A common solution, although not without its problems, was to incorporate grandparents and other relatives into the parental visit. When this proved impossible the wishes of children and relatives were sometimes ignored.

The Children Act 1989 places a duty on local authorities to ascertain the child's wishes before making decisions which affect them. Social workers said they went to considerable trouble to ensure that children's views were heard and much emphasis was placed on involving children in decisions which concerned them. However, children and young people's priorities can change rapidly and social workers found there were times when children wished to alter contact arrangements set by the courts. For example, some children found that daily contact, although initially welcome, became difficult to sustain because it interfered with new aspects of their lives. Social workers were then faced with a dilemma. Do they go back to court to change the contact arrangements, an action likely to have an adverse affect on the child? Or do they leave things as they are and thus ignore the child's wishes? One successful solution was to find a middle road and, through negotiation with the guardian ad litem, gain the agreement of both child and family to informally change the arrangement.

The supervision of contact

Supervised contact was not restricted to care order cases. In some social work offices parents were "persuaded" to accept accommodation with supervised contact as an alternative to care proceedings. Social workers admitted that this meant families were more likely to view the intervention as punitive rather than supportive, but felt the strategy was justified because it prevented children entering care. This practice suggests that "accommodation" is not always portrayed to families as a service to support children and families.

The supervision of contact placed a considerable burden on social services resources and involved a variety of staff. Although all the study local authorities used social workers, social work assistants and family centre staff to supervise contact, there were special arrangements too. One authority employed "contact officers" who were assigned once contact arrangements have been established. Their duties might include supervising contact, arranging visits and escorting children or parents to and from contact venues. Senior management held a number of reservations about their roles, responsibilities and a need for training. Nonetheless it was widely acknowledged that the use of contact officers was key to the high levels of contact this authority was able to sustain. Indeed, field social workers admitted that they 'could not function without contact officers'.

When social workers were themselves involved in supervision the toll on their time was considerable, especially in cases involving two or three contact sessions a week or long journeys (for example, to enable one child to see his mother on a monthly basis entailed a round trip of 400 miles). Nevertheless social workers were enthusiastic about the importance of nurturing family ties.

Not all supervised contact was carried out by local authority staff. In straightforward cases and those where there were no security issues, foster carers frequently assumed this responsibility. Alternatively in a few cases social workers arranged for parents and children to meet at the home of relatives with the expectation that they would ensure the child's safety.

Many social workers expressed mixed feelings about using foster carers and relatives in this manner. Some thought the responsibility for supervision should not be delegated to untrained personnel. To expect relatives such as grandparents to supervise contact could place them in an unacceptable position, their loyalties torn between their child and grandchild. However, in cases where foster carers or relatives were adequately trained, supported and "supervised", social workers believed the practice could work very successfully. Foster carers were seen by many social workers as an underused resource.

Contact which necessitates supervision has an element of risk. In these cases a coherent picture of what occurred might be hampered when sessions were covered by different individuals or when escort staff failed to pass on their experiences. Social workers felt there was a need for clear guidance on information recording and sharing.

Timing of contact

Parents and children naturally wish contact at times to suit them – after school, at weekends and on festive occasions. In line with Guidance and Regulations 6.7, when contact did not require supervision social workers encouraged foster carers to negotiate with families and children visiting arrangements to suit all parties. When this worked out social workers' role was purely supervisory. Such arrangements, however, could become problematic with time because as the foster child settled in and bonds were established, carers increasingly wished to involve the child in their day-to-day activities. Contact sessions which disrupted these plans were increasingly resented. In other cases foster carers were not prepared to assume responsibility for contact.

To improve the situation, social workers believed foster care training should place greater stress on the facilitation and management of contact. The maintenance of contact between a foster child and birth parents was not a priority for many carers.

When children are in care and contact has to be supervised, "out of hours" contact is more difficult to arrange because it has to compete with emergency support and preventive interventions. A possible solution proffered in one district was for more flexi-time workers who would be responsible for contact.

Venues for contact

Visits by the parents to the child in his foster home, residential home or in the family home are the most usual forms of contact. They can provide continuity for the child in that setting and opportunities for the parents and carers to meet. (The Children Act 1989, Guidance and Regulations Vol 3:6.18, 1991)

The foster home

In line with the Guidance and Regulations, a common venue for contact was the foster home. In most cases social workers felt this arrangement worked well. However, there were occasions when this was not possible or suitable because of difficulties in ensuring privacy, the behaviour of the birth family and the effect of visits on carers' lives:

- When children need "looking after", relationships with their birth family have often been turbulent (Triseliotis *et al*, 1995; Packman and Hall, 1998). Consequently, contact can be an emotional, traumatic and embarrassing experience for both parents and children, and privacy is essential. Foster homes, however, often include other children and are active places with few opportunities for children and parents to meet in peace and quiet.

- In some cases the foster carers did not want contact to take place in their home, particularly when birth parents had a history of mental illness, drug or alcohol abuse or physical violence. But even where such extreme circumstances did not exist, not all foster carers were willing to have their homes "invaded". Once again social workers saw the solution in terms of foster care training.

- When foster carers were willing to assume responsibility for contact arrangements social workers thought the burden must be carefully monitored and carers supported and supervised. Indeed, it was not unknown for carers looking after two or three children to have at least one parent or family visiting every day. The problem is exacerbated when separated parents or relatives visit at different times, or visits with siblings "looked after" elsewhere also need to be arranged. Social workers were aware that using the foster home for contact placed severe restrictions on families, particularly in cases where more than one child was looked after.

The family home

It was generally acknowledged that most children and families want contact at home. But arranging home visiting for children younger than ten years was not routine practice among any of the social work teams. Although many teenagers kept in touch with their families by casual visits after school or at weekends, such free and easy contact was not as common for younger children. Irrespective of whether the child was in care and contact had to be supervised or simply accommodated, social workers tended to shy away from home visits unless rehabilitation was planned. Several of the social work teams believed home visits could leave children confused. The comments of one social worker reflect their feelings: 'It would give children mixed messages. They'd wonder why it's safe to go home to see mum every day but not to live here.'

Social workers also worried that if young children went home for contact visits they would not be able to cope or seek appropriate help should anything go wrong.

Alternative places

> However, other venues may have advantages for some children and in some circumstances. Outings are one example. (The Children Act 1989 Guidance and Regulations Vol 3: 6.18, 1996)

When, for whatever reason, social workers decided contact should not take place at home and using the foster home was not possible, finding suitable alternative venues was difficult. Although social services offices were generally avoided, a range of other local authority facilities, including day centres, family centres, under-fives units and therapeutic facilities, were employed. All were felt to have drawbacks. For example, therapeutic facilities were frequently used for Memorandum Interviews and could be stigmatising, while the busy atmosphere of day and family centres was not always congenial to privacy.

In addition to these sites some social workers sought out more

259

unusual venues to suit the needs of individual families. For example, one family met at the Salvation Army hostel, elsewhere a family was brought together at the contact site set up for divorced families, and one district was able to take advantage of a rentable room at their local library.

"Outings" were thought to offer many benefits: they provided a neutral and pleasant atmosphere, demonstrated the commitment of social services and gave both family and children a "treat". Social workers reported organising contact in shopping centres, fast-food stores, parks and during activity-based trips, all of which they had been able to fund (see Schedule 2 (16.1)of the Children Act 1989). These types of arrange-ments were said to be appreciated by all parties and proved particularly helpful in promoting harmonious contact.

Conclusions

The discussions with some 300 social workers from six local authorities suggest the Children Act 1989 has had a noticeable impact on contact arrangements involving foster children and their families. There is much evidence to indicate that social workers go to considerable lengths to ensure that regular contact with parents is maintained, even in cases where children are not expected to return home quickly.

A major problem highlighted by the discussions was balancing the wishes of children and families with both the working hours of social workers and the need to protect children. Families want to see each other when it suits them and preferably at home, while social workers' time is restricted and home visits for children younger than ten years are viewed with caution. Although this attitude to home visits may be justified when children are in care and contact is supervised, there is little to suggest that practice differs when children are accommodated. Social workers talked of long-term accommodation as a last resort measure and not as part of a package of services which could be used to support children and families (see the Children Act 1989, s 20 (1)). To set long-term accommodation within the context of family support would encourage a more imaginative attitude to contact where occasional visits home and to relatives might be part of the plan. Thus children would be encouraged to keep in touch not only with their parents (and this often means only mother) but also with their wider kin, friends and home neighbourhoods.

To ensure that children and families meet regularly appears to be the primary aim of most contact arrangements. The benefits are seen in terms of keeping families in touch so that children know who they are and where they come from. Although this is commendable, more could be done. Research has shown that relationships between children and their families are frequently poor at the point when long-term accommodation is required. Contact sessions could be used in a purposive way to improve filiation. To do this would require direct work with children and families and has resource implications. Nonetheless research on leaving care suggests that when family relationships fail to improve, care leavers are particularly isolated and dependent on social services, an outcome which also has cost implications (Biehal *et al*, 1995; DoH, 1996).

References

Aldgate J, 'Identification of factors influencing children's length of stay in care', in Triseliotis J (ed), *New Developments in Foster Care and Adoption*, Routledge & Kegan Paul, 1980.

Biehal N, Clayden J, Stein M and Wade J, *Moving On: Young people and leaving care schemes*, HMSO, 1995.

Berridge D and Cleaver H, *Foster Home Breakdown*, Blackwell, 1987.

Department of Health, *Focus on Teenagers: Research into practice*, HMSO, 1996.

Department of Health, *The Children Act 1989, Guidance and Regulations, Vol 3: Family Placements*, HMSO, 1991.

Fanshel D and Shinn E B, *Children in Foster Care: A longitudinal study*, Columbia University Press, 1978, USA.

Hess P M and Proch K O, *Contact: Managing visits to children looked after away from home*, BAAF, 1993.

Millham S, Bullock R, Hosie K and Haak M, *Lost in Care: The problems of maintaining links between children in care and their families*, Gower, 1986.

Packman J and Hall C, *From Care to Accommodation*, The Stationery Office, 1998.

Rowe J, Cain H, Hundleby M and Keane A, *Long-term Foster Care*, BAAF/Batsford, 1984.

Thoburn J and Rowe J, 'Research: a snapshot of permanent family placement', *Adoption & Fostering*, 12:3, pp 29–34, 1988.

Triseliotis J, Borland M, Hill M and Lambert L, *Teenagers and the Social Work Services*, HMSO, 1995.

Wedge P and Mantle G, *Sibling Groups and Social Work*, Gower, 1991.

Section VI
Education, health and development

Foster carers and social workers are expected to promote the development of looked after children. If asked whether they are concerned about the "whole child", nearly all would doubtless answer, 'yes, of course'. But it has been suggested that social workers in particular have tended to be preoccupied with children's emotions and behaviour, to the neglect of other aspects of development such as education and health (Jackson, 1989). This is not to suggest that children's relationships, feelings and actions are unimportant – quite the contrary. Careful attention to these should not only help children directly, but also form a basis for progress in other areas of life (Rutter and Rutter, 1993). Nevertheless there has been growing evidence that this is not enough. Outcome studies of children in care have shown that *on average* they often compare very poorly with their peers on most dimensions of development, though of course there have always been important exceptions (DoH, 1991; Sellick and Thoburn, 1996). Although much of the responsibility for poor outcomes can be attributed to adverse initial circumstances, it appears that foster and residential care experiences all too rarely help children make up the difference. The sharing of responsibilities between foster carers, social workers and parents may result in no one taking an overall perspective or consistently undertaking specific tasks like attending school meetings (Parker *et al*, 1991).

Although research on children in care before 1990 had considered educational progress alongside other measures, schooling had hardly ever been the focus. A seminal study which began to rectify this omission was carried out by **Aldgate *et al* (1993)**. The authors noted that in the 1980s, educational matters and continuity of schooling had been given low priority in placement planning and review. Their study showed that social workers concentrated on attachment, physical needs and links with birth families, with children's educational attainments scoring very low in their rankings. School matters were often discussed during social work visits and reviews, but seldom did this lead to specific action to enhance school achievement. Absence of significant behaviour problems was taken as a sign that all was well. Nearly all foster carers saw schooling as one of their prime responsibilities. They took an active interest in homework, reading and so on. Despite this commitment, the children were not catching up. Both foster carers and social workers had high expectations about the ultimate academic achievements of the children, but did not show understanding of the specific input required to make that possible. Aldgate *et al* concluded that many of the children needed remedial or other extra *academic* assistance. The home environment provided by foster carers was good, but not sufficient by itself.

Other work, particularly by Fletcher-Campbell (1990; 1998), has pointed to the need for much greater mutual understanding and co-operation between social workers and teachers. The former need to be more attuned to school curricula, demands and progress, while teachers can be helped to be more aware of the specific needs and sensitivities of children who are looked after. This should be supported by joint inter-departmental policies and collaborative structures at management and case planning levels (Fletcher-Campbell, 1998; Borland *et al*, 1998). Academic achievement and social success at school, or the support of an interested teacher, can be vital factors in improving children's self-esteem and helping them overcome adversity in their early lives (Fonagy *et al*, 1994; Gilligan, 1997).

Only one-fifth of the social workers interviewed by Aldgate *et al* 'placed health issues high on their agenda' (p 27). Further information about gaps in health knowledge and communication were identified by **Butler and Payne (1997)**. They carried out an audit of initial medical examinations in one Welsh county. They noted that, although these are required by statute, their main purpose has not been made clear. Butler and Payne suggested a broad remit for medicals, going beyond a minimal check for illness along the lines of the old 'freedom from infection' certificates. The writers recommended a full history-taking and assessment, plus exploration of health-related behaviour and safety issues as appropriate.

The audit established that only half of the sample of 100 children looked after by the local authority were identified on the community health records as having that status. All of these had been offered an appointment of the statutory medical, but only half of the appointments were taken up. This meant that overall only one-quarter of the children had been examined. The medicals had dealt adequately with physical growth and current development, but most gave little attention to family and developmental history. No record indicated that worries expressed by the child had been discussed. The authors concluded that more systematic procedures of information sharing are required and that medicals should be seen as having a broad health promotion function. They also expressed the hope that the Looking After Children system would help improve matters (see below).

A second analysis of statutory medicals was carried out in a London borough by **Mather *et al* (1997)**. Analysis showed that significant medical information was missing in about a quarter of the cases. Many foster carers, social workers and older children had only partial knowledge of the child's immunisation record.

Just under half the children were referred for attention to physical or behavioural problems. Unlike the Butler and Payne survey, this study identified that significant numbers of adolescents had received health education advice. This may reflect a difference in recording rather than clinical practice.

Mather *et al* also reported on findings from a questionnaire survey and group discussions carried out by the Who Cares? Trust (Fletcher, 1993). The young people saw little purpose in routine medicals, were mostly reluctant to discuss their concerns with a doctor and often refused to attend. They tended to see medical help in terms of medication for illness and did not regard their emotional health, eating habits or sexual behaviour as matters for consultation with a doctor. Many voiced concerns that health professionals (and social workers) could not be trusted to keep confidences. Yet many of the same young people clearly had emotional problems, such as depression and low self-image. The authors concurred with Butler and Payne that health needs should have more concerted attention, but expressed doubts about the value of routine medical examinations. They proposed that young people should be given opportunities to discuss their concerns (which usually include a health component) with a person of their choosing at a suitable time.

During the 1980s it was increasingly realised by policy-makers and academics that child care practice had tended to neglect important aspects of development, including not only education and health but also other very important features, notably identity. The Department of Health sponsored a project which examined assessment and outcomes (Parker *et al*, 1991). Ultimately this led to the development of what became known as the Looking After Children (LAC) system (Ward, 1995). This consists of a set of forms which are intended to record key information about the child and his/her needs, and about plans, decisions, actions and reviews. The aims are not confined simply to recording, since the materials are expected to promote better communication among all the parties concerned with the child, improve the assessment and meeting of need, and eventually contribute to strategic planning for looked after children.

Originally the LAC system consisted of Action and Assessment records. A different type of record was prepared for children of different age groups, with each covering seven dimensions:
- health;
- education;
- family and social relationships;
- emotional and behavioural development;
- identity;
- self-presentation;
- self-care skills.

Later on additional records were devised to cover such matters as essential information, placement agreements, care plans and reviews.

In many ways the LAC system has been very successful. Variants have been adopted in a number of countries (Jones *et al*, 1998). On the whole feedback from social workers about usage of the forms has been positive, though there have been complaints about the amount of work entailed. Scrutiny of completed forms indicate that some are very full and informative, but others are incomplete or inadequate (Moyers, 1997; Wheelaghan *et al*, 1999; Bell, 1999). The system has been subject to critiques. For example, it has been suggested that the items in the records are largely based on a white middle-class view of development. Also the use of standard questions and tick-boxes can be seen as reflecting a broader trend in child care policy and management which is prescriptive, fragmenting and dehumanising (Knight and Caveney, 1998; Garrett, 1999). In defence of the system, Jackson (1998) has argued that the contents of the records represent commonly shared aspirations for children and help to ensure that children's needs are met.

Phillips and Worlock (1999) described how the LAC system had been implemented in one London borough, with particular attention to the role of foster carers. Managers and planners in the social work department were attracted by the integrated and comprehensive nature of the system. Once the materials had been introduced, it was realised that training and implementation had concentrated too much on social workers, with foster carers marginalised. Yet foster carers (and residential staff) proved to be knowledgeable and enthusiastic about the use of the records. Thenceforth, foster carers were included in training and were encouraged to use the Action and Assessment Records with young people. Some gave positive feedback about the clarity and helpfulness of the forms for talking to children and young people and for child care reviews. Although the LAC system has its faults and critics, it seems set to be a very important influence on assessment, communication and planning for most British foster children in years to come.

20 Social work and the education of children in foster care

Jane Aldgate, Anthony Heath, Matthew Colton and Michael Simm

Jane Aldgate is Professor of Social Work at Leicester University. Anthony Heath is Official Fellow of Nuffield College, Oxford. Matthew Colton is Lecturer in Applied Social Studies at the University of College of Swansea and Michael Simm is Principal Social Worker, Children's Services, Oxfordshire Social Services Department.

This paper was published in Adoption & Fostering, 17:3, 1993.

One of the major advances in the monitoring of children's progress introduced by the Children Act 1989 was the much-needed attention given to health and educational issues (see DoH, 1990). In assessing the potential of foster carers, the *Guidance and Regulations Volume 3* on *Family Placements* (DoH, 1991a), social workers are required to consider 'the applicant's attitudes and expectations in relation to education' (p 26). This includes the encouragement of special talents and interests and the 'capacity to develop an understanding of particular educational methods, settings and services which they may not have encountered before. Could the applicant cope with providing any necessary support to a child with special educational needs?' (p 27). Furthermore, any reviews of children in foster care have to consider the educational arrangements made for the child. Special attention is given to children's needs at critical points in their educational career, for example, in the period leading up to GCSE preparation. Here, it is suggested, top priority should be given to continuity of education if children have to change placements.

These new requirements are in stark contrast to the absence of interest in official guidelines pre-1989. The *Guide to Fostering Practice* (HMSO 1976) and the pre-1988 Boarding Out of Children Regulations give no attention to education. Additionally, research on statutory reviews in the early 1980s also revealed the low priority given to educational matters and the frequent exclusion of teachers from these events on the grounds that their presence would breach confidentiality for the child (McDonnell and Aldgate, 1984).

Jackson sums up the pre-Children Act 1989 position in her 1987 monograph (p 7):

Almost all the meagre references to education and schools relate to the problem of attendance or classroom behaviour. Nowhere is there a sense of school as a central part of a child's life, or education as the key to his future.

Little therefore is known about how social workers perceive education within their repertoire of activities on behalf of foster children.

The Oxford study on the educational progress of foster children

This article discusses some of the findings from an ESRC-funded study on the educational progress of children in long-term foster care to identify the nature and extent of social work activity and attitude towards the educational progress of these children. The aim of this study has been reported at length elsewhere (see Heath *et al*, 1989; Aldgate, 1990).

Briefly, the study investigated the educational progress over three years of 49 foster children of middle school age in the care of one county authority. This was a remarkably stable group of children for whom the average length of stay in their current placement was six years. Many expected to stay there until adulthood. The children's educational performance and current homes were compared with a contrast group of children living in their own families who had never been in accommodation or care but whose families were clients of the social services department. By comparing the foster children with others at the same schools from similar backgrounds, we hoped to unveil some of the myths which had surrounded the attainment of children looked after by the local authority by comparison with those living in the general population. We interviewed the primary carers of the children, their teachers and their social workers, and the children themselves. We measured their attainment in English, maths and verbal ability on standardised tests which are commonly used in schools nationally, and also looked at their behaviour.

Social workers and the education of foster children

This article concentrates on the social work contribution to the foster care system. There are three main areas of investigation reported here:

- The place of education within social workers' activities in relation to foster children.
- The practical application of the corporate parenting role in foster care and its impact on children's performance at school.
- The expectations of social workers, carers and teachers in relation to children's education.

Education and social work activity

Firstly, social workers were asked about their priorities: 'In planning for a child in foster care, how do you rank the following areas of work?' The first choices of social workers from the predetermined lists developed in consultation with practitioners are shown in Table 1. (Throughout this article, we have reported the findings in percentages for ease of reading, but it is important to remember that our sample is small – 49 children – so figures only give approximations of proportions.) The table shows that by far the most popular activity was work on children's attachments (cited by 42 per cent of social workers), followed by attention to physical needs and the promotion of self-image, a high priority activity for only one-fifth. The maintenance of links was ranked first by 11 per cent of social workers. Educational matters ranked highly with only two per cent while none placed top priority on the development of children's special talents. An almost identical picture emerged from analysis of the lower rankings, with educational issues and the promotion of talents coming bottom of the list of priorities.

How can these rankings be explained? It is hardly surprising that social workers gave maximum attention to attachments and children's physical needs and development. There has been much criticism in research of multiple changes of placements (e.g. Berridge and Cleaver, 1987; DHSS, 1985; DoH, 1991). The search for stability underpinned the whole permanency planning movement in the 1970s and 1980s. That

Table 1

Social workers' rankings of care activities for looked after children

Helping children make successful attachments	42%
Attending to children's physical needs and development	21%
Helping children acquire a sense of self-esteem	21%
Helping children maintain links with their birth family	11%
Attending to children's educational attainment	2%
Helping children develop special talents	–
Missing data	3%

an unstable, uncertain environment may be damaging to children's ability to form attachments has also been consistently stressed in recent research (see for example, DHSS, 1985; DoH, 1991c). Additionally, social work training has traditionally emphasised attachment theory so that it is a natural part of the social worker's knowledge base (CCETSW, 1991).

It might have been expected that attention is paid to children's physical needs since social workers bear the legacy of many child abuse enquiries about children who have died from physical abuse or neglect. However, there is a difference between paying attention to health matters to prevent abuse and including health in the general promotion of a child's welfare. This is reflected in our results, with only one-fifth of workers placing health issues high on their agenda. It is noticeable that the general health of children in care has been given little prominence in child care literature or in regulations prior to 1989 and has recently been raised as a subject of some concern (Parker *et al*, 1991; CCETSW, 1991).

The promotion of self-esteem has also been a neglected area (DHSS, 1985; DoH, 1991c). It is therefore of interest that in our sample only one-fifth of social workers put priority on the enhancement of self-esteem. Jackson (1987) believes that social workers have given little attention to promoting children's self-esteem and points to the relationship between educational success and the development of a positive self-concept. As Table 1 shows, among our social workers, there was even less attention paid to the nurturing of special talents or encouragement of educational attainment than to self-esteem in general, although a case could be made for the enhancement of the latter by promotion of the former. Subsequent exploration (table not shown) revealed that in fewer than a quarter of cases had the Boarding Out allowance been used for educational purposes. For these ten children, money had been spent on music lessons in six cases and on school trips for the rest.

As Parker *et al* (1991) suggest, such compartmentalising of a child's attributes may be perceived as rather peculiar by many parents but is a feature of social work research. Our findings are supported by a large sample study by Knapp and his colleagues who compared social workers' objectives and the achievements, and found that only 16 out of 285 objectives listed by social workers related to education. Similarly, although half the children were said to have school-related problems only six were considered to warrant educational improvement as part of the solution (see Parker *et al*, 1991). Regret about lost educational opportunity also permeates accounts of young people who have grown up in care (Festiger, 1983; Stein and Carey, 1987; Stein, 1990; Garnett, 1992).

Corporate parenting and education

Why does education seem to get such a low priority when children are being looked after by foster carers? As Parker *et al* (1991) suggest, this lack of attention to education contrasts 'markedly with the attitudes of concerned parents' (p 88). Concerned parents are to be found in every part of society. The recent study by Tizard *et al*, for example, (Parker *et al*, 1991, p 89) found:

> ... that 80 per cent of parents, mainly working class, thought that the choice of the child's first school was important and over half had visited or considered schools other than the one the child finally attended. Pre-school literacy and numeracy were related to parental teaching independent of social class. The child's progress in infant school was strongly influenced by the amount of parental contact with and knowledge about the school, again independent of social class.

Some problems may occur when parental responsibility is shared between social worker, foster carer and parents. Although children may have the benefit of highly committed social workers and foster carers at any one time, as Jackson suggests, children may suffer from 'the lack of personal investment in them as individuals, extending over a lifetime, which is the normal experience of people brought up in their own families' (Jackson, 1987, p 26). We thought it would be useful to test out Jackson's view by exploring the roles and relationships in the foster care system with special reference to education.

Boarding Out visits

One obvious way in which social workers exercise their role in foster care is to visit the child and the foster family regularly. Such visits provide a potential forum for discussion of educational progress. Previous studies on long-term foster care have often commented on the quasi-adoptive nature of some of the very long-term placements (George, 1970; Triseliotis and Russell, 1984; Rowe et al, 1984). Earlier surveys have also indicated that social workers did not always adhere to the regulations and that visits lapsed (see, for example, McDonnell and Aldgate, 1984).

It was therefore heartening to find in our study that social workers were more vigilant in fulfilling the Boarding Out Regulations (1955 Regulations were in operation at the time of the study) in relation to long-term care arrangements Although the average length of stay in the current placement for our children was six years, over 90 per cent of social workers visited at least three monthly while almost two-thirds visited monthly or more frequently. No social worker visited less than six monthly. It did seem that social workers and foster carers were talking together on a regular basis about the children for whom they were jointly acting *in loco parentis.*

What did they talk about? We ranked social workers' answers to a range of subjects chosen to represent some of the main areas that Boarding Out visits might ordinarily cover. According to the social workers, children's general progress was the most popular topic mentioned by 88 per cent. Discussion of care plans was also high on the agenda for two-thirds of workers (67 per cent). Contact visits from parents was a fairly frequent topic (48 per cent), not surprisingly since well over two-thirds of our children had contact with birth families. More event- or need-driven topics, such as sorting out behaviour problems and discussing additional boarding allowances, were given a lower priority and possibly reflected more individual circumstances. Behaviour problems were mentioned by 26 per cent of workers and money matters by 20 per cent. It was clear that discussion of children's educational progress was usually included in the Boarding Out visits for almost three-fifths (58 per cent) of social workers but, as will be shown, there was a discrepancy between this general discussion and more specific activity.

Statutory reviews

Another important forum for input about educational achievement and progress is the statutory review, given even more power by the Children Act 1989. Our research was conducted just prior to the Act.

Several social workers saw their formal involvement at the review being the most appropriate and least intrusive forum for their input on education. When asked to comment on how the monitoring of educational progress should be arranged between social workers, parents and foster carers, a typical comment was:

I prefer to monitor a child's educational progress through reviews where all parties are able to discuss and evaluate educational information. It seems particularly unfair to me for a foster child to be seen to be different by his or her peer group if a social worker is the party to make contact on parents' day. Obviously, information about the child is necessary to aid planning but it must be gathered in a sensitive way.

Those who wished to delegate the day-to-day monitoring of educational matters to foster carers did so to reduce the artificiality of corporate parenting and to promote for the child an atmosphere of normality. A typical comment was:

I feel the foster parents should be the front-line people monitoring the children's progress. This is much better for the child who does not like to feel "different" from his or her peers. Feedback can be given then to social workers and parents unless there are severe problems when a social worker may also need to become more involved.

The reliance on statutory reviews to influence children's well-being has not been without problems in the past because of inconsistent input and accountability for subsequent actions (Sinclair, 1982; McDonnell and Aldgate, 1984). It was heartening in the Oxford study to see that expectations of teachers' involvement had changed considerably since the time of these earlier studies. Eighty-two per cent of social workers said they would expect a teacher or head to be present at the review. In 85 per cent of cases social workers would also expect to include written material from schools either directly, or incorporated into a report by themselves. We found it surprising that social workers were less inclined to include in their reports information from foster carers about children's educational progress. Under half said they would report on this (49 per cent). Policy in the authority studied was that foster carers should be present at reviews which might account for the absence of their written contribution. Nevertheless, the fact that carers' views were not always included on paper could undervalue their considerable knowledge.

Shared parental responsibility and education
The issue of corporate parenting was explored further with both foster carers and social workers by asking how they managed the division of parental responsibility on specific issues. We were concerned to investigate the division of labour in relation to care plans, school matters and any behaviour difficulties children might have. Unfortunately, the resources and scope of the study did not permit us to elicit the views of the birth parents to complete the picture of shared parental responsibility.

The results were somewhat unexpected, with a fairly strong difference of opinion between foster carers and social workers on how decisions should be made about the specified areas of children's lives. It should be borne in mind that our foster children were unusual in that they had stable placements with an expectation of stability until the age of majority. This may have influenced perceptions.

Firstly, we asked whose job it was to make long-term plans for the foster child's education and career. Three-fifths of foster carers (60 per cent) thought the decision should be theirs alone; 37 per cent that it should be a joint decision between foster carer, social worker and, if possible, parent. The rest (two per cent) thought plans should be made by social workers. By contrast only ten per cent of social workers thought this decision should be solely made by foster carers and the remaining

Table 2
Views of social workers and foster carers on key care issues

Making long-term plans

	Carers	Social workers
Carer alone	60%	10%
Joint decision	37%	90%
Social worker only	2%	–
p<0.001		

Choosing schools for foster children

	Carers	Social workers
Carer alone	80%	41%
Joint decision	20%	59%
Social worker only	–	–
p<0.001		

Visiting schools

	Carers	Social workers
Carer alone	90%	67%
Joint decision	10%	33%
Social worker	–	–
p<0.001		

Helping children in trouble with the police

	Carers	Social workers
Carer alone	51%	8%
Joint decision	49%	82%
Social worker only	–	10%
p<0.001		

90 per cent thought the decision should be made jointly. The difference in proportions thinking the decision should be made by foster carers alone was significant at the .001 level.

Foster carers also expected that social workers would delegate to them the choosing of their foster child's school. Eighty per cent of foster carers thought this decision should be theirs and 20 per cent thought it should be made jointly with social workers. By contrast, only 41 per cent of social workers expected foster carers to choose a suitable school and 59 per cent thought it should be a joint decision. Once again the difference in proportions was significant at the .001 level.

The majority of foster carers (90 per cent) also expected that they alone would be responsible for visiting schools to discuss children's progress. The remaining ten per cent thought this should be shared with social workers and sometimes parents. Two-thirds of social workers (67 per cent) expected foster carers to visit schools and talk to teachers on parents' days without their intervention (consistent with another finding, not detailed here, that well over half of the social workers had not visited children's schools in the last year), but the remaining third (33 per cent) thought that these parental duties should be shared. Here, the difference in proportions was significant at the .01 level.

Finally, we asked about how responsibility would be divided if children were in trouble with the police. Foster carers divided the responsibility between themselves and jointly with social workers almost equally (51 per cent dealing with problems alone and 49 per cent jointly). A minority of social workers (10 per cent) thought the responsibility was theirs alone, but the majority (82 per cent) thought that the matter should be dealt with jointly. Only eight per cent said they would expect foster carers to sort out problems alone. The difference in the proportion of views on joint responsibility in relation to the police was significant at the .01 level.

Our findings show a clear discrepancy between the perceptions of foster carers and social workers about the corporate nature of their role. The foster carers' views strongly reflect findings from previous studies about the wish of carers to become as like as possible to ordinary parents. There was, however, one major deviation from former studies which we have reported on elsewhere (see Aldgate, 1990): the inclusiveness of birth parents in the foster placements. Most foster carers felt well-attached to their foster children and saw them as part of their family. This attachment seemed to be unaffected by the presence or absence of parents.

The social workers seemed to perceive their role very much within the expectations laid down in Regulations both pre- and post-1989, but the evidence suggests that there were some tensions in translating the ideal into practice. There is clearly an issue about interpreting how the statutory requirements may be fulfilled. The data gives an impression that there is some confusion about division of labour. We can only speculate how the different perceptions of the specific aspects of parenting investigated may have affected the working partnership between carers and workers in real terms but, clearly, the discrepancy in expectations between workers and carers in developing and carrying out care plans for foster children is an area demanding further practice guidance.

Parental attitude and educational attainment

Apart from the important issue of sharing the parental responsibility for foster children, we also wished to explore the attitudes which underpinned that activity in relation to children's educational progress. It has long been held by educational sociologists that parental attitude and encouragement about education in the general population is a significant factor in the promotion of children's attainment (Halsey *et al*, 1980; Parker *et al*, 1991). Clearly, one might hope that a loving foster home could offer children a chance to flourish.

As reported elsewhere (Heath *et al*, 1990), our foster carers were "model parents". They participated a great deal in their children's day-to-day education. They attended school events regularly, discussed children's progress with teachers, helped children with homework, encouraged them to borrow books from the library and took children on educational leisure activities. They were far more active in these realms than parents in the comparison group. But those who support the parental interest lobby would have been disappointed to find that this stimulating environment had little effect on children's attainment in its own right. Our foster children were doing little better than the comparison group of children.

Counteracting the past

It may well be that long-term foster children are a special group who need more than concerned parents to counteract their past disadvantage. It has been suggested that 'just being in care is not usually in itself a primary cause of educational failure. It is rather that children bring their educational problems in to care with them and too often care experience does little to ameliorate these deficiences.' (DoH, 1991c, p 9).

In our study, it was of interest that the children who had come into the care system because of suspected child abuse or neglect had markedly lower scores on our standardised tests of attainment than the children who had come into care for other reasons, irrespective of age at admission or number of changes of placement (see Aldgate and Heath, 1992).

Expectations great or small

There is a further area which has been raised as significant in relation to children's educational achievements: parental expectations. Given the corporate nature of parenting for children in foster care, we thought it important to explore this area with both social workers and foster carers and compare their views with those of teachers.

Firstly, we asked both foster carers, social workers and teachers for their assessment of children's current educational performance. There was a fairly high degree of congruence between social workers and foster carers but a lower rating of performance by teachers of the highest and lowest performers.

Table 3

Perceptions of current educational performance of foster children

	Social workers n = 43	Foster carers n = 49	Teachers n = 49
Performance level			
Above average	28%	35%	20%
Around average	51%	41%	37%
Below average	14%	24%	35%
Don't know	7%	–	–

As Table 3 shows, 35 per cent of foster carers thought children were doing well at school as did a slightly lower percentage (28 per cent) of social workers. Fewer teachers (20 per cent) thought children were doing well. Just over two-fifths of foster carers (41 per cent) thought their children's performance was average compared with half the social workers (51 per cent) and 37 per cent of teachers. Around a quarter of foster carers (24 per cent) and a third of teachers (35 per cent) estimated a lower than average performance, but only 14 per cent of social workers put children in this category. The rest were not sure. Of course our numbers are small and therefore percentages may not always be accurate but they do suggest that social workers may have a tendency to take an unduly optimistic view of children's performance. It is impossible to give clear reasons for these differences since this is beyond the scope of the data collected. However, the optimism from social workers could reflect Jackson's view that social workers tend to conflate educational performance and behaviour problems. An absence of behaviour problems and the low profile of social worker visits to schools might account for this. The NFER study had a similar finding: that social workers did not believe children were underachieving and held views rated by the researchers as 'subjective and unreliable' (Fletcher-Campbell and Hall, 1990, p 112).

The findings are of interest because low expectations of carers, teachers and social workers is a reason put forward for the low achievement of foster children (Jackson, 1987), a view hitherto validated by research evidence. In his important outcome study of long-term foster care, for example, Triseliotis found, 'Almost all the foster children terminated their education at 15 . . . The former foster children's aspirations were broadly within the aspirations and expectations of their foster parents' (Triseliotis, 1980, p 152).

The foster carers in the Oxford study were certainly not "high fliers" (only four were graduates) but some were educationally ambitious for their foster children. While around a quarter (24 per cent) were simply willing to wait and see what happened, only ten per cent thought their foster children should leave school at 16. Almost two-fifths (39 per cent) expected children to stay on until they were 18 and take "A" levels and a further 27 per cent thought children might go on to higher education. In the absence of detailed data about foster carers' circumstances in comparison with carers in earlier studies, we can only speculate on why our population seemed more educationally ambitious for their children than those in earlier studies. It may be that our foster carers are not representative of others or it could be that attitudes towards education have changed generally over the last few years. This is certainly an area warranting an update from research.

Social workers were even more optimistic about future attainment than they had been about the present. They expected all the children to gain some qualifications and a high proportion, over three-fifths (63 per cent) to gain at least five GCSEs. Just under one-fifth of the children were expected by social workers to gain "A" levels (18 per cent) and half of these "A" level children were expected to go on to higher education.

There seems little in these findings to suggest that expectations were too low. If anything, social workers were over-optimistic about the foster children's performance, if their potential was to be judged by the standardised tests of attainment we employed in the study. Three-quarters of the foster carers also had expectations of high attainment for their foster children.

Implications for practice

Piecing the mixed evidence together: that, although social workers discussed education at statutory visits, they put educational progress and the promotion of special talents low on their list of priorities; that they rarely used the Boarding Out allowance for educational purposes; that less than half had visited school in the previous year; and that they tended to separate self-esteem from educational attainment, it seems likely that, in practice, they might also have delegated educational matters to foster carers to a large extent. This would help explain the social workers' over-optimism about children's current and future performance, based possibly on their lack of detailed knowledge about attainment and on a tendency to equate absence of behavioural problems with acceptable attainment. It would also help to explain the foster carers' wish to handle day-to-day matters on their own since this reflected the status quo.

Such a strategy would certainly be viable if the children did not have educational difficulties. With the professionalisation of foster care, there is also a strong case for carers being clearly mandated to take responsibility for specific issues. There is, however, danger in taking educational progress for granted. The divergence between the views of teachers and social workers suggests a need for far clearer channels of communication between them so that the true position of children's attainment can be established, or there should be a clear delegation of this duty to carers with the expectation that they will take the initiative to report back to social workers at specified and regular intervals. The Children Act 1989 emphasises a corporate local authority strategy to provide a context for such a dialogue. If this duty is taken seriously, the educational needs of looked after children are likely to receive more attention from social workers and teachers. It remains to be seen how far the new arrangements for self-governing schools will be an inhibiting organisational factor in the struggle to improve inter-disciplinary liaison.

There is a tension, too, between trying to create for a foster child as normal an environment as possible and ensuring that children's educational needs are met. Because education is so important offering children extra help should, in our opinion, outweigh any worries about the stigma that may attach to remedial help.

Our study suggests that children's educational problems may be long-standing, having their origins in early childhood before they were accommodated or in care. Remedial help may well be needed over a long period of time. It is therefore important that strategies for educational compensation are begun as soon as a child has the status of being looked after by the local authority. The Children Act 1989 urges placements to be made to promote continuity of family and education. There needs to be a strong emphasis on educational attainment in care plans and in the written agreements required by law for looked after children.

Careful assessment and monitoring should be mandatory. The adoption by social workers of the newly developed Looking After Children Assessment and Action Schedules, developed for the Department of Health (DoH, 1991c) for children of all ages, are a good place from which to begin (see also Parker et al, 1991). They place an emphasis on accountability for action which may solve some of the problems of division of corporate parenting, provided that all those sharing parental responsibility are fully aware of, and in agreement with, the actions that need to be undertaken to promote children's welfare.

Above all, there needs to be a change in attitude, both in social work practice and in training, so that the education of children looked after has high priority with both managers and workers. The view that children need to recover emotionally from bad life experiences before they can move on to new achievements must be challenged. It should be set beside the view that educational achievement could be a factor in building confidence and self-esteem. While we would not wish to suggest that attention to children's attachments should be in any way reduced, the low priority accorded by social workers to education should surely now be reversed if the principle of promotion of welfare is truly to have meaning for all children accommodated or in care long-term.

References

Aldgate J, 'Foster children at school: success or failure', *Adoption & Fostering*, 14:4, pp 38–48, 1990.

Aldgate J and Heath A F, *The Educational Progress of Children in Foster Care*, Report to the ESRC, 1992.

Berridge D and Cleaver H, *Foster Home Breakdown*, Basil Blackwell, 1987.

CCETSW, *The Teaching of Child Care Social Work in the Dip SW*, CCETSW, 1991.

Department of Health and Social Security, *Social Work Decisions in Child Care*, HMSO, 1985.

Department of Health, *The Care of Children: Principles and practice in Regulations and Guidance*, HMSO, 1990.

Department of Health, *The Children Act 1989 Guidance and Regulations*, *Vol. 3, Family Placements*, HMSO, 1991a.

Department of Health, *Patterns and Outcomes in Child Placement*, HMSO, 1991b.

Department of Health, *Looking After children: A guide to the Action and Assessment Schedules*, HMSO, 1991c.

Festinger T, *Nobody Ever Asked us: A postscript to foster care*, Columbia University Press, 1983, USA.

Fletcher-Campbell F and Hall C, *Changing Schools? Changing People? The education of children in care*, National Foundation of Educational Research, 1990.

Garnett L, *Leaving Care and After*, National Children's Bureau, 1992.

George V, *Foster Care Theory and Practice*, Routledge & Kegan Paul, 1970.

Halsey A H, Heath A F and Ridge J, *Origins and Destinations: Family class and education in Britain*, Clarendon Press, 1980.

Heath A F, Colton M and Aldgate J, 'The educational progress of children in and out of care', *British Journal of Social Work*, 19:6, pp 447–60, 1989.

Jackson S, *The Education of Children in Care*, University of Bristol, 1987.

McDonnel P and Aldgate J, 'Review procedures of children in care,' *Adoption & Fostering*, 8:3, pp 47–51, 1984.

Parker R A, Ward H, Jackson S, Aldgate J and Wedge P (eds), *Living Away from Home: Assessing outcomes in child care*, HMSO, 1991.

Rowe J, Hundleby M and Keane A, *Long-term Foster Care*, BAAF/Batsford, 1984.

Stein M and Carey K, *Leaving Care*, Blackwell, 1986.

Stein M, *Living Out of Care*, Barnardo's, 1990.

Triseliotis J, 'Growing up in foster care and after', in Triseliotis J (ed), *New Developments in Foster Care and Adoption*, Routledge & Kegan Paul, 1980.

Triseliotis J, 'Foster care outcomes, a review of key research findings', *Adoption & Fostering*, 13:3, pp 5–13, 1989.

Triseliotis J and Russell J, *Hard to Place: The outcome of adoption and residential care*, Heinemann, 1984.

21 The health of children looked after by the local authority

Ian Butler and Heather Payne

Ian Butler is a Senior Lecturer and Research Fellow in Social Work at the University of Wales, Cardiff. He was for many years a social work practitioner and manager in residential, field and day care services for children. Recent co-authored books include "Getting into Practice: Social work with children and families" (1997), "A Case of Neglect? Children's experiences and the sociology of childhood" (1996) and "Children Speak: Children, trauma and social work" (1994). Heather Payne is Senior Lecturer in Child Health, University of Wales College of Medicine.

This paper was published in Adoption & Fostering, 21:2, 1997.

Introduction

Implicit in all forms of parenting is a concern for the health of the child. For most parents, the nocturnal peek in at the cot is the beginning of a lifetime of well-meant, if sometimes unappreciated, concern for the physical well-being of their offspring. For the child brought up by a "corporate" parent such as the local authority, these primary and primal concerns may be less personally felt and less assiduously pursued. In this article, we report examples of failure to carry into practice specific requirements of the Children Act 1989 that bear on the health of children looked after by the local authority.

---

[1] Children "looked after" by the local authority include all those children provided with accommodation as part of a voluntary arrangement with the child's carers as well as those children formally in the care of the local authority by order of the court. For definitional purposes no distinction is made between looked after children according to the manner of their accommodation.

The health of the looked after child

The general duty of the local authority in England and Wales to the looked after child is to 'safeguard and promote his welfare' (s 22 (3) (a) Children Act 1989). In this context 'welfare' is not defined but by inference from other of the Act's provisions, it can be held to include a consideration of the child's health needs. This interpretation is made explicit in the formal Regulations and Guidance that support the Act.

Given the unarguable importance of a child's health to his or her general well-being, it is surprising that we know comparatively little about the health of children looked after by the local authority, possibly because, in Kahan's view:

*Little importance has so far been attached to either routine informa-
tion gathering, medical examinations or analysis of what could be
known.*

There is evidence from research into the outcomes for children in public care which suggests strongly that 'deprivation is a common factor among all types of children who enter care' (Bebbington and Miles, 1989). As such, we might infer that there is a *prima facie* cause for concern given that there is a known association between social deprivation and poor health generally. For example, the association between low birth-weight, postnatal mortality and socio-economic status is well established (Townsend and Davidson, 1982; 1992). In reviewing the sociography of child health in the UK more broadly, Ennew (1994) notes that while class is the dominant factor:

*. . . the gender and ethnic origin of the parent who is seeking state aid
are also important factors in determining a child's health status.*

The over-representation of children from the most economically dis-advantaged sections of the community and the over-representation of black children in public care should be sufficient to engage a heightened interest in the health needs of the looked after population. Indeed, one can trace a concern with the health of children who enter care against a background of deprivation to the very origins of public provision for children and in the recurring skin and eye infections that marked out the occupants of the metropolitan workhouse and the district school (Pinchbeck and Hewitt, 1973).

More recently, *The Short Report* (HoC, 1984), an important influence on the Children Act, expressed its concern over the health of children in public care, attributing part of the reason for its concerns to 'failures in liaison between social services departments and the various parts of the NHS' (para 330). The subsequent work of Bamford and Wolkind (1988) on the health of children in care, led unequivocally to the conclusion that:

... *we have neither a clear knowledge of their physical state on reception nor any idea about changes in health that may occur while they are in care.*

In addition, Utting, in his 1991 survey of various reports from the Social Service Inspectorate, stated that:

... *there was evidence that the process of health assessment generally was haphazard and the use of medical services was largely in response to illness.*

The DoH went even further:

... *far from remedying existing deficiencies ... periods in public care have further* impaired *the life chances of some children and young people because of poor educational achievement, uncorrected health problems and maladjustment* [our emphasis].

How and why the health needs of a particularly vulnerable group of children are found to be addressed in such a way that their life chances are actually impaired is illuminated briefly in Kahan's work (1989) and more recently in work on assessment of outcomes in child care (Parker *et al*, 1991). For example, it is suggested that the passage of the burden of health care from parents to other carers may result in the loss of both factual and intuitive knowledge, derived from the parents' previous daily and intimate contact with the child. The knowledge lost is not only that of the child's normal state of health and the minor daily signals whereby a parent is sensitive to any change in a child's health, but also that of her or his health history.

Given that increasing estrangement from one's family of origin is an attendant risk for all children looked after by the local authority, lost knowledge relevant to the child's health is not always recoverable. This is particularly so given the division of responsibility for health care between social worker and either residential or foster carer. In the words of Parker *et al*:

> *No one person may see it as their job to carry out the daily monitoring which most parents do without thinking.*

The active promotion of a particular child's health, for example, through good dietary nutritional practice, may be on the agenda of no one who has actual day-to-day care of the child. Work by Blaxter (1981) and Mayall (1986) suggested that parents carry the largest share of responsibility for the health of children with only occasional assistance from health care professionals. Such professionals are both unused to and unfamiliar with the role of carrying that responsibility for the health of a particular child over an extended period.

'Systems so perfect that no one will need to be good' (TS Eliot)

We have reported Kahan's suggestion that previous processes of routine information gathering, including medical examinations, have produced little to illumine the state of health of children in public care. In such circumstances it may be surprising to find detailed, formal guidance in place to address known risks and to help counteract deficiencies in the delivery of services to such children.

In relation to looked after children, formal Regulations (DoH, 1991, (b) (c) (d)) require the local authority, *inter alia*:

- Before the placement of a child, to inform the relevant health authority and the child's own doctor of the arrangements it intends to make or has already made (DoH, 1991, (b) Regulation 5);
- Upon placement, 'to ensure that arrangements are made for the child to be examined by a registered medical practitioner and require the practitioner who has carried out the examination to make a written assessment of the state of health of the child and his need for health care' (DoH, 1991, (b) Regulation 7);
- Throughout the period of his or her accommodation, to maintain

records of key aspects of the child's health history and 'details of any . . . medical examination of the child and of any medical or dental need of the child' (DoH, 1991, (c) Sch 2 para 20);

- To review, at least annually, depending on the age of the child, by means of a medical examination and a written assessment 'the state of health of the child and his need for health care' (DoH, 1991, (d) Regulation 6).

In the light of previous experience and perhaps in tacit recognition that establishing a thorough regulatory framework may prove insufficient, formal guidance from the DoH exhorts social workers 'to play an active role in promoting all aspects of a child's health' (DoH, 1991, (d) para 1.95). The guidance goes on to state, in the context of the residential care of children:

. . . staff need to adopt a very vigilant attitude towards the health of children in homes. Their health should be carefully and continuously monitored and medical advice should be sought promptly when causes of concern are identified. Regrettably there is sometimes a poverty of expectation about the standard of health children in homes should enjoy. The health of a child in a home should be promoted with the same assiduity as would be the case for a child living with caring parents.

In the context of foster care, a similar (though somewhat more terse) exhortation is to be found:

Responsible authorities should act as good parents in relation to the health of children looked after or accommodated by them. Health care implies a positive approach to the child's health and should be taken to include general surveillance and care for health and developmental progress as well as treatment for illness and accidents.

Specific guidance, however, amounts to no more than a paraphrasing of the Regulations.

Nonetheless, the need for both exhortations suggests continuing deficiencies in practice. In this context, the "looked after medical" represents an important opportunity to introduce and incorporate the health status and needs of children into the broader social work plan for the child. Moreover, data revealed by a careful analysis of such medicals may also provide indications of possible strategies for the development of practice and policy on broader fronts in relation to the whole population of looked after children. The following report of an audit of such medicals in one local authority area shows that such opportunities continue to be missed.

An audit of medical examinations of looked after children

The specific purposes of the audit which is the subject of the remainder of this paper were to see whether Regulations covering initial medical examinations were being followed, and to establish a basis for a review of medical, and later social work, practice in this area. The county studied is mainly an urban area with a total population of approximately 300,000. Around 6,000 children are born each year and about 700 children are looked after by the local authority at any one time. All medical examinations of looked after children are carried out by doctors of the community child health services. Other counties have differing arrangements, some using exclusively community child health services, some using exclusively general practitioners, and others using a combination, depending on local arrangements.

Because there were clear expected standards of practice laid down in Regulations and Guidance (DoH, 1991, (b) (c) (d)) it was appropriate to use the process of audit as a tool. Audit has been incorporated into medical practice in recent years as a mechanism for self-assessment and self-improvement. Audit answers the question: 'Are we doing what we should be doing?' or even 'Are we doing what we think we are doing?'. The key features of audit are standard setting by means of peer group review. This ensures acceptability of the process as the standards are self-imposed by a peer group of professionals, rather than being externally imposed. The steps in the audit process may be represented as follows:

The audit cycle
↓ choose topic
↓ set standards by peer group review

⬇ measure practice
⬇ compare practice with standards
⬇ implement any necessary changes
⬇ repeat measurement and comparison to ensure changes have had the
   desired effect

Thus the audit process can also be seen as a tool for the management of change, as it involves the professionals in the evaluation of their own work, gives them ownership of problems and the means to identify solutions. As it is self-imposed, it is relatively non-threatening and acceptable. It should be emphasised that the reported audit was at this point solely medical, although the natural progression would be to a multidisciplinary audit once the purely medical issues had been tackled.

Audit of medical contact
The first question asked was: 'Are all the children who should be seen being seen?' Given the statutory nature of the "looked after medical examination", the standard set for the purposes of audit was 100 per cent. A random sample of 100 names was selected from a list of all 693 children looked after by the local authority. The community health records were then checked for evidence of an up-to-date medical examination. Of 100, only 51 (51 per cent) were correctly identified on community health records as children looked after by the local authority. Of the 51 so identified on community health records, all had been offered appointments for the statutory medical within eight weeks of the due date but only 25 (50 per cent) attended the appointment. Thus, in all, only a quarter of the medicals had been performed, compared with an expected audit standard of 100 per cent and despite this being a formal requirement not an "optional service". It was clearly necessary to examine possible reasons for such a large discrepancy.

Some of the sample were children placed "out of county", usually with foster carers. The rate of these placements was approximately 11 per cent at the time. However, as the community health department had not been told this was the case in the majority of cases, the child's Community Notes (containing information about immunisations, developmental assessment, health problems) had not been forwarded and were thus unavailable in the county of residence. It was unclear in these circumstances who would be responsible for arranging medical examination in the placement occupied by the child, either now or in the future.

These findings also highlighted problems in the routine mechanism for passing information about admission to care or accommodation from social services to health services in the particular area studied. The eight districts of the county each had a different system for this, all of which were based on telephone messages, imperfectly executed, and with no clear procedure for passing on details such as a change of address. The use of pro-formas prepared by British Agencies for Adoption and Fostering (BAAF) for this (and other purposes) is not, to our knowledge, very widespread which raises doubts about their perceived usefulness in practice. (It must be acknowledged, however, that elsewhere in the UK practice will have achieved higher standards and more assiduous procedures for recording and scrutinising information of this sort.)

The poor attendance rate of those who were offered an appointment was also a cause for concern. There were no differences in the rate of attendance between children looked after by the local authority but placed with their parents, and those placed with foster carers or in children's homes. Each had an equally poor rate of attendance.

Part of the explanation for this may have been the low priority given to "looked after medicals" over many years, not only by the social services department but also by the community child health service. In the community child health service, such medicals had been explicitly placed low down on a list of work priorities. Appointments were likely to be offered at unpopular times in school holidays, and were liable to be cancelled at short notice in the event of need for cover for a higher priority clinic. A review of the appointment letters showed them to be confusing and not giving appropriate information about the nature of the appointment being offered.

Quality of medical contact
The next focus of the audit was to examine the quality of those medical contacts which did take place. The question to be addressed was: 'Of the children looked after by the local authority, who were seen for examina-

tions and what had been achieved?' This naturally led to the question: 'What is the purpose of the medical contact?' Legislation, guidance and regulations are nowhere explicit about the role and purpose of medical advice. They refer severally to 'medical need', 'health need', 'medical examination', 'state of health' and 'need for health care', without presenting a clear and coherent account of these overlapping but distinct issues.

We would suggest that the "looked after medical" has all too often been administered as a "freedom from infection" procedure, with no clear focus on the broader interests or welfare of the child. This again is a consequence of the lack of a clear role for medical advice. In that a medical consultation can be for a number of purposes – to diagnose disease, to give immunisations, to screen for illness, to give treatment or offer advice – the content and purpose of a consultation is unique and is determined by the participants and their circumstances.

Assuming that the desired model for this contact is orientated towards safeguarding and promoting the welfare of the looked after child, as indicated by the terms of the Children Act 1989, the purpose is thus not simply to ensure the absence of illness but to promote health in its wider sense, as a state of positive physical, psychological and emotional well-being. This is a broad remit which will include the medical history, family medical history, examination of physical and mental state, and developmental and emotional assessment of the child or young person, as well as the exploration of age-appropriate health issues such as substance use or safe sex and harm minimisation techniques.

In fact, the areas that were satisfactorily dealt with in the medical examination were the relatively straightforward physical and sensory characteristics. The audit standard applied to determine adequacy was 'more than 60 per cent' of the sample. While arbitrary, such a standard allows for the fact that findings which are unexceptional are often not recorded. However, given the nature of the intervention, it is clear that there is room for improvement, as Table 1 suggests.

Table 1

Areas adequately dealt with at medical

N = 51		
Heart	51	(100%)
Weight	45	(88%)
Vision	45	(88%)
Development	45	(88%)
Hearing	38	(75%)
Height	36	(71%)
Immunisations	34	(67%)
Speech	32	(63%)

Table 2 shows the areas that had been agreed to be significant during the audit discussion but which were not satisfactorily dealt with in the medical examination (i.e. less than 60 per cent of sample).

Table 2

Areas not adequately dealt with at medical

N = 51		
Legal status	4	(8%)
Care history	11	(22%)
Family history	19	(37%)
Developmental history	23	(45%)
Growth centile	26	(51%)

Where age and developmentally appropriate:

Contraception discussed	0 of 7
"Wishes and feelings", including health worries discussed	0 of 20

NB: Growth centile was plotted with previous measurements in none of the records, for the simple reason that a centile chart was not included in the file. This administrative oversight was easily corrected.

Implications for local practice

There were five implications drawn from these findings, which have brought about significant changes in local practice with regard to the whole system of supervision of health care for looked after children:

- that the shift in ethos and approach to the looked after child required a new written pro-forma which allowed the appropriate recording of data;
- that the term "medical examination" was an inappropriate model and an off-putting term and should be altered to "health check";
- that the consultation should assist and empower the child to develop appropriate responsibility for his or her own health in an age appropriate way;
- that health information about the child (such as allergies, relevant family medical history) is vital and needs to be passed on to current carers and health attendants using a continuous record that travels with the child; and
- that the consultation should result in the production of a "health care plan", a jargon-free, problem-based report, listing actions required and who is to take them, sent to the social worker, to dovetail with and inform the overall care plan.

Discussion

The process of medical audit provided a mechanism whereby we were able to identify some major deficiencies in the way the health care oversight for children looked after by the local authority was being provided in one area. However, it also identified that some of the problems were not simply those of the community health service, but would need co-operation between health and social services if they were to be tackled.

In our case, the results of the audit are being shared with social services and the process is being informally extended by peer group discussion of mutual problems in jointly providing a service for the same target group. However, the formal structures for the several agencies with a concern for the health of the looked after child are, by statute and regulation, substantially in place. These may become more sharply focused with the development and implementation of statutory Children's Services Plans but the inertia is not entirely a bureaucratic one. It is also a question of attitude.

The responsibility for promoting and protecting the health of children looked after by the local authority as a group is another issue that arises from this study. Taking a broad, epidemiological view of health outcome in this group of children and young people gives valuable insights into possible ways of improving their universally poor health status. For instance, the immunisation rate among children looked after by the local authority should be as good, if not better, than the general population. However, because of poor record-keeping we were unable, in this case, to determine an accurate immunisation rate for those children looked after by the local authority. Once such information systems are in place it will be possible to monitor health outcomes, not just processes.

Control of asthma, age at recognition of developmental problems, age of fitting hearing aids for congenital hearing impairment, notifications of measles and pertussis, immunisation cover, control of insulin dependent diabetes all have significance for health, and the British Paediatric Association recommends their measurement as reliable indicators for health status of populations of children. Targeted populations should include looked after children.

Monitoring these indicators to identify and (if possible) reverse any adverse influences on health is clearly desirable, although at present this is not a well-defined responsibility for either health or social care professionals. The introduction of concepts of child health and development into social work training might go some way towards alleviating this problem, although there is currently great pressure on the curriculum.

At the point of placement, it should be a matter of administrative routine to convey to the proposed carer key health information concerning a child. This should be in portable form given that any child is likely to experience several placements and may contain a reminder of the statutory requirement for a health check and a latest date by which one should be sought. In the case of children placed with foster carers, care would need to be taken so that the routine monitoring of the foster child's health was not carried out in such a way as to disadvantageously mark him or her out from other children in the household. The Assessment and Action Record forms derived from Parker's (1991) work, which are becoming universal in practice, will supply further means to achieve these objectives although they cannot supply the will any more than any existing pro-formas.

If each social services department had a designated doctor for substitute child care (a similar, and possibly extended role of the designated doctor for child protection) then this function, as well as the overview of advice and policy on health promotion issues such as smoking, smoke alarms, seat belts, etc. to substitute carers, could be provided in a way which could truly promote the health and welfare of the looked after child. It is encouraging to note that the job descriptions of some newly appointed community paediatricians include reference to their role in relation to looked after children.

In the case of children living with their own parents, as we have suggested, the concern with their child's health is a primary and primal one. Current practice would suggest that similar urgency is not felt in regard to children in public care. Greater awareness among professionals of the importance of a child's health to her or his general well-being would help, but strong local awareness and advocacy by those with the day-to-day care of children would help even more.

Note

We have elaborated our analysis of the original data and reported more detailed findings in "Neither Seen nor Heard: Process and outcome in the health of children looked after by the local authority", (Ambulatory Child Health: The Journal of General and Community Paediatrics 4, pp 165–72, 1998).

We note also that recent government policy initiatives have made particular reference to the health care needs of looked after children. The 'Quality Protects Initiative' (DoH, 1998) is a strategic planning process designed to ensure that services for children are 'well-managed and effective'. As part of its specific objectives (Objective 4.2) to improve the quality of service to all children in need, it requires local autorities (inter alia):

To ensure that children looked after enjoy a standard of health and development as good as all children of the same age living in the same area with respect to the following indicators:

- *take up of medical examinations required by statute;*
- *growth and development assessed through health surveillance for children under five;*
- *take up of immunisations.*

The more recent White Paper, "Modernising Social Services" (1998) also notes that while many children in the public care 'have significantly greater health needs than their peers in the community they have greater difficulties in getting access to services' (p 57). In both instances, it remains unclear how the fine detail of this heightened awareness of the health needs of looked after children is to be carried into meaningful practice. While we welcome both initiatives, we would remind practitioners of the line from T S Eliot in our original article. We still need 'good people' as well as good systems.

References

Audit Commission, *Seen But Not Heard: Developing community child health and social services for children in need, Vol 2*, Audit Commission, 1994.

Bamford F N and Wolkind S N, *The Physical and Mental Health of Children in Care: Research needs* (two papers), ESRC, 1988.

Bebbington A and Miles J, 'The background of children who enter local authority care', *British Journal of Social Work*, 19:5, 1989, cited in DoH, *Patterns and Outcomes in Child Placement*, HMSO, 1991.

Blaxter M, *The Health of the Children: A review of research on the place of health in cycles of disadvantage*, SSRC/DHSS Studies in Deprivation and Disadvantage, Heinemann, 1981.

British Paediatric Association, *Outcome Measurements for Child Health*, 1992.

DoH, *Patterns and Outcomes in Child Placement*, HMSO, 1991a.

DoH, *Arrangements for Placement of Child (General) Regulations 1991*, SI 890, HMSO, 1991b.

DoH, *Children's Homes Regulations 1991*, SI 1506, HMSO, 1991c.

DoH, *Review of Children's Cases Regulations 1991*, SI 895, HMSO, 1991d.

DoH, *The Children Act Guidance and Regulations*, Vol 4, *Residential Care*, HMSO, 1991e, p 7.

DoH, *The Children Act Guidance and Regulations*, Vol 3, *Family Placements*, HMSO, 1991f.

Ennew J, 'Childhood as a social phenomenon: National Report England and Wales', *Eurosocial*, 36:16, European Centre for Social Welfare Policy and Research, p 17, 1994, Austria.

House of Commons Second Report from the Social Services Committee 1983–1984 ("The Short Report"), *Children in Care*, HC 360–1, HMSO, 1984.

Kahan B, 'The physical and mental health of children in care', in Kahan B (ed), *Child Care Research, Policy and Practice*, Hodder & Stoughton/Open University, 1989.

Mayall B, *Keeping Children Healthy: The role of mothers and professionals*, Allen & Unwin, 1986.

Parker R, Ward H, Jackson S, Aldgate J and Wedge P (eds), *Assessing Outcomes in Child Care*, HMSO, 1991.

Pinchbeck I and Hewitt M, *Children in English Society, Vol 2*, Routledge & Kegan Paul, 1973.

Townsend P and Davidson N, *Inequalities in Health Care: The Black Report*, Penguin, 1982.

Townsend P and Davidson N, *The Health Divide*, Penguin, 1992.

Utting W, *Children in the Public Care: A review of residential care*, SSI/HMSO, 1991.

22 The statutory medical and health needs of looked after children
Time for a radical review?

Mary Mather, Jane Humphrey and Jenny Robson

Mary Mather is a Consultant Community Paediatrician for Greenwich Healthcare Trust. She is the Honorary Secretary of the Medical Executive of BAAF and Medical Adviser to the Greenwich Adoption and Permanency Panel. She has been involved in both local and national training on the health needs of looked after children. She is also a member of the Department of Health Reference Group reviewing the implementation of "Quality Protects". Jane Humphrey is a Staff Grade Paediatrician with the same Trust and Jenny Robson is Development Manager for the Who Cares? Trust.

This paper was published in Adoption & Fostering, 21:2, 1997.

There are an estimated 60,000 children in public care – together they would almost fill Wembley Stadium. They are looked after by the 176 local and unitary authorities of England and Wales.

Many children and young people enter public care from an environment where they may have suffered physical, emotional or sexual abuse. They come from an unpredictable world and are often stuck at some early stage of development because they have been deprived of the nurturing experiences and relationships which promote their development.

Until very recently, this group of children has not had a high priority in strategic planning for either health, education or social services. As far as health is concerned, research into their needs has been very limited and publications thin on the ground, even in dedicated journals. This is despite the existence of increasing evidence to suggest that health care, as it is presently organised, fails most of these children while the service which is being offered to them is undervalued and often rejected.

For the medical practitioner involved in the care of these children, there is frequently a stark contrast between the services offered to this group and that given to every other child patient. Those doctors who remember the FFI (Free From Infection) inspections will no doubt vividly recall the "extra" added onto the end of an out-patient clinic spent seeing "normal" children and their caring, anxious parents. A subdued, unresponsive child, invariably accompanied by a social worker who knew virtually nothing about her or him, would be undressed, checked for bruises or infestation; a stethoscope would be waved in the general direction of the chest, she or he would be duly declared "free from infection" and the appropriate form would be signed. The child then disappeared, never to be seen again by that doctor or clinic. This almost veterinary procedure did nothing for the child, the doctor, the social worker or indeed human dignity and thankfully has been abandoned. Interestingly, the usefulness of the process was never questioned or audited at the time.

However, the contrasts between arrangements for children living with their families and those fostered in residential care continue. The looked after child is all too often only registered as a temporary patient with the foster carer's General Practitioner (GP). Thus the child receives acute or urgent treatment, but the preventive care, health surveillance and immunisations offered to every other child in the practice are effectively denied to those most in need. Serious undiagnosed medical problems continue to be found at adoption medicals carried out on children who have spent many years in care. For children coming into care, there is no equivalent to the comprehensive BAAF medical forms which ensure the collation of medical information prior to adoption.

The Children Act 1989, the accompanying regulations and guidance, as well as the Looking After Children Project, require that all looked after children have a programme of health care and health education. All children should have a medical examination soon after they enter public care, with regular follow-up medicals every six months for children under two and every 12 months for children over two years of age. Recently, the Action and Assessment Records have been introduced nationally with the intention of improving both the information gathering and the care planning for looked after children. The long-term effects of these innovative records will need to be carefully monitored. However, it is probably true to say that no other group of children in the country has such stringent safeguards around their health, reinforced by legislation.

If these statutory regulations had been carried out as recommended over the last 40 years, then each health authority in the UK would have invested considerable medical time and resources in this particular group of children. Yet, despite this investment, the health needs of looked after children are poorly met, poorly co-ordinated and unmanaged. They remain a uniquely deprived and disadvantaged group. *The National Child Development Study* by Lambert (1983) showed that children in care have many health problems. A study of accommodated children by Packman and Hall (1995) found that one in ten looked after children suffered varying forms of ill health and twice as many had non-acute medical needs, such as hearing loss, poor eyesight or impaired mobility. National figures for looked after children suggest that the average take-up for the statutory medical is about 25 per cent (Cleaver, 1996). Despite the statutory nature of these medicals and the health resources invested in them, there is very little published data about both the efficacy of the medicals themselves and the outcomes for the child.

Why should a system with so many legal safeguards, and to which a large amount of health service resources are devoted, produce such an unsatisfactory situation for both the consumers of the service and for doctors and social workers? In an attempt to try to understand this paradox better, this article firstly reviews a purely medical approach by looking at the medical examinations of looked after children carried out over a two-year period. We then consider the views and needs of the young people themselves. Young people in care rightly have views and aspirations about the services they need and deserve. We believe it is absolutely essential to understand this element if substantial progress is to be made in improving the health outcomes for looked after children.

An analysis of statutory medicals in Greenwich

Between 1993 and 1995, 219 medicals were carried out on 194 different children by the community doctors from the Community Child Health Services, Greenwich Healthcare Trust. A standardised medical form was devised so that the information could easily be recorded and analysed.

In addition, GPs who undertook these medicals and were identified by requesting payment were also asked to complete the same form. An analysis was conducted into the children's health status and health needs from the completed forms. The doctors were specifically asked to record when health information was not available from the person attending with the child. This analysis revealed significant data about the children but also showed a worrying absence of important health information in those caring for the child. The uptake represented close to 25 per cent of the estimated looked after child population for the borough.

The 194 children consisted of 107 boys and 87 girls. Forty-five children (23.2 per cent) were under five years of age, 87 children (44.8 per cent) were 11 years and over. The GP was unknown in ten per cent of the cases. The apparent lack of GP involvement emerged as a recurring theme in the inner city area of this London borough. This is worrying, as in the future GPs will become increasingly responsible for the commissioning of health services in their locality. There is a very real danger that this group of children could be even more marginalised by this development.

Details of the birth history were unknown in 56 children (28.9 per cent). Thirty-eight children (19.5 per cent) had "an abnormal" birth history including prematurity, instrumental delivery or time on a special care baby unit. Of the 121 children, where parental information was available, 37 (30.6 per cent) had a background of chronic parental ill health or parental learning difficulty. It appears from this limited study that a significant number of looked after children are disadvantaged from birth by problems which either separate mother and child at birth or interfere with a parent's ability to care for that child. We are also aware, largely from anecdotal evidence, that the needs of children are often given a low priority by physicians and psychiatrists who care for their parents. This is an area which deserves further study; the admission of a parent into a long-term programme of medical or psychiatric treatment may have catastrophic consequences for that patient's child, which may not be fully appreciated by professionals more used to dealing with adults.

The full immunisation status of the child was unknown to the foster carer or the social worker in 91 per cent of the children, although some partial information was available for most children. Parent-held child health records have improved this situation for younger children, but a concerning number of older children do not know what infectious diseases or immunisations they have had in the past.

Of the 142 school-aged children, 82 (57.8 per cent) had educational problems and 24 (16.9 per cent) were statemented as having special educational needs. For only one-third – 50 (35.2 per cent) – was school progress said to be normal. Behaviour problems emerged as a major concern in 88 (45.4 per cent) of the children in the study, while 22 (11.3 per cent) were receiving formal therapeutic intervention from the child mental health services.

Following these medicals, just over half of children (114) were referred for further assessment, advice or treatment. Just under half (48 per cent) of these referrals were regarding vision, hearing or dental problems or for help with behaviour difficulties. Forty-four adolescents received advice about alcohol, smoking, drugs or safe sex, although invariably these behaviours were already established at the time of the medical. Adolescents as a group were particularly likely to refuse to attend a medical and were especially resentful of being examined.

There is little that is startling or unique about this depressing picture. The statutory medical generally has a poor uptake, is a low priority in health care and forms part of a system which is not well co-ordinated. As the health service moves towards a more primary care-led system, there is a danger that the health care of these children may become even more fragmented, with frequent moves meaning frequent changes of GP.

Strenuous attempts to improve the uptake of these medicals are unlikely to improve the health of looked after children unless professionals, carers and, most importantly, the young people themselves see them as relevant to their needs.

The consumers' view

Young people's views about their health needs and their opinions of statutory medicals were sought in a survey and in a series of group discussions. Key points from the findings of these two studies are reviewed in the rest of this article. At the end of 1992, a questionnaire developed by the Who Cares? Trust was completed and returned by over 600 service users (Fletcher, 1993). This was followed up in 1995 when the same Trust ran a series of consultation groups with young people in public care, to discuss their health needs and concerns, in an attempt to inform the health development programme for the Trust. Each group consisted of six to eight young people, aged 13 years and over, with all the groups including a mix of males and females and both black and white participants. Most of the young people had been looked after for periods of more than two years and some had been in and out of residential or foster care many times. The concerns and needs focused on by these young people were modest and spoke volumes about the system's failure to address their needs.

Having medical examinations made little sense to many of the young people. Few knew they had any choice about whether or not to have one, and those who did frequently refused. Medicals were not seen as an opportunity to discuss health needs and concerns. All had experienced a lack of opportunity or encouragement to discuss and promote basic health care. These young people regarded a visit to the doctor as purely about getting medicine because they were ill. The idea of asking for advice on general health care, sexual health, acne or eating disorders was not on their agenda.

Confidentiality emerged as being of serious concern to the young people in both health and social work settings. Many said they did not trust their doctors to keep whatever they said or requested confidential. There was, in addition, a fear of discussing health concerns with GPs and other health professionals owing to a lack of sensitivity about the particular situation in which looked after children find themselves. The fact that medical reports are sent to their social workers and that anything that they said was likely to be discussed at the next planning meeting or review emerged as a major deterrent to seeking medical care. Many voiced concern that intimate details about their health and well-being were discussed and disseminated as if everyone had a right to know. Some young people expressed the view that often meetings were conducted as if they were not present.

They talked overwhelmingly about depression, isolation and the lack of a trusted adult with whom they could discuss personal health matters.

Most were struggling with unresolved issues of loss, bereavement and separation. Against this background it was extremely difficult to take a proactive approach to health care. As one young woman (aged 14) said, 'If you feel so bad about yourself and what has happened to you, what does it matter if you take risks with your health anyway?'

The young people seemed to lack basic health care information. They wanted information about diet, eating disorders and exercise, confidential contraceptive guidance and clear advice on drugs. Most found it difficult to access the appropriate information. Although they had some knowledge about these issues, they got it mainly from television, magazines and from each other. Communication with their carers about such matters seemed to be mainly about the rules regarding what they could and could not do. There was a real lack of opportunity for discussion and debate about the impact of risk-taking behaviour. They said those who cared for them were too embarrassed to help them think through the issues.

For those in residential care, rest and sleep were of particular concern. There was a lot of pressure, particularly from the older age group, to stay up, stay out and join in. For others, bedtime had very traumatic associations but few were able to talk to anybody about these feelings. Several young people referred to the fact of being surrounded by adults who smoked, saying that they had not smoked prior to being looked after, but had started due to peer pressure and the fact of living in an environment where smoking was the norm.

Conclusions

Increasingly within the health service, there is a drive towards effectiveness, and evidence-based medicine and outcomes. There is also a very appropriate movement to include the views of consumers in the development of services. However, in the case of the routine medical for looked after children, the main consumers appear to have been the social services department and the medical profession. The young people and their parents have been largely excluded from this process. Consequently, systems have developed which are not relevant to the needs of this very disadvantaged population. We suggest that the following should be included in any debate on the future of looked after child medicals:

- There needs to be more emphasis on the health of the looked after child and less on the medical examination. Apparently mundane health problems are not mundane: hearing, vision, immunisation and dental care are all important health issues. Like any good parent, it is better to address these problems early in the child's life than to tackle them in adolescence or when the young person leaves public care.

- Children and young people in public care have a right to health and health care services. Article 24 of the UN Convention on the Rights of the Child states that 'young people have a right to good standards of health and to services which promote their health'. These rights include open access to health care, to absolute confidentiality (unless they are at risk of abuse) and the right to refuse both medicals and medical treatment.

- Young people should also be able to be seen by a doctor of their choosing – a doctor who is sensitive to that person's individual circumstances and has some knowledge of the context of public care.

- Good parents place a high emphasis on preventive health care, particularly at an early age, encouraging children to be aware of the importance of being fit and staying healthy. Most parents ensure that their children, especially when young, are fully immunised, have regular dental examinations and checks of their hearing and vision. As a child enters adolescence it becomes less easy for parents to intervene. Local authorities who are looking after children must adopt this model. All children entering the care system should have a comprehensive holistic assessment of their physical health as well as their social, emotional and educational development. Unfortunately this may only happen if the child is placed for adoption. This assessment should include the complete collation of the child's medical background and family history. Out of this assessment package should flow a care plan with emphasis on health education and development. The number and frequency of the medicals for the child can then be tailored to this plan.

- Older children and teenagers are the group most likely to refuse a medical. They should be encouraged to take part in a similar process of assessment, leading to a report which will be given to the young people themselves and discussed fully with them. Part of this process would be to reassure them that the assessment will not be repeated unless there is a good reason to do so. Adolescents make up a high proportion of looked after children. Their collaboration with assessment and treatment is vital (Sinclair *et al*, 1995; Cleaver, 1996).

- Above all, the stigma of being in public care and the issues of bereavement, loss and trauma need to be addressed. The development of self-confidence, a positive sense of identity and self-esteem must be nurtured. It is only then that these young people will feel able to take a responsible attitude to their own health.

While some agencies are developing strategies to ensure that the health needs and concerns of the young people they look after are more appropriately addressed, there is still a very long way to go. Health professionals, social workers, teachers, carers and parents need to work co-operatively on health and welfare issues. The young people concerned must feel they can both identify with and trust the individuals who are charged with their health care. Only then will there be any change in the poor health outcomes for looked after children.

Note

Since this article was written in 1997, looked after children are finally being recognised by both national and local government as a priority group for action. In 1998 a number of important publications, particularly the "Utting Report", highlighted the damage which children in the care system continue to suffer. In response, the Government announced a whole range of initiatives that will reform the public care system over the next three years.

All children have the right to health, and a healthy childhood. Childhood is a period of continuous growth and development and health in childhood therefore means meeting the needs of a child not only for physical health but also for developmental, emotional and social growth. For all parents the health of their children is very important. Children in the public care system must have the same rights to health as other children. They often enter care deprived of the opportunities for healthy growth and development. They must not continue to be further disadvantaged by inadequate substitute parenting.

If children are to leave public care having achieved their maximum potential, then local authorities and health authorities will need to provide more innovative health services in the future. Looked after children need to be active, informed participants in their own health care. They need to be offered health care that incorporates confidentiality, choice and a lack of discrimination.

The key message of this article remains the challenge for the future. The stigma of being in public care must be addressed and the issues of bereavement, loss and trauma dealt with effectively. If this is not done, then it will be difficult if not impossible to create an environment in which young people are able to take a responsible attitude towards their own health.

References

Cleaver H, *Focus on Teenagers*, HMSO, 1996.

Fletcher B, *Not Just a Name*, Survey by the Who Cares? Trust and the National Consumer Council, 1993.

Lambert L, 'A study of the health of children in care, using information derived from the *National Child Development Study*', National Children's Bureau Report to the Social Science Research Council, 1983.

Packman J and Hall C, *Draft Report on the Implementation of s 20 of the Children Act 1989*, Dartington Social Research Unit, 1995.

Sinclair R, Garnett L and Berridge D, *Social Work Assessment with Adolescents*, National Children's Bureau, 1995.

23 Implementing the Looking After Children system in RBK&C:
A big step forward for children and foster carers

Malcolm Phillips and Dave Worlock

Malcolm Phillips is the Team Manager for Short-term Fostering in London's Royal Borough of Kensington & Chelsea and Dave Worlock is Planning and Development Manager with the same Borough.

This paper was published in Adoption & Fostering, 20:4, 1997.

Can introducing a new set of forms ever lead to anything other than mountains of work and extra headaches for social workers? In the case of the Department of Health's integrated materials for Looking After Children, the answer is emphatically 'Yes!', but only if implementing authorities are able to learn from previous mistakes.

This article traces some of the gains for one London Borough from participating in the process – led by the Department of Health and Dartington Social Research Unit – of designing, revising and implementing the Looking After Children (LAC) materials. The paramount purpose of the LAC system is to improve the outcomes for all looked after children. At the same time, the materials are helping to maximise the direct involvement of children/young people and their parents.

However, another outstanding gain in the Royal Borough of Kensington & Chelsea (RBK&C) is that we learned how to place foster carers and residential social workers at the centre of the whole planning and review process, rather than on the periphery as happened at the beginning. This means that it is no longer necessary nor desirable for the child's social worker to be expected to "do everything".

311

Where do the gains come from?

The LAC materials were launched in May 1995 with the help of Sir William Utting and Virginia Bottomley. Our first year's experience of using the final version of the materials has indicated that the biggest gains are yet to come. The materials are simply tools, the real value of which stems first from the excellent opportunities they provide for assessment and action in each child's individual case and, secondly, because they facilitate research and development throughout services for children and families.

With some 80 per cent of local authorities in England and Wales now implementing all or part of the LAC system, we will eventually be able to share and learn from compatible data collected on a national basis. RBK&C is one of 12 authorities consulting with Dr Harriet Ward of Dartington Social Research Unit about how data from the LAC materials can be used as management information. Computerised versions of the LAC materials will greatly assist this development. International initiatives have already begun. (Readers interested in the research into the use and possible implementation of the LAC system should refer to Ward, 1995.)

What are the LAC materials?

The materials include two groups of forms: the *Planning and Review Forms* for use with all looked after children; and the *Assessment and Action (A&A) Records* which are normally used with children who have been looked after for six months or longer. The *Planning and Review Forms* comprise:

- an Essential Information Record;
- a Placement Plan (Part 1) Placement Agreement;
- a Placement Plan (Part 2) Day-to-day Arrangements;
- a Care Plan;
- consultation papers (for child/young person, parent, carer); and
- a Review Form.

These forms provide the framework for collecting and sharing all the information, and making all the agreements required by the Children Act 1989 and its associated regulations. Creative care planning for looked after children depends upon their "corporate parents" writing down the same kind of information which parents in the community keep in their heads. Certainly foster carers cannot do their job properly if important facts are not made known to them.

The age-related *A&A Records* are booklets designed to encourage communication between all the partners involved in the care of the child. They are used to assess systematically the child's progress in relation to the care they receive and to changes or improvements in plans.

The six *A&A Records* were the original core materials of the LAC system. They cover the following age ranges:

* under one year;
* one and two years;
* three and four years;
* five to nine years;
* ten to 14 years; and
* 15 years and over.

The first versions of these forms were devised following the report of the DoH's independent working party (see Parker *et al*, 1991). The much improved and colour-coded final versions are used to compile a comprehensive picture of an individual child's developmental progress across seven key dimensions: health, education, identity, family and social relationships, social presentation, emotional and behavioural development, and self-care skills.

The local response in Kensington & Chelsea

Prior to the Children Act coming into effect in October 1991, RBK&C had revised all its procedures in respect of looked after children in accordance with the requirements of the Act, with its accompanying regulations and guidance. In particular this required the development of pro-formas for Care Plans for looked after children, and new Review Forms.

Early in 1992 two developments occurred. First, we were starting to think about the need to review our new procedures and pro-formas for looked after children; we knew our first attempt would not be perfect and that we would have to revise them on the basis of experience.

Secondly, we received a box of materials from the DoH including: *A&A Records, Planning and Review Forms,* and a basic facts sheet, together with the book *Looking After Children: Assessing outcomes in Childcare* (Parker *et al,* 1991).

The small group responsible for reviewing and revising our recently developed procedures and forms looked at the DoH materials and concluded it would make a lot of sense for us to use them, for three reasons:

- The research findings and issues in *Assessing Outcomes in Child Care* rang a bell with people.
- The advantage of these materials was that they offered a package that was integrated, i.e. the different elements were all linked.
- We felt this was likely to become a nationwide system, so it made sense for us to be part of that now rather than go down a separate path.

In May 1992, the Head of Children and Family Service and the Service Managers Group agreed to implement the *A&A Records* and other materials within the department. An Implementation Group was set up with the clear task of enabling implementation on 1 January 1993. This group included three locality team managers, a deputy officer in charge of a children's home, a training officer, a Child and Family social worker, a fostering link worker and a planning officer.

In July 1992, a half-day conference was held for Children and Family managers and practitioners. The main speaker was Professor Sonia Jackson from the University of Swansea who had been a member of the DoH Working Party. This conference introduced managers to the thinking and research behind *A&A Records* and how they can be used to improve practice and outcomes.

Training, delivered by members of the implementation group (mostly managers), began during October and November. Members of the group worked in pairs and led one-and-a-half hour workshops with staff teams in their own offices. While residential staff were to receive this training, no plans were made for foster carers to receive training *prior* to implementation. It was planned to do training sessions during foster carers' support groups early in the new year.

Guidelines were produced for staff on how to use the *A&A Records.*

At this stage all the emphasis was put on it being the social worker's role to complete each record, although we assumed the foster carer would be present.

We later learnt the error of this approach. There was no real concept of partnership and the sharing of tasks; it had simply been envisaged that the child's social worker would do everything important in looked after children cases. Part of the point of the *A&A Records* is to assess the quality of care the child is receiving, which we had interpreted as meaning that the carers couldn't monitor themselves.

Implementation and evaluation

During January to May 1993 the children's social workers were asked to indicate how the records could be enhanced and to comment on their usefulness in improving our understanding of the child's needs and in planning future action. The social workers were also asked to give their assessment of what the carer, parent and child or young person thought. Foster carers were not asked directly.

Generally, the feedback was very positive (37 evaluation forms were completed). One of the interesting comments made in six of the 37 cases was that 'It can be embarrassing for the social worker to ask the carer about issues of diet, place to do homework, appearance . . .' Our view of this was that children's social workers were uncomfortable about being perceived by the carer as questioning the quality of care they provide.

All comments were fed back to Harriet Ward who was doing the developmental work on the LAC materials. This was the start of an ongoing relationship with Dartington Social Research Unit whereby we continued to provide feedback about all the materials over the next few years. We also kept staff up to date by publishing two newsletters during 1993, sent to all staff informing them about what was happening with the LAC materials, locally, nationally and internationally. Copies were not sent to foster carers.

A launch seminar on Plans and Reviews was held on 16 February 1994. Its purpose was to help people understand and focus on why planning and reviewing are essential elements of good practice in work with looked after children. Ruth Sinclair from the National Children's

Bureau was the main speaker. The seminar attracted 70 staff – managers and practitioners – but again we hadn't thought to invite any foster carers.

Introduction of revisions

Dartington developed a second draft of the "white forms" (later to be known as the *Planning and Review Forms)* based on comments received from the five piloting authorities. Changes included a new Care Plan and Placement Plan (Parts I & 2). The *A&A Records* were still in their original form.

During February/March 1994 half-day training sessions on the revised materials were arranged for all locality, residential and Family Placement Unit (FPU) staff in their individual team settings. The training was delivered by members of the Looking After Children Project Implementation Group (LACPIG), all of whom were managers, now including the team manager for short-term fostering.

We were still training different groups of staff in isolation from each other. Training for foster carers was limited to their monthly support groups. In other words we didn't give priority to foster carers at that time, either in terms of their role in using the materials or their training needs.

A second version of the LAC materials (including a "disability" supplement) was formally piloted during April to September 1994. Feedback was given to Dartington, with a view to a final version being produced in spring 1995.

Recognition of missing links

In April 1994 LACPIG reviewed the training and noted that:

> *Seventeen foster carers in the short-term team's monthly support group have looked at the package. They had no problem in understanding the system and liked the way the forms were laid out.*

The question that arose was 'Why are we seeing foster carers as peripheral to the implementation plan for the LAC system?'

In June the same year, LACPIG agreed to introduce 'a greater role for fostering link workers and residential workers in chairing the initial planning meetings; team managers should give social workers permission not to do everything'. Our feedback to Dartington requested that Placement Plan Parts 1 & 2 have space for fostering workers to sign.

Foster carers move in from the periphery

Preparation for implementing the final version of the materials began in October. LACPIG was working on several issues, including the concern expressed by social workers that there was still too much for them to do, and the dawning realisation that here and in other local authorities, the carer is in many cases the best person to complete sections of the *A&A Record* with the young person.

The enthusiasm foster carers and residential social workers had demonstrated for the LAC materials, particularly the *A&A Records,* now began to provide solutions to several challenges. Our new guidelines for using the records stated:

> *The whole idea of the* Assessment and Action Record *is that all the key people are involved in its completion in one way or another The emphasis is on partnership, so the child/young person, parent, carer and child's social worker should all share their views and engage in discussion about the particular points raised.*

By December 1994, our detailed implementation plan had to be sent to the Social Services Inspectorate. With regard to training we now had no hesitation in proposing to train staff and carers in mixed groups comprising social workers, foster carers, residential carers and FPU staff (up to 20 per group).

Our reasoning for the mixed groups was that it was crucial for the different partners in the corporate parent role to hear each other's perspectives and understand their different needs and priorities. The best way was to communicate face to face. The focus would be on the principles and thinking behind the materials, thus avoiding a bureaucratic approach to filling up forms.

Foster carers share responsibility as lead trainers

Training would now be delivered by mixed pairs, comprising a locality social worker and either a foster carer or residential social worker. Part of the reason for having front-line practitioners and carers as trainers was to prevent the trainer *vs* trained conflict which can arise with professional trainers, or trainers who are managers. We wanted the message to be 'Look, we're in this together. We are partners, equals, and need to learn and sort out together how we can use the materials to help children.' LACPIG also wanted to model the partnership between carers and social workers as one of the keys to the effective use of the LAC materials. Suggestions included:

- Foster carers and residential workers could take the lead role in working through the *A&A Records* with young people, and in most cases are the most appropriate people to be doing this.
- There is greater scope for involving FPU link workers and residential social workers in the completing of Placement Plan Part 2 (day-to-day arrangements), such as setting up and chairing planning meetings.

During May to June 1995, nine training days were provided for mixed groups of Children and Family social workers, foster carers, residential social workers and FPU link workers. A further two training days for foster carers in the Refugee Project were conducted in the Amharic and Tigrinia languages. All this training was led by well-prepared pairs drawn from a group of four foster carers, four Child and Family social workers and one residential social worker. A manager from LACPIG briefly attended the start of each training day to "own" responsibility for the overall implementation, including the snags. The same manager returned at the end of each day to collect feedback and answer questions. In addition, two half-day training sessions were run for administrators.

As promised, all the feedback (whether critical or complimentary) was collated and presented to a half-day workshop for all Child and Family team managers, Officers in Charge, Service Managers and Heads of Service. A ground-breaking development in that session was that two young people who had spent many years in the care system were the main speakers. The managers agreed on some 29 actions they needed to take in response to the feedback from the young people, carers and staff.

Responding to front-line feedback

Our procedures (computerised) were revised in response to reported difficulties and more emphasis was put on partnership between the social worker, carer, FPU worker and others, and the importance of negotiation about who is the best person to do what. For example:

The child's social worker is not expected to do all the tasks described in these procedures. His or her role is to co-ordinate the process and to make sure that the tasks and actions are completed by the most appropriate person. The most appropriate person might be the foster carer, residential social worker, parent, FPU link worker or the child's social worker, all of whom are partners in the process of caring for the child/young person. The needs of the particular child/young person and the circumstances of each individual case will determine who is the most appropriate person to do a particular task, and this should be negotiated by the partners involved.

The final version of the LAC materials was successfully introduced, on target, in July 1995. A colourful newsletter, with a covering letter from all the trainers, was subsequently sent to all Child and Family staff and *all* foster carers. This reported on all the training sessions, including the collated feedback. As requested during that training, blank sets of the LAC materials were sent to all foster carers.

In addition, revised flow charts (colour coded) for planned and unplanned placements, and the review process were circulated to all Child and Family staff and *all* foster carers. Our "user-friendly" flow charts have been very popular within RBK&C, and with colleagues in other authorities.

Follow-up workshops

Following feedback during the main training about the need to widen the partnership concept, a workshop on the LAC materials was held in January 1996 for educational professionals. One headteacher reported that in preparation for a Review a looked after child had already chosen her class teacher as the person to sit with her and complete the education dimension in her *A&A Record*.

Soon afterwards seven half-day workshops were held for social workers and carers to evaluate how things were going, share experiences and problem-solve. The trainers were new pairs of well-prepared carers and social workers. Half-day management seminars were held in February and March in order to produce Action Plans for the future maintenance and development of the whole LAC system, for instance monitoring individual cases, collating data on all our looked after children, and induction training for all new staff and carers.

On 31 March 1996, LACPIG ceased to exist. RBK&C has subsequently established a new group with a longer-term brief and wider membership, called the Looked After Children Policy Steering Group.

Assessing the benefits of implementation

To summarise, there are no easy answers in the quest to ensure good outcomes for children but we have identified many gains from implementing the LAC system. Key examples are that the materials:

- focus clearly on the needs of the child or young person;
- recognise the complexities and challenges involved in the public care of children;
- help children or young people and parents to get involved;
- recognise foster carers and residential workers as key players in the planning and review process;
- facilitate an active partnership between all the key players;
- ensure clarity about what needs to be done and who is doing it;
- do not simply add to an authority's paperwork but replace it with a carefully researched and integrated package, setting new national standards; and
- provide excellent opportunities for aggregating information and facilitating future research.

The last word belongs to carers and young people

Fred Fever, a young person who spent many unhappy years in the care system of another agency, told managers in RBK&C that bad experiences can only be avoided by the full implementation of the LAC materials:

They are of no use if the truth is not recorded . . . they are of little value to children and young people if they themselves are not involved in the process . . . the Assessment and Action Records will be of little value if they are not used properly.

In the mixed training sessions foster carers were generally very positive about the materials:

Reviews get done more effectively rather than just going through the motions.

The new forms are good because there's more space to "talk" on them.

Feedback also showed that challenges still remain:

Give foster carers blank sets of the materials so they can become familiar with them.

Issues of ethnicity must be adequately tackled or this can be a barrier to partnership.

Nothing happens if social workers do not adhere to timescales.

Many foster carers in RBK&C quickly became advocates of the LAC materials. Madeleine Klein, a short-term team foster carer, made the following remarks:

The language on the forms is straightforward and direct. The questions are "child-friendly" so children of four or five years can understand and enjoy helping to complete the records.

Parents and relatives want to know everything that has happened to the child and this shows them how decisions are come to.

It stops things being taken for granted.

The social worker can use the form to criticise the standards of care but this is right because it is for the benefit of the child.

If this system was used in years gone by, many of the children would not have grown up confused about their background and what happened to them.

Several carers have offered training and advice to colleagues here and in other authorities. In the words of Tereza Glai, a carer in the Refugee Fostering Project:

Don't rush; go at the child's pace. Foster carers can pick the right time to work on the forms. Talking about the questions in the records can gently open up sensitive issues. Working together on the records strengthens a healthy relationship between the young person and the carer.

Social workers and foster carers must keep the record safe and secure. It's the child's life.

References

Parker R, Ward H, Jackson S and Aldgate J (eds), *Looking After Children: Assessing outcomes in childcare*, HMSO, 1991.

Ward H (ed), *Looking After Children: Research into practice*, HMSO, 1995.

Section VII
Endings

For some children fostered on a long-term or permanent basis, in one sense the placement never ends, as the children become members of the family for good. They may well stay into early adulthood and retain close links even after making a home of their own. This is the exception, however. After most placements, children return home. This is generally a satisfactory ending, though some restored children are abused and some are accommodated again later (Farmer and Parker, 1991; Bullock *et al*, 1993). Children may also be adopted from foster care or move on to another kind of placement.

The impact of such changes on children is reasonably well known (Fahlberg, 1994). Little has been written about foster carers' responses. **Strover (1996),** herself a foster carer, shed some insight on this from a study she had carried out. She interviewed ten couples and one single carer in Northern England. Also questionnaires from 40 foster families were analysed. Understandably the respondents preferred placement endings which were planned and not rushed. A number had felt unhappy about decisions to move children back home or on to new families. They also felt they had little say in what happened. Nearly all of those interviewed regretted that they received little or no information about the child's progress after leaving. Words or letters of appreciation by social workers were much valued by foster carers, but they received these only occasionally. In general the foster carers in the study were looking for more recognition of their feelings, knowledge and role. Among the suggestions for changed practice were routine follow-up discussions, written acknowledgement of the work done and provision of information about children they had cared for.

The dissatisfactions recorded by Strover suggest a lack of true partnership between foster carers and social workers in many instances. If one or more placements ends unsatisfactorily from the foster carers' viewpoint, then they are likely to reconsider whether it is worthwhile carrying on. **Triseliotis *et al* (1998)** provide a rare glimpse into the reasons why some foster carers do give up that role. Based on a study of half of Scottish fostering agencies, they estimated that the annual rate of loss of foster carers is just under ten per cent. For about a fifth, the reason for ceasing to foster was age or ill health, while a small number of others had only fostered with a view to adopting, so they stopped once the child was adopted. A further one in ten changed jobs or residence. More than half of those who gave up were affected by dissatisfaction with the service provided by the agency or by problems with a child or parent. These were often related, since a common complaint was that social workers did not give enough support to deal with difficulties in the placement. Not uncommonly, it appeared that agencies were unaware of dissatisfaction and attributed the cessation of fostering to practical factors. Most of the foster carers who stopped had several years of experience, suggesting the loss of a significant resource.

24 How foster parents experience social work with particular reference to placement endings

Angela Strover

After university Angela Strover lived and taught in Australia and India for six years during which time she had two children. She then lived in Leeds for 20 years with her present partner, her two and his three adopted children. There they fostered ten children "permanently" (some of mixed heritage) and others briefly. For various reasons they have educated 13 of their children at home for between six months and nine years. In 1993 Angela completed a Master's Degree in Social Work. In 1992 the whole family began renovating a derelict cottage in Swaledale where she, her partner, John, and four teenagers now live.

This paper was published in Adoption & Fostering, 20:4, 1996.

During my 15 years as a foster parent I often felt quite dissatisfied when children left us. Therefore when I did a Master's Degree in Social Work at York University, I decided to investigate the experiences of others like myself. I deliberately use the term foster parent rather than foster carer as I believe the essential skills needed to care for foster children are those of parenting. My interest was in foster parents' relationships with these children rather than with members of their birth families. This does not mean that I regard being a foster parent as in any way superseding the role of birth parents; rather it is a role which should complement theirs.

When reviewing the literature there seemed to be a lack of material regarding social workers working with foster parents at the ending of placements. The effects on foster parents seemed seldom to be considered. Yet in *A Study of Those who Cease to Foster* (Portsmouth Social Services, 1975), it was said that 'A foster parent is expected to love and be ready to lose the child.' This report concluded that the role of the foster parent is not always made clear, the foster parent being half client, half colleague. It seems, therefore, that social workers may not always be clear about their role *vis à vis* foster parents while the latter's role may be even more ambivalent owing to the parent/worker relationship they have with the foster child/client. Unlike many other professional workers, foster parents can, and indeed often need to, become emotionally involved with the child in care. Findings are often unsatisfactory and continuity of contact can be important. Though writing specifically about adolescents, Downes (1992) asserted: 'If foster parents help with the arrangement over the end of the placement their continuity of care and concern is demonstrated.'

One agency, Barnardo's, tried to offer planned post-ending support. In their Specialist Family Project in Edinburgh they worked with six families in time-limited placements where the end was built in from the start. They encouraged foster parents to continue visiting the children after the ending of placements. They found that:

> The key practice point to emerge from this study was the need for continuing support for families, even where the end of the placement is properly managed and co-ordinated and in line with initial plans.
> (Practice Paper, 1989)

Three of the six families felt that, at the time of the child's departure, they had not fully acknowledged their own distress, feelings of loss and worries about the children's future. The social work role was well defined and included the need to be very sensitive to the possible needs of the foster parent and to take the initiative where appropriate. In this project foster parents expressed a mixture of feelings, including "sadness", "relief" and "satisfaction at a job well done". Downes (1982) described it as part of a social worker's role to further this sense of job satisfaction, writing: 'I suggest that field social workers could play an important part after placements end in reassuring foster parents of their value.'

In the Barnardo's time-limited placements, what was absent in contrast to where a placement breaks down was the destructive sense of guilt that Berridge and Cleaver found in *Foster Home Breakdown* (1987). They wrote, 'With few exceptions foster parents had indisputably made considerable investments in their relationships with children . . .' but also that 'most foster parents who were interviewed held themselves, usually unjustifiably, responsible for the downfall of the placement'.

Berridge and Cleaver found that social workers were often very uneasy about continued contact with foster parents in these cases and that this is reflected in an "all or nothing" attitude in which foster parents are often viewed by social workers as a set of discrete packages rather than an integrated experience. Yet they found that, particularly for older children, a 'configuration of relationships can be satisfactorily negotiated' so long as the roles occupied by the adults do not become confused. They see no reasons why relationships with former foster parents should not be nurtured and say that their evidence suggests that children can benefit a lot when carers continue to demonstrate an interest in their welfare. With the child's agreement, and obviously not necessarily in all circumstances, they urge continuity of contact.

Similarly, Downes (1992) acknowledged that hostile endings can be powerfully undermining, but the outcomes are better if they are followed by the young people being "welcomed back": 'The social worker may need to actively encourage meetings between adolescents and foster parents.'

Nature of my study

The study consisted of two parts: a small sample of personal interviews and a questionnaire survey. My sample consisted of ten pairs and one single foster parent. I personally recruited five and the other six responded to a request for volunteers sent out in Division One of Leeds social services on my behalf.

In an attempt to find out how typical or untypical this sample was I asked them to complete a quick general questionnnaire on their experience. This same questionnaire was sent to 91 other foster parents in the Division so that responses from the two samples could be compared. Forty questionnaires were returned in time to be used.

I also invited all the foster parents concerned, both in my sample study and in the questionnaire survey, to make a list of do's and don'ts for social workers.

The interviewees

Table 1 gives an overview of the 11 sets of foster parents in my study sample, the duration of placements, the length of their experience and the number of children and social workers each had had. Also, from their responses to the questionnaire I was able to estimate their overall level of satisfaction with the social work service they had received.

In order to check bias in my interview sample I compared answers on the brief questionnaire to those I received from the 40 other foster parents in the same area. In the question about the ending of placements the control sample scored 57.1 per cent in a measure of satisfaction while my study sample only scored 37.5 per cent, one of the greatest differences between the two groups. It may be then that they were partially motivated

Table 1
An overview of responses

Interviewees	Fostering type(s)[1]	Years experience	No. of children	No. of social workers	Level of satisfaction[2]
FPI	all	30	160	50	18.2%
FP2	all	26	over 100	'too many'	52.5%
FP3	L,T	2	5	6	55.6%
FP4	all	14	11	12	43.75%
FP5	all	11	20	10	59.1%
FP6	S	14	over 80	over 200	39.6%
FP7	S	5.5	7	6	26.1%
FP8	S,T	14	over 40	over 40	50%
PF9	S,T	3	15	8	57.3%
FPIO	L,T	14.5	9	over 12	10.4%
FPII	L	3	2	5	62.5%[3]

[1] L = Long term, S = Short term. T = Time limited.
[2] FP11, who were the most satisfied of the foster parents interviewed had had no experience of endings.
[3] The responses to the questionnaire were weighted as follows:
very satisfied 4 points; *satisfied 3* points; *about equally satisfied and dissatisfied* 2 points; *rather dissatisfied* I point; and
very disappointed 0 points. I then calculated the scores as a percentage of the total possible score (that is, the score if everyone was completely satisfied).

by a need to make their dissatisfaction known, as well as an awareness of the need to improve social work practice.

Summary of findings from interviews with foster parents

After the first baby left I cried buckets and roared for a week. Then you get another phone call asking you to do it again.

Planning and preparation for placement endings
When asked how they felt about the endings of placements, they all considered it "good" when endings were planned, phased and with foster parents actively involved. Rushed endings had often left them feeling they had let the child down and thus they too were upset. An opportunity to accompany children to a new placement and subsequently to visit gave pleasure when it was made possible.

With regard to preparations for endings they all felt the ending needed to be a planned part of the placement so that foster parents and children were both prepared for the move. Not, as one said, 'You just get told the baby will leave next week'. They felt they should be able to work with the social worker and not just be left to do it on their own. Eight foster parents described situations where placements of pre-adoptive babies of children "freed" for adoption while in their care had been left to "drift". Mutual attachment had become so strong that they had often wanted to adopt them themselves. In such circumstances attempts to force endings caused great distress yet it was, as they pointed out, not they who had let the placement drag on. Five foster parents felt that without planning or preparation for the ending of a difficult placement, where there is no end in sight, you tend to feel the strain more. This can contribute to a breakdown.

I enquired whether their opinion about the best ways of handling an ending was asked for or considered. Generally, they did not feel part of a team but they did value and appreciate occasions when their views had been sought and considered. It was often hard when they were not consulted and half the sample were able to cite very sad consequences of their views being ignored and subsequent placements breaking down. One concluded: 'Right from the start we thought it wouldn't work.' Children had been uprooted for the sake of a "policy", only to return or go elsewhere – far more disturbed as a result.

By "policy" they usually meant the pre-arranged plan that social workers had for the children in their care. Some foster parents had also been informed that it was not the policy of the area to allow or encourage foster parents to adopt children placed with them or to allow more than a certain number of foster children within a family. This last restriction caused one couple to conclude: 'They should not judge us by themselves.' This couple felt that over the years they had amply demonstrated their abilities through fostering a large number of children.

One foster mother told me how she was still in touch with a former foster child who was very unhappy in an adoptive placement where both the child's and the relatives' wishes had been ignored. They had wanted to foster her long term and both the child and her relatives had also wanted this. The ex-foster mother remarked ruefully: 'But no, the policy was adoption.' Similarly, another remarked: 'They should have gone for what they'd got', rather than 'be dogmatic to the point of destruction'.

The majority agreed with this. They felt that rigid adherence to policy got in the way and jeopardised the security that the child had acquired with them. For the child's sake they felt that each case should be judged on its merits.

When asked if there was anything else they would like to say on the subject of endings, one couple with thirty years' experience of fostering said they felt there was a great need for more sharing of responsibilty and planning for young adults leaving care. In their experience the ending of long-term placements had often been left entirely up to them. They knew that these young people would need them for a long time yet and they felt trapped. One social worker had actually said, 'If you can't cope, turn them out', but they knew they couldn't do that. Planning had simply not been undertaken or followed through.

Follow-up information and discussions
I asked them how much follow-up information they were given. None of the group felt that any real effort was made to give them further news of the child or children once they had left. Indeed one said, 'The only news you get is when they turn up again.' All found this lack of follow-up information very hard to accept and had often wondered how children

had subsequently fared. Some had found out by chance and some entirely through their own efforts, for example, by visiting schools. One couple who had fostered over 80 children said they would have liked to have known of the outcome of their work in order to get more "job satisfaction". The few exceptions to this lack of follow-up were greatly appreciated.

Asked whether they were given the opportunity to discuss how placements had gone, nobody had experienced follow-up discussions as a matter of course. One couple said that after a difficult placement: '. . . It left us looking for help and suggestions . . . it was an unhappy time.' Only where the foster parents got on very well with the social workers did such discussions occur, and then only informally. In one case a crisis and breakdown in the placement had led to such a discussion and the foster parents thought that without it they would not have been able to continue fostering. Some felt that post-ending discussions might help to demonstrate that foster parents and their work are valued. A couple who had fostered close to 100 children stated that in none of these cases had the social worker discussed with them how the placement had gone. They pointed out that a foster parent has a child for 24 hours a day and so is bound to have knowledge of the problems involved – valuable information which might well be useful to social workers and future carers. Some felt that this absence of follow-up discussions was indicative of the general lack of support and interest in them as people.

Just to be left angry or upset at the ending of placements was painful. All said they had felt the need for "comfort" at such times and for their feelings to be recognised. One couple said, 'We were left in limbo with nothing'; and another, 'When a child leaves, you have a feeling of a big emptiness'. However, discussions did not take place as a matter of course, even when the placement had been traumatic. One foster mother in particular regretted not receiving any words of comfort or praise when a nine-year-long placement of a child with special needs had suddenly come to a traumatic end. Four of the sample suggested that follow-up discussions might be a useful form of counselling, especially where placements had broken down.

Recognition

The instances when they had been genuinely thanked or praised for their work were very much appreciated. Comments made at reviews had often made them feel valued. One couple recounted with pride how at the end of a review they had been sincerely thanked for their work in general. Yet it was clear that very few letters of thanks had been received considering the number of children and length of time involved. Six foster parents who had a total of over 90 years' fostering experience with nearly 400 children received only ten letters of thanks between them. The remaining five received none. Three of the letters were to the same foster parent about the same child. She remarked: 'I thought the letters were wonderful and I felt like framing them.'

Sometimes people felt distinctly unappreciated. One couple said they felt like 'an item to be used', 'part of the fixtures and fittings'. They thought social workers really needed to know far more about what it is like to be on the receiving end of social work practice. The foster mother said sadly: 'The child is taken back when *they* see fit.'

Finally, I asked whether the social worker ever discussed with them their role in the placement and what both sides had learnt from it, and whether this was helpful. Responses included: 'We have never been asked what we learnt from a placement', and 'Have social workers nothing to learn from foster parents?' Only one couple had ever formally discussed what they had learnt from a placement, but this was with their link social worker not that of the child. Two had discussed it informally, whereas six felt social workers did not have time for such things although all felt that they had experience worthy of recognition. None had been given the opportunity to discuss the social workers' role in the placement.

Questionnaire findings

Foster parents' specific requests

Below is a summary of the do's and don'ts for social workers which I asked all the foster parents to write on the back of their questionnaires. Twenty-six did so. Grouped together, their suggestions make a powerful statement as to how they wish to be treated by social workers. I arranged them under headings, noting the number of people who made comments alongside. These were the headings, with examples of comments:

- Be professional and/or simply good-mannered (22)

Keep appointments and be on time. Our time is important too.
Don't give details of access, etc. at the last minute.
Remember you are in our home.

- Give us the practical help we need and are entitled to (18)

Be aware of foster carers' requirements and entitlements.
A social worker wouldn't work for nothing; don't expect us to go for weeks without an allowance.

- Keep in regular contact and show you care about us (17)

Show you care for both foster carers and children.
Always find time to listen to foster carers; they often need to "offload" to someone.

- Respect our work and knowledge (16)

Listen to us, especially when it comes to children leaving us.
Ask foster parents about kids; we have them longer than you see them.
Treat foster parents as part of a team.

- Share information (16)

Involve foster parents and tell us what to expect when a child is in therapy.
Tell me how the children that have left me are getting on.
Be honest when placing a child.

- Give us confidence in your competence and common sense; don't just go by the book (16)

You cannot place a child from a book.
Don't latch on to the latest theory (you need a catholic approach to problems).
Accept that it is not wrong to become emotionally involved with a child.
Have a sense of humour.

- Remember we are human and have lives and families of our own (10)
Don't assume that foster carers are infallible. We need breaks sometimes but are expected to carry on.
Realise that foster parents have some life of their own.

Implications for social work and placement endings

In general my findings based on the study sample's responses support what came out of my review of the literature. They highlighted what makes for a successful ending by providing numerous examples of bad ones and clear indicators are given of what is lacking in these.

Are there then any reasons why social workers neglect placement endings and their follow-up? Much has been written about good social work practice with reference to "termination" with clients and there have been reminders that workers, too, will be affected by these endings. Wasserman (1974) wrote that:

> *When termination is involved the practitioner needs to be aware that within the transference between client and worker, earlier experience related to separation and loss will be involved.*

Do social workers then, perhaps unconsciously, avoid the painful process of facing up to feelings of loss? Is this avoidance made easier by the fact that a foster parent's position is ambivalent, especially as they are not regarded purely as "clients" and would not want to be? Yet if the therapeutic effects of a placement are not to be undone, it would seem important that the ending is well managed and that both client (child) and worker (foster parent) have their feelings and needs acknowledged.

My small sample strongly suggests that for the sake of the children and for their own satisfaction the end of a placement should generally incorporate:

- time for planning and preparation in which they, the foster parents, are crucially involved;
- opportunities for foster parents to be able to show continuity of caring;
- follow-up discussion of the placement in which their knowledge and feelings are given due weight and respect;

- the availability of continued support and counselling after the ending;
- written acknowledgement of the work they have done; and
- opportunities for foster parents to be able to acquire follow-up information about the children they have cared for.

There is, of course, the huge practical problem of making time for such things. In practice social workers are almost invariably having to devote themselves to more pressing problems and are, if not overworked, working to capacity. They would need extra time, space and information; more social workers might well be called for. Also in practice, as most foster parents know only too well, once a child has left they are usually asked to take on another within a very short time, if not immediately. Therefore foster parents often cannot, any more than social workers, afford the luxury of pausing to assess their situation, needs, feelings or future requirements. Yet placements, even if they do not break down, are seldom problem free. How much valuable feedback information may be being lost is hard to judge.

Social workers may have reservations about continuing contact between child and former foster parents, as mentioned by Berridge and Cleaver (1987). Apart from special schemes, such as the work Downes (1992) describes with professional foster parents and adolescents in time-limited placements, foster placements are usually forced to be a set of separate "packages". Downes saw the role of the social worker as 'aiming to maximise the likelihood of the alliance between foster parents and adolescents surviving the end of the placement'. Outside of such schemes social workers might have more inclination and opportunity to give children an "integrated experience" if foster parents themselves were given more time to ensure that continuity of contact is constructive. As one foster parent interviewed said, 'It is important not to foster distrust in a child'. Although it may seem obvious that people should not just simply disappear out of children's lives, there does not seem to be any provision for counteracting this.

The financial implications of giving foster parents the opportunity of a child-free respite in which a retainer fee is paid may make such a suggestion seem unrealistic. However, if as Herbert Laming (Chief Inspector of the Social Services Inspectorate) says, 'Foster carers have become the cornerstone of child care in this country,' surely extra finances for such schemes should be made available nationally so that foster parents are better cared for. This would not only be constructive and therapeutic for everybody concerned, but could also prove financially beneficial if fewer foster parents gave up fostering. Personally I was relieved and glad to stop short-term fostering and concentrate on our long-term placements.

A respite would enable feelings of loss and guilt to be faced, would allow foster parents to visit children recently in their care, contact their own link social workers, discuss their own needs as well as the child's, and generally sort out future requirements and the passing on of any necessary information. It would also allow the children recently in their care to come back and visit without the feeling that their places had been taken. Given this scheme, children or young people could be spared the feeling, cited by Downes (1992), of 'the family boundary closing impenetrably behind them'. One adolescent remarked to me that the foster parents he had only just left did not want him any more as 'a new boy had moved in'.

Berridge and Cleaver (1987) wrote that 'Despite the fact that several couples had seen many children come and go their sense of loss remained significant'. Social workers would not expect a bereaved person to go through the same experience time and time again, with little support or sympathy, without some damage being done. Thus it would seem that the management of separation is very important for the foster parent, as well as for the child.

In my view the key to a good relationship between social workers and foster parents, as perhaps for all relationships, is mutual respect. But respect has to be earned and will develop if both social workers and foster parents feel that each is doing their job well. The summary of do's and don'ts gives social workers a succinct and forceful guide on how foster parents wish to be treated by them.

References

Berridge D and Cleaver H, *Foster Home Breakdown*, Blackwell, 1987.

Downes C, 'How endings are experienced in time-limited placements of difficult adolescents', *Journal of Adolescence 5* (December), pp 379–94, 1982.

Downes C, *Separation Revisited*, Ashgate, 1992.

Hunter A, 'Models of effective partnership', *Family Placement Theory*, Barnardo's Practice Paper, 1989.

Portsmouth Social Services, 'A study of those who cease to foster', *British Journal of Social Work,* 1975.

Wasserman S L, 'Ego psychology', in Turner F (ed), *Social Work Treatment*, Free Press, 1974, USA.

25 Foster carers who cease to foster

John Triseliotis, Moira Borland and Malcolm Hill

John Triseliotis is Emeritus Professor at the University of Edinburgh and Visiting Professor and Senior Research Fellow at the University of Strathclyde. Moira Borland is Research Fellow at the University of Glasgow and Malcolm Hill is Director of the Centre for the Child & Society at the same University.

This paper was published in Adoption & Fostering, 22:2, 1998.

Introduction

In recent years concern has often been expressed that there is a looming crisis in fostering as a result of difficulties in recruitment and retaining carers (see NFCA, 1997). Issues of supply and demand have often featured prominently in fostering literature over the last 50 or so years, but specific information has been lacking. In particular little is known about who ceases to foster and why. The only published research known to us on the matter is what came to be known as the "Portsmouth study", carried out some 20 years ago (Jones, 1975), and Gregg's (1993) study also based on samples drawn from a single agency in England. In addition, Pasztor and Wynne (1995) provide a summary of American studies on the subject. The dearth of studies in this area is illustrated by the fact that Berridge's (1997) excellent review of foster care research for the Department of Health makes reference to only one study which was part of more extensive research carried out within a single English authority (Cliffe and Berridge, 1991).

We report on this issue from a much larger study which was prompted mainly by concerns about the supply and demand of foster carers in Scotland. The study was set up in 1996 with the twin aims first, of establishing who the carers are and second, identifying the policies, structure and organisation of the fostering services in the 32 local authorities and one voluntary agency. The two parts of the study were designed to complement each other. The key aims were:

- To examine the characteristics, motives and social circumstances of those who foster and seek explanations concerning the retention and loss of foster carers; describe the experience of fostering, including contact issues between parents and children; and evaluate post-placement support and general experiences of the fostering service;
- To identify the policies, organisation and structures of the new social work departments for fostering, including the agencies' fostering needs, recruitment approaches, the preparation, assessment and training of carers, continued placement support to children and carers, the assessment of children and the matching processes followed, financial arrangements and monitoring mechanisms.

Phase one of the study, which was carried out in 1996, identified the characteristics and life-styles of active and former carers and, more important, how they perceived the operation of the fostering services in 16 Scottish local authorities and in one voluntary agency. This article reports findings from this phase, but with the main focus on the former carers and why they gave up fostering. Where appropriate, data are contrasted with similar information from active or continuing carers. Knowing the former carers' views of why they ceased to foster, though only one of a number of aspects that have to be taken into account, nevertheless provides valuable feedback for agencies in developing their fostering services. The perspective of the agencies was pursued during the second phase of the study which took place in the summer period of 1997.

Sampling methods

Identifying exact figures of who ceased to foster and why was far from straightforward. Not all of the sampled authorities had accurate lists of those who ceased or, if they had, the lists did not always give the reasons why these had stopped fostering. Furthermore, modern systems of information technology had hardly been used to keep up-to-date information on issues of supply and demand, foster carer availability, preferences and so on. The implications for policy making, planning and monitoring arising from the absence of such basic information are obvious.

After a rather complex and laborious process, including tapping the memories of staff, we were able to piece together what we think is a reliable picture of those who ceased to foster in 1994 and 1995 and why. We are confident that in relation to two-thirds of the agencies featuring in the study we were able to obtain fully accurate information. With the remaining one-third we may be over- or under-estimating losses by about one per cent.

Methods of data collection

Information on carers who ceased to foster was obtained in three ways:
- *Postal questionnaires* Of 216 former carers identified by the 17 agencies, postal questionnaires were sent out to 201 of them. (No questionnaires were sent to 15 carers who had been de-registered following mainly allegations of abuse.) Of the questionnaires sent out 97 (or 49 per cent) were returned. (One arrived too late to be included in the analysis.) The response rate was less satisfactory than the 74 per cent obtained from continuing carers.
- *Agency records* Information was also obtained from staff and agency records on why the 216 carers gave up fostering. Eventually a picture was compiled on 149 (or 69 per cent) of the original 216 who withdrew or who were asked to withdraw. Data from this exercise were invaluable in helping to check with the replies received from carers through the postal survey.
- *Personal interviews* Personal interviews were also held with 27 former foster carers who ceased to foster. These were randomly selected after excluding those who left fostering because of retirement. The interviews provided in-depth material which helped again to act as a check on the statistical data and on information obtained from staff and records. This form of triangulation has helped to provide a more accurate and consistent picture of why these carers gave up fostering.

The proportion who gave up fostering

During the two-year period preceding the start of the study, the 17 agencies had incurred a total loss of 216 carers. Between them the same agencies had 1,184 active foster carers, so the annual loss was around nine per cent. Translated into national figures for Scotland this would result in an annual loss of around 160 foster carers in relation to a total of about 1,900 fostering households. As was to be expected, there were variations between agencies. The lowest loss of four per cent was experienced by the only voluntary agency featuring in the sample which had 51 active carers on its books. The highest loss of 13 per cent was incurred by a middle-sized agency with almost 100 active foster carers.

Our figures are similar to those reported from a recent survey carried out by the National Foster Care Association (NFCA) of English local authorities. The agencies in that study who answered the question on losses reported an overall eight per cent loss, with a quarter of these experiencing more than ten per cent (Waterhouse, 1997). No explanation was given about the nature of the losses. In contrast, the Portsmouth study, though poorly documented as far as actual numbers were concerned, identified an annual loss of around 27 per cent (Jones, 1975). Some American studies suggest up to 50 per cent losses within the first year of fostering (Pasztor and Wynne, 1995). With no previous Scottish studies to compare with, we cannot say whether these findings represent an improvement or not.

Background characteristics

The study contrasted a number of personal and background characteristics shared by former and continuing carers such as marital status, number of own children, religion, housing, ethnicity, health, educational qualifications, employment and social class. No significant differences were found between those who ceased to foster because of dissatisfaction with some key aspect of the operation of the fostering service and the active ones, except that those who ceased were more likely to:

- Have poorer health at the time of giving up (female carers);
- Have somewhat larger families and more own dependent children;
- Be active worshippers (female);
- Hold non-manual occupations (female);
- Have larger houses.

Unlike Jones (1975), this study found no significant differences between age at recruitment and ceasing to foster.

Motivation to foster

When it came to their stated motivation to foster, no discernible differences could be identified between former and continuing carers. The same concerns and interests had attracted both the former as well as the continuing carers. Even certain differences found between female and male carers that were identified in the active group persisted within the group who ceased.

Overall, and except for those who enter fostering with a view to adoption or because it suits their family's circumstances at a particular time, looking for the carers' motives as a key reason for ceasing to foster does not appear to be a productive line of enquiry. It is possible that better methods of preparation and selection in the last decade or so have led to greater uniformity in the type of person who comes into fostering now.

The foster children

The study also contrasted the number and type of children fostered at any one time by continuing and former carers, the ages of the children, sibling groups, children with mental or physical disabilities fostered, type of fostering undertaken (including community care schemes for adolescents), difficulties presented by the children, breaks and holidays taken. No significant differences were again found except that former carers were more likely to:

- Be fostering under five-year-olds;
- Have had fewer breaks;
- Say they were not undertaking the kind of fostering they preferred;
- Have had more difficulties with parents over contact.

Why carers ceased to foster

We now turn to the more vital question of why these former carers gave up fostering. Table 1 presents side by side the primary explanations offered by the surveyed former foster carers and those stated by fostering staff/social work records.

While the main reasons for which foster carers cease to foster are diverse, there are also a number of consistent patterns which can be grouped into two broad categories: (1) internal factors connected with the fostering services; and (2) external factors.

1. Internal factors connected with the operation of the fostering services included:

- Outright dissatisfaction with the operation of the fostering services;
- The children's behaviour;
- Impact of fostering on own family/no privacy;
- Burn-out/stress/no respite;
- Allegations;
- Biological parents' behaviours.

The above areas of dissatisfaction amounted to 57 per cent of all the responses. If we were to add those who said they had left because of ill-health resulting from the stress of fostering, then around three-fifths of carers left because of some aspect connected with the operation of the fostering services. These reasons did not always have to do with the behaviour or attitudes of social workers or the agency. A large part of it was related to the general implications arising from caring for some very problematic children. There was no evidence to suggest that those who ceased were fostering more problematic children compared to the rest. The Portsmouth study too found that about half the responses of those who ceased were in some way connected with the operation of the fostering services (Jones, 1975), albeit withdrawals were much higher in that study.

On this basis the fostering services in Scotland can expect to have an annual loss of around six per cent (between 80 and 100 carers) who leave because of dissatisfaction with fostering including the children's problems and for having had no placement. In contrast Gregg (1993), based on his study of the carers of a single agency in England, claims that for foster carers ceasing to foster is 'a natural process'. Furthermore, though the social work support they received could have been improved, it was generally appreciated and found to be helpful. Inevitably studies based on single agencies simply show what is happening in that agency and findings cannot be generalised.

2. External factors included:
   - The adoption of the foster child;
   - Illness/retirement;
   - No space or needing to work;
   - Moving house.

Retirement and illness featured in almost a fifth of the responses offered (eight retired and four withdrew because of illness). With one exception, the 17 carers (or 18 per cent) who withdrew after adopting the foster child were some of the most satisfied with the fostering services. Other key explanations offered by carers included moving house, the need to work or no space. A few had been fostering for the sole reason of fostering only one child known to them. Once this was completed they withdrew.

Levels of congruence found between former carers and fostering workers/records

Though there were a number of similarities in the explanations offered by former carers and social workers of why carers ceased to foster, there were also notable differences. Fostering workers significantly under-estimated the proportion of carers who withdrew because of dissatis-faction with the fostering services, the foster children's behaviour, stress and parental interference. They "exaggerated" the numbers of those who left because of moving house and/or the need to work, illness or retire-ment and 'own request' (see Table 1).

The most glaring difference between the two groups was the much higher proportion of carers to fostering workers, who said they had left fostering because of outright dissatisfaction with the operation of the fostering services (26 per cent to two per cent). It could be argued that those who returned the postal questionnaire or spoke to us were not a true representation of all those who ceased to foster and that the fostering workers' views were more representative. We tried to check this by comparing the levels of congruence (where we had the names) between the views expressed by social workers and those of former foster carers. Where foster carers gave as their main reason for with-drawing the 'lack of social work support', the 'attitudes and behaviour

Table 1

Why carers ceased to foster based on the views of former carers and fostering workers/records

Explanations	Former f/carers' primary reason		Fostering staff's primary reason	
	N	%	N	%
Dissatisfaction with the service	25	26	3	2
Retirement or illness	18	19	32	22
Adopted the foster child	17	18	19	13
Children's behaviour	16	17	8	5
Needing to work, move, no space	14	15	30	20
Impact on own family, no privacy	12	12	13	9
Stress, no respite	10	10	6	4
Allegations	5	5	17	11
At own request or had enough	–	–	12	8
Biological parents' behaviour	4	4	–	–
End of unique placement	2	2	4	3
Other (bereavement, no placements)	5	5	5	3
Total	128*		149	

* The percentages are based on multiple responses and do not add to 100.

of social workers' or 'the activities of the social work department', fostering workers tended to say the carers had withdrawn 'at their own request', 'own decision' or that 'they had had enough, or 'because of work commitments'.

It seems that in part carers' real reasons for ceasing to foster were not conveyed to fostering staff or adequately recorded. In other instances social work records used generalised explanations like 'own request' and 'own decision' which obscured the problem.

We can also make some comparisons between the explanations offered by the former carers who gave up because of factors associated with fostering, and those offered by continuing ones when describing times they felt like giving up. There were many similarities between the two. Both spoke about children's problems, chronic lack of social work support and related issues concerning the operation of the fostering service, including stress and effect on own family. On the basis of these findings, the difference between the two groups was one of degree rather than of substance. Eventually the pressure or a crisis become too much for some individuals, tilting the balance towards withdrawal.

Working relationships with the fostering services

Next we contrasted the perceptions of former foster carers with those of active ones on the quality of relationships with the children's social workers, link workers and the agency as a whole. The ratings of satisfaction offered by the former carers were, as expected, below those of continuing ones. The same applied when it came to the levels of support and whether expectations had been met or not.

However, it was thought that to obtain a truer picture all those carers who gave up for external reasons should be left out of the analysis, which should concentrate instead on the 50 carers who left because of definite dissatisfaction with some key aspect of the operation of the fostering services. These form the basis for the next section.

The overall picture that emerges from Table 2 is that just over half the former carers rated their relationship with the social workers and the agency as 'good', or 'very good', but the rating for 'very good' was notably lower. As we say in the main report, carers were very discriminating between 'very good' and 'good'. Somewhat more favourable ratings were given to relationships with the link workers. However, compared to continuing carers, former carers rated all three types of relationships significantly lower. Perhaps it was to be expected that, as far as relationships were concerned, former carers would feel more disillusioned compared to continuing ones.

Much of the dissatisfaction of the former carers with the children's social workers centred around the latter's failure to visit often enough or provide sufficient background information on the child, being unresponsive to requests for help and support when the children were being difficult, being unappreciative of their efforts and not being available when needed. Typical comments included: 'no support from child's social worker'; 'could have done with more support'; 'lack of commitment from certain social workers'; or 'poor matching'.

Worse in the eyes of the carers were telephone calls or other messages

Table 2

Contrasting the rating of relationships between continuing and former carers who left because of dissatisfaction with some aspect of the fostering service

Relationship level	Relationship with social workers		Relationship with link worker		Relationship with agency	
	Cont.	Former	Cont.	Former	Cont.	Former
Level	%	%	%	%	%	%
Very good	46	31	68	40	37	18
Good	32	22	22	31	45	36
Neither good nor bad	13	14	8	20	13	26
Poor	6	18	1	7	4	12
Very poor	3	14	1	2	1	8
Total	100	99	100	100	100	100

never being returned or being told the social worker was always somewhere else and unable to come to the phone: 'calls to child's social workers not being returned'; or 'being left to cope on our own'.

There were a variety of other comments suggesting that as carers they had very little say in what happened to the children and there was little recognition of them as members of a working team or as partners.

Support

Another comparison made between the two groups of former and continuing carers was in the amount of support received.

The pattern found with relationships was repeated here but more strongly. Significantly, fewer former than continuing carers described the level of support as 'very good' or 'good'. Correspondingly, more former carers described support as neutral ('half and half') or as 'very poor' to 'poor'. Former carers repeated some of the comments made earlier, especially infrequent visits, unavailability and unresponsiveness to requests for help. Nevertheless many were satisfied with the support contact but still gave up.

When asked to say whether their overall expectations of fostering had been met, only 29 per cent of those who gave up because of dissatisfaction with the fostering services said that they had. This contrasted with just over half of active carers who said their expectations were fulfilled. Their main explanation for the apparent disappointment was of fostering turning out to be much harder than they had expected and the lack of support from the fostering services.

Fostering experience

We also compared former and current carers' characteristics, and views on the service, in relation to their length of service. Carers who ceased to foster had an average of 7.5 years of fostering experience compared to 7.0 years of continuing ones. Even taking account of only those who ceased because of dissatisfaction with some aspect of the work of the fostering services, their fostering experience still amounted to an average of 7.3 years. It cannot be said, therefore, that those who withdraw do so only after a short period of caring. Just under half had fostered for less than five years, but over a quarter had fostered for more than ten years (see Table 4). In fact only nine per cent had fostered for less than a year compared to 40 per cent found by Jones (1975). However, almost all those who gave up before the first year was over were the ones who were dissatisfied with the fostering service.

The large percentage of carers leaving after a year prompted Jones (1975) to write that 'there is little to be gained from higher recruitment of foster parents if large numbers of recruits cease to foster only after a

Table 3
Levels of support as perceived by continuing and former carers

Level	Continuing %	Former %
Very good	37	12
Good	35	20
Neutral	18	40
Poor	7	16
Very poor	3	10
Total	100	98

short period as an active foster parent' (p 41). There is no answer, perhaps, to the question of how long carers should be expected to foster before they give up. Would the perception of themselves as doing a professional job or having a career make any difference, or does the demanding nature of the job impose its own time-limits? As we say in the main publication, carers on the whole do not see themselves as making a career out of fostering.

Factors that triggered the final decision

Apart from those who retired or stopped fostering because of other external factors, the decision by the rest of the carers to cease fostering was not usually taken lightly. In the view of many, the situation had been building up over a period of time, but the final decision was usually triggered by some recent event such as action or inaction by the social work services, the behaviour of the placed child, deterioration of health, the need for a break or the end of a placement. Typical comments illustrating the precipitating factor included: 'disillusionment with the social work department'; 'trying to argue with social workers for better matching'; 'lack of support'; 'child's bad behaviour increased', 'the end of placement seemed a good time' or 'we could not take any more; our health and our family's life were affected'.

While the majority said that once they decided to stop nothing would have made them change their minds, there were a few who indicated that changes in attitudes within the social work services might have stopped them from giving up. Typical comments included: 'with more support'; 'if the social work department's attitudes were different'; and 'changes in the social work department'.

Some of the above comments were repeated when asked what, if anything, might bring them back to fostering. A number mentioned changes in the operation of the fostering services, more space in their house, better health, better pay and better conditions of service or after their adopted child settled down. The total numbers of possible returnees, assuming their grievances were attended to, did not amount, however, to more than ten per cent of all those who ceased to foster.

Table 4

The number of years former carers had fostered compared with continuing carers

No. of Years	Former carers		Continuing carers	
	N	%	N	%
0–5	45	48	418	52
6–10	25	26	179	22
11–20	23	24	170	21
21–30	2	2	34	4
30+	–	–	5	1
Total	95*	100	806	100

*One missing

Summary

The annual loss of foster carers for all reasons found among 17 agencies in Scotland was around nine per cent. There were variations between agencies but these were not usually high, suggesting a uniform practice across the country. The annual losses sustained for reasons relating to the operation of the fostering services amounted to almost six per cent or between 80 to 100 carers lost annually across the whole of Scotland. In England, with over 20,000 carers, this percentage would amount to around 1,000 carers lost each year. The losses are much lower than those found in the Portsmouth study some 20 years ago (Jones, 1975). Former carers fostered for an average of 7.5 years which may not seem low, though some agencies in the sample demonstrated that they could keep their carers longer.

There was no evidence that the majority of foster carers gave up easily. The reasons why they withdrew were diverse, but almost three-fifths were related to some aspect connected with the operation of the fostering services and the rest to external factors. Background characteristics and declared motivation were in most respects similar to those of active carers. The eventual decision to cease fostering by those who are dissatisfied is a culmination of four main interacting factors:

- A past history of unresponsiveness and unavailability of social work support;
- The child being more difficult than expected;

- Unresponsiveness to requests for help and support during the most recent crisis;
- Impact on own family.

The lower than expected losses should not lead to complacency. Many of the dissatisfactions expressed by those who ceased to foster were also shared by a significant proportion of continuing foster carers and require urgent attention. They include infrequent social work visits, unavailability of social workers, the stand-by service covered by staff who are not knowledgeable about fostering, absence of partnership, lack of information on the children's background, the children being more difficult than expected, stress arising from the fostering task and low pay. Meanwhile, fostering staff may have to establish more accurately and also properly record the main reasons for which carers give up.

Note

More details covering the first phase of the study on continuing and former carers appear in the publication *Fostering Good Relations: A study of foster care and foster carers in Scotland, Part I*, available from the Scottish Office Central Research Unit, 21 South Gyle Crescent, Edinburgh EH12 9EB.

The study was financed by the Social Work Services Group of the Scottish Office and co-ordinated by the Central Research Unit.

References

Berridge D, *Foster Care: A research review*, The Stationery Office, 1997.

Cliffe D and Berridge D, *Closing Children's Homes*, National Children's Bureau, 1991.

Gregg P, *Why do Foster Parents Cease to Foster? A study of the perceptions of foster parents*, M. Phil. Thesis submitted to the University of Southampton, 1993.

Jones E, 'A study of those who cease to foster', *British Journal of Social Work*, 5:1, pp 31–41, 1975.

National Foster Care Association, *Foster Care in Crisis*, NFCA, 1997.

Pasztor E M and Wynne S F, *Foster Parent Retention and Recruitment: The state of the art in practice and policy*, Child Welfare League of America, 1995, USA.

Waterhouse S, *The Organisation of Fostering Services*, NFCA, 1997.

26 The implications of recent child care research findings for foster care

Roger Bullock

Roger Bullock is a Senior Research Fellow at the Dartington Social Research Unit. Since this article was written the Unit has continued to undertake research in child care and recent publications relevant to foster care are: "Parental Perspectives in Cases of Suspected Child Abuse" (1995); "Children Going Home: The reunification of families" (1998); "From Care to Accommodation: Support, protection and control in child care services" (1998); and "Prevention and Early Intervention with Children in Need" (1999).

This paper was published in Adoption and Fostering 14:3, 1990.

The past decade has seen the publication of a number of child care research studies. Programmes of work commissioned by the Department of Health and the Economic and Social Research Council have produced new information on several aspects of the child care system, such as the effectiveness of services, processes of decision-making, long-term outcomes, clients' perspectives and statistical trends. Much of this has important implications for foster care. For example, there are research findings on long-term placements, as in Rowe, Cain, Hundleby and Keane's scrutiny, and fostering breakdown has been explored by Berridge and Cleaver. Foster care has also been viewed in its wider child care context, as in the Dartington Unit's study of the family links of children in care or in Rowe and colleagues recent analysis of children's placements while away from home.

In this material, several themes are significant for understanding the contribution of foster care to child care services, both now and in the future. Seven of these will be explored in this article, the first concerning the heterogeneity of child care cases.

The heterogeneity of child care cases

It is clear from all the research studies that, although children in care share a common legal status and nearly all spend a period away from home, they differ widely in all other respects, such as their personal and family characteristics, reasons for admission and their care placements. Thus, children's entrances to and exits from care vary, as do their subsequent experiences. While certain sub-groups of children can be identified, such as abused children or those beyond parental control, no single group dominates the total care population. Indeed, children and families often find themselves stigmatised by groundless assumptions that because an admission to care has occurred, abuse or control must be an issue. In fact, the most common reasons for entry result from temporary breakdowns in family care, such as when a parent falls ill or enters hospital.

Given this variety of child care cases, foster care, which is the main alternative to care by the child's own family, has to fulfil a wide range of tasks and functions. These vary from nurturing an abandoned baby or containing a serious offender to the temporary care of a child whose mother is having another baby. Foster care, therefore, is not a single approach and its variety needs to be acknowledged in the recruitment, training and support of foster carers.

A wider perspective on children's needs

The recent research findings have also increased our understanding of the needs and situations of separated children. We know from *Lost in Care* that 60 per cent of younger children enter care with siblings. For them, the social work task is meeting the needs of a group of separated children who are related in some way rather than that of providing for *the* child in care. In addition, although it is little explored, nearly all children have a considerable extended family even though it is more dislocated and spread across different households than is the case for the general population. Thus, the pyschoanalytic emphasis on the relationship between individual children and their parents, which dominated child care theory in the past, has been widened to include broader kinship networks and has been complemented by sociological and ecological perspectives. Our views on children now include the child's health, education, friendships, family links, gender, race and sexuality. Children are also increasingly seen as functioning in their local communities, so schools, peers and the heritage of their locality need to be considered. Perhaps only social class, particularly important in British society, is denied the attention it deserves.

These changing views have influenced our thinking about the continuity we seek for separated children. It is no longer sufficient just to provide an alternative family, hoping that other benefits will automatically follow. Foster carers increasingly have to promote continuity in the lives of children, a responsibility that involves pursuing the child's interests in a wide range of areas.

The place of foster care in children's care careers

This increasing concern with continuity requires that foster placements need to be viewed in the context of a child's whole care career. In matching placement to child and in seeking motivation to continue our efforts, we often forget that much happens to separated children before and after fostering. Many children, for example, experience residential care before moving to a family and many leave for hostels, bed-sitters and so-called independent living. This variety in children's care careers highlights the relationship between fostering and other social work interventions. Instead of resting on an uncritical belief that our particular contribution is the child's salvation, we need to forge closer links between foster care and the services that precede it, admit its casualties and shelter its leavers. Again, this has considerable implications for foster carers. On the one hand, contingency plans may be necessary to reduce harm in the event of placement disruption, while on the other foster parents need to anticipate long involvements in young people's subsequent lives.

However, any suggestion that care contributions may lose their significance over time does not justify poor standards in the short-term. The recent research emphasises the significance of pre-care planning, admission processes and subsequent decision-making for favourable outcomes. Viewed in the context of a life-time, one's first days in care may seem a distant memory, but how important for child and family can be the competence of those early carers. A bad initial experience might well affect a child's life chances.

Realistic expectations of fostering

All of the research studies reveal considerable gaps between child care intentions and achievements, discrepancies which, if anything, are widening as fostering now encompasses children with all kinds of special needs, such as those with disabilities, remandees and AIDS sufferers. In reality, there are rarely sufficient placements available to offer much choice of placement and foster carers' expertise in one area can too readily be extended to cover a pot-pourri of difficulties requiring specialist approaches. We need, therefore, to acknowledge the limitations of our interventions, be they the high breakdown rates revealed by Berridge and Cleaver for older children or the limited gains made by very difficult adolescents fostered after leaving Youth Treatment Centres, as found in a recent Dartington study. Yet, at the same time, we need to give hope to those who live and work with separated children and to support them in situations where failure and disappointments are intrinsic to specialist work.

The relationship between carers and social workers

As fostering has expanded to include older children and those with special needs, the roles of foster carers have needed to change. Professionals no longer bring children unannounced to foster families for care and tending, to stay as long as those who know best decide. With more complicated child care cases, and with increasing responsibilities thrust on them, foster carers cannot remain passive.

If we want people to take disturbed or disabled young people into their homes and expect them to promote these children's health, education and family links, foster carers have to be partners rather than agents of social workers. They have to be involved in reviews and in framing contracts; they must be given responsibility to negotiate the styles of placements with children and families and they must contribute to decisions about children's futures. Such arrangements are essential if foster carers are expected to share confidential information, such as abuse revelations, or to undertake therapeutic work with children's families. Foster carers will always be the majority of those who tend separated children in care, but tending alone is no longer sufficient. As a Canadian social work teacher, Kathleen Kufeldt, has described, they need to be 'parents plus', the plus being the ability to apply their parenting skills to other people's children.

Foster carers' contributions to children's care careers

The longitudinal research studies of Packman and Dartington which chart children's care experiences over time both stress the significance of key moments in the child's career. At reception there is bewilderment, guilt and anxiety, while in the first few weeks family contacts can be lost. When children move, social and educational networks can be broken, and so on. At all these points, foster carers are important, whether it be in reducing stress, handling parental visits or preparing children for departure. One of the functions of research is to relate past, present and future events in children's lives in a way that is not always apparent at the time decisions are made. Appropriate actions by foster carers can do much to mitigate the risks faced by children at each stage.

As research has a habit of bringing us down to earth, perhaps we need to settle for smaller gains, noting the contributions of each child care approach, rather than being doctrinaire. Research comparisons of different child care interventions are, unfortunately, scant, but one message from those that are available is the need to consider clients' views on the provision we offer. Does a small residential unit ever feel the same as a large foster home? We see them as distinct parts of the child care service, but children's perspectives may suggest otherwise, as Kahan's interviews with young people who have grown up in care have shown.

Demographic and economic trends

In considering the future of foster care, two factors, one demographic and the other economic, cannot be ignored. The number of adolescents is set to rise by one-third in the 1990s and, as residential provision has been curtailed, many of those needing to live away from home will be fostered. The demand for places, particularly for older children, is set to rise. However, it is also forecast that in southern Britain, at least, there will be a serious labour shortage. It seems that people of all ages will be wooed into employment, causing social services to compete with trade and industry for the time and skill of foster carers. This combination of a growing demand for foster home places and increased employment opportunities must affect the recruitment, maintenance and motivation of those willing to take children into their homes.

Conclusions

Recent child care research has produced many new findings about services and interventions with separated children. Seven themes highlighted in the studies relating to foster care, both now and in the coming decade, have been identified here in the hope that the implications of findings, which may not seem immediately relevant to fostering, become apparent.

Note

Considerably more evidence has become available since this article was written. There have also been important policy and practice developments. The research overviews produced by the Department of Health – 'Patterns and Outcomes in Child Placements', 'Child Protection: Messages from Research' and 'Caring for Children Away from Home' – expand the points made with new information and elaborate analyses. The issues raised have also been incorporated into legislation and guidance and in practice initiatives, such as the "Looking After Children materials" and "Quality Protects".

References

Berridge D and Cleaver H, *Foster Home Breakdown*, Blackwell, 1987.

Dartington Social Research Unit, *The Care Careers of Young People Leaving Youth Treatment Centres*, 1989.

Department of Health and Social Security, *Social Work Decisions in Child Care: Recent research findings and their implications*, HMSO, 1985.

Kahan B, *Growing Up in Care*, Blackwell, 1979.

Kufeldt K, 'In care, in contact?', in Hudson J and Galaway B, *The State as Parent: International research perspectives on interventions with young persons*, Dordecht, Kluwer, 1989, Netherlands.

Millham S, Bullock R, Hosie K and Haak M, *Lost in Care*, Gower, 1986.

Rowe J, Cain H, Hundleby M and Keane A, *Long-term Foster Care*, BAAF/Batsford, 1984.

Rowe J, Hundleby M and Garnett M, *Child Care Now: A survey of placement patterns*, BAAF, 1989.

Stein M and Carey K, *Leaving Care*, Blackwell, 1986.

27 The foster child: the forgotten party?

Kathleen Marshall

Kathleen Marshall is a solicitor, child law consultant and Visiting Professor to the Centre for the Child & Society, University of Glasgow. She was formerly Director of the Scottish Law Centre. She chaired the Edinburgh Inquiry into Abuse of Children in Care which reported in February 1999. She has written and presented numerous papers on aspects of child law and children's rights.

This paper was published in Adoption & Fostering, 15:3, 1991.

I am going to begin this article with the observation that, in our society, children are the pawns of adult concern. They are not "forgotten". They are essential components of the great game of life – but they are moved in accordance with adult rules, for adult ends, and in accordance with strategies which may well change from game to game. Not forgotten, but forgotten as "parties" to the actions of the adult world.

When parental relationships break down, onlookers may well observe that the adults involved become so caught up in their own battles and their own hurt that they are blinded to the effect on the child. This is not necessarily the result of shameful egocentricity. The child may be so much loved that it is too painful for the parents to contemplate that what they are doing is hurting him or her.

Decisions about a child are, by law, supposed to be centred on the child's best interests. But it is often "best interests" as perceived by a range of adults without the child's view on the matter being ascertained. The child, as such, is not forgotten; the child as party to the proceedings too often is.

It often takes an outsider to point this out. The parents are too involved. A sympathetic solicitor, a conciliator from the Family Conciliation Service, a social worker or health visitor or teacher might notice what is happening and suggest to the adults that they modify their perspective on the situation.

Who defines the child's "best interests"?

But it is not just in family relationships that the child can become the forgotten party. It can also happen in our child care system. And it is possibly almost as hurtful for operators of that system to acknowledge what has happened as it is for the hurting parents.

The child care system has, after all, been designed with children in mind, with children as the focus. Professionals operating the system have often devoted their lives to working for children. They are bound to become defensive when it is suggested that the system leads to the unnecessary suffering of children. One need only think of the snorting reaction that accompanied the introduction of safeguarders in the children's hearing system. This was seen as a foreign concept foisted on Scotland by the inadequacies of the English child protection system, exposed by the Maria Colwell case. Safeguarders were seen by many as unnecessary because:

- 'We are the ones who safeguard the child's interests,' said the children's panel members.
- 'We are the ones to safeguard the child's interests,' said the social workers.
- 'We are the ones who safeguard the child's interests,' said the reporters.

And that is not even to mention the parents.

The system is geared to protecting the child's interests. But what about the child's views? What about the child as party to what is happening? As an actor in, rather than as an object of the proceedings?

It is not enough to talk about "interests" as perceived by the adult world, we must also talk of "rights", of the right of the child to have his or her views elicited, respected and taken seriously.

There are difficulties in this. It is not a simple matter. There are issues about, for example:

- Do children have to be a certain age before they are involved in decision-making?

- Do we have to consult and involve a two-year-old?
- Can we be sure that the child's views are *informed* views?
- Does the child really understand the situation?
- Is it right to place on children the burden of the power of choice?
- Is it ethical to pretend that there are options, when there may appear to be none?
- Are there *really* none? Or are we just unwilling or unable to provide them?

Changing the rules

It is important to balance assessment of interests with respect for rights. Children don't change much from generation to generation. Their basic needs and wishes do not differ, but our perception of them does. Our assessment of best interests is affected by a number of factors:

- legal requirements;
- the prevailing deference to the notion of "parental rights";
- resources (cash);
- resources (people – staff and foster carers), fashions or "movements" in childcare:
  - children tell the truth/children fantasise;
  - rescue and permanency *versus* rehabilitation;
  - blood ties and identity *versus* clean break;
  - child as party of the family, served by integrated social work departments, *versus* child as an individual protected by children's departments and child advocates;
  - foster carers as substitute parents *versus* foster parents as semi-professionals;
  - foster care *versus* institutional care.

I am not suggesting that these "fashions" are erratic and fickle, nor that the contrasts are stark and rigid, but we do change the rules; we do change the strategies, and we move our pawns accordingly.

Fashions are not just fickle. They respond to what has gone before – to recent experience. The pendulum keeps on swinging, searching for an elusive balance. All the more elusive, for the fear of condemnation when a mistake is made. If parents are protecting their own wounds, professionals in the child care system are protecting their vulnerability. Fear of the consequences of action or inaction leads to a mentality of "cover my back" and an unwillingness to indulge in healthy risk-taking.

In a recent case which came to the attention of the Scottish Child Law Centre, a young person in foster care had made and retracted allegations of physical abuse against his carers. 'I just wanted to see if they really wanted me,' he said. 'I didn't mean it'. He had phoned all over the UK to get someone to help him stay 'in my nice home', as he put it. He had a new social worker, who had a new senior. Neither of them knew him and neither appeared willing to risk leaving him in the placement.

For foster carers too there is uncertainty. The child has not been re-defined – his or her needs remain the same – but the role has. Is the child to be treated as "one of the family" with all that entails within that particular family's culture? Or is he or she to be treated in accordance with a series of child care regulations? Do the foster carers know what is expected of them in this new relationship? And does the foster child know what is expected of him or her? If there is an agreement between the carers and the local authority, is the child party to it? Does it even recognise the concerns of the child?

Certainly if I am staying with friends or relatives, I feel more comfortable if it's clear that it's OK to make myself a cup of coffee when I feel like it, take a bath, or get my own cornflakes, rather than wait for breakfast to be served. On the other hand, I'd feel a little put out if I went to stay with a friend and was handed a copy of the rules of the house. The dilemma must be all the more acute for foster children – transient members of temporary families. How do they know, or how do they find out where they stand? Do they have an opportunity to influence these matters?

The route into foster care

The route into foster care might be classified as "voluntary" or "compulsory". If it is a compulsory measure, in Scotland it will most likely have come through the children's hearing system. This at least gives the child specific rights to appeal decisions and call reviews at stated intervals.

If the child enters care through some of the other compulsory modes, his or her right to participate and object is less clear. Children committed to care under the matrimonial, guardianship and adoption legislation, and children detained in places of safety, do not have the relatively simple option of appealing a condition of the supervision requirement or calling for a review. They are not parties to the decision.

Children in "voluntary" care are in a similar plight. "Voluntary" for whom? For the parents? Yes, most likely. For the authority? Yes – although it can be regarded as a duty. But for the child – not necessarily. Voluntary care can well be compulsory so far as the child is concerned, without the legal safeguards built into a system which recognises the need for clear regulation of compulsory measures of care. Once in care, there is a route "in" for children through the boarding out and fostering regulations, which contain among the particulars required to be ascertained before a placement is made:

the child's wishes and feelings in relation to fostering in general or proposed placement with a foster parent as the case may be, including any wishes in respect of religious upbringing.

This requirement does not apply to cases of emergency placement and placements made within six weeks. However, it is worth noting that, whatever other requirements may be dispensed with, section 20 of the Social Work (Scotland) Act 1968 *always* applies, obliging the local authority, in reaching any decision relating to a child in care, to ascertain as far as is practicable, the wishes and feelings of the child regarding the decision and give due consideration to them, having regard to his or her age and understanding.

So here we have two requirements to consult the child – one written into the boarding out and fostering regulations which *usually* applies, and one within the body of the Social Work (Scotland) Act 1968, which *always* applies. To what extent this principle is recognised in practice, I am not qualified to say.

So the conclusion so far as the route into foster care is concerned is that, even if the child is not party to the decision to enter into care as such, he or she should be party to any decision about a foster placement. This is not to imply that the child has a veto, but it does mean that his or her wishes must be ascertained and taken seriously.

Moving into the foster home

There is a motto to the effect that: 'To grow is to change. To grow perfect is to have changed often.'

If that is true, then some of our most perfect human specimens must be the products of our child care systems. For many of them have had to change very often indeed – more often than most of us would believe – and in ways which require an exercise of the imagination to comprehend.

How *would* one set about fitting into a new family? Are you meant to be one of them, or be apart? What do you call your new foster carers? Mr and Mrs? Aunt or Uncle? First names? Or even Mum and Dad?

What's the routine in the house? Are you supposed to get up early? Fix yourself breakfast? Help with the chores? Come home at a certain time? Can you just use *any* of the shampoo in the bathroom, or does it sort of belong to anyone? Do they have a rule about not flushing the toilet at night?

More important – do they really want you there? Do the birth children of the family want you, resent you or regard you as a curiosity? Do the adults want you, or are they just in it for the money?

Do we devote enough attention to the need to recognise and maintain the child's identity? Does the child really need to change schools, breaking established friendships, or would it be better to spend some time and resources on keeping him or her there, even if this means a bit of travelling?

Does the child need to change foster carers? Every now and again, we hear of cases where short-term foster carers want to keep the child but can't because of their age or race or other factor regarded as significant.

I know I'm probably treading on dangerous territory here, for I am not a social worker, nor a psychologist, and I have never studied these matters in depth. But, as an outsider, so far as these decisions are concerned, I do sometimes feel uneasy when I hear of a young child being removed from an apparently happy situation to one which is a better match on paper, where the statistics for success will lie in his or her favour.

Research is based on broad and general surveys, and reaches broad and general conclusions. It is useful for making broad and general provision, in building up appropriate resources and making good general decisions. But our duty, in conscience and in law, is to look at the welfare of each child as an individual. We should not be deterred from making appropriate individual decisions by fear of setting a precedent or breaching a sacred rule. Rules, they say, are for the guidance of wise men, and the obedience of fools. That maxim applies equally to fostering decisions. I would stand by the right of the child to have his or her welfare the criterion for any decision, and I would advocate a flexible attitude to even our most worthy principles in order to achieve this.

Moving home and family involves an obvious break in identity, but there are other less obvious angles to this which are also important. What about the child's property for example – the toys, bikes, clothes and other familiar items that are left behind? Can we soften the blow by identifying what is important to the child, by seeing it as the *child's* property rather than the parents'? I heard recently about one foster child who wrote to his birth mother asking for his bike. 'After all,' he said, 'it belongs to me. You gave it to me for my birthday.' The mother felt unable to help, as the bike was still at home with a violent father whom she was unwilling to approach. I don't know whether that little boy ever got his bike. It would seem a bit "over the top" to sue for its return. And yet, it was as important to him as a car or a CD player is to someone of more mature years. We need to build into the system the notion that children have things that belong to them, that they want, that they need as one of the underpinnings of individual identity.

Identity may really be the root of the problem. The child should not feel obliged to fit into each new home like a member of the family. It *is* hard to get the balance between making this assumption and presenting "the rules of the house". But it seems reasonable to suggest that just as information is supplied to foster carers in terms of Regulation 23 of the boarding out and fostering regulations, so should information be supplied to the child about the family with whom he or she is going to stay: information on the family's background and attitudes, the foster carers' motivations for taking the child on, the wishes and feelings of the birth children of the family about foster care. And so far as those elements are concerned which contain a possibility of negotiation, should not the foster child also be party to this agreement? This could apply for example to:

- arrangements for contact with the birth family;
- educational, medical and dental matters;
- financial arrangements.

What does the child feel that he or she needs that is not being catered for? If care is for the benefit of the child, if section 20 of the 1968 Act is to be respected, and children's wishes and feelings ascertained and taken into account, it seems a nonsense to consider making these decisions without involving the child – and involving the child, not just as a gesture, as a concession to new-fangled ideas about involving children – but as a right, as a *party* to the agreement.

Living in foster care

The first point I want to make concerns the financial arrangement between the local authority and the carers. There is a certain murkiness around about who gets paid what. I am thinking mainly of the situations involving placements with a relative under a supervision requirement from a children's hearing. The boarding out regulations in Regulation 9 authorise the payment of allowances to 'foster parents'. 'Foster parent' is defined in Regulation 2 as 'a person approved by a care authority in accordance with Regulation 7'. This has been interpreted as excluding those relatives who have not gone through the whole approval procedure, involving the fostering panel.

Last year I was receiving enquiries from relatives who explained that they were not getting fostering allowances because they were relatives, and not approved foster parents, and were not getting child benefit on the basis that the child was officially "in care".

As a stop-gap, I suggested remedies such as resort to section 20 of the 1968 Act for assistance from the local authority, and even felt it necessary to refer some to what appeared to be a relevant charity for assistance. But that was clearly not the ideal solution. I believe that some success has since been obtained in the child benefit field, and that some authorities at least make some payments to relatives, but clearly this is a situation that requires further investigation.

The important point here is that, in all of the legal talk about the interpretation of regulations, it is very easy to forget that in the middle of it all there is a child with needs. One relative telephoned who was concerned at the financial implications of looking after a child under supervision, but was afraid to make a fuss in case the child was taken away from her. The fear may have been unjustified, but it was real, and for so long as it was real, she was unwilling to raise it with the authorities, preferring instead the anonymity of a telephone advice line. We *must* provide adequate allowances as a matter of right in respect of these children.

Holidays and staying away from the foster home, are another issue. Birth parents may object to a foster child going on holiday with a foster family. This can be a source of disappointment and bitterness for the child. Do we defer too much to parental wishes in this respect? Do we consult the child? Are we clear about the extent to which we can accept the child's agreement as sufficient? If not, should this be clarified?

Where children are subject to children's hearings supervision requirements, it is important to ensure that conditions are flexible enough to allow the child to go on holidays, and, unless demonstrably inappropriate, to do the normal things a child likes to do, such as staying overnight occasionally at a friend's house, or at scout camp. We must ensure that compulsory care for a child does not effectively amount to incarceration at one address.

What are we afraid of? That the friend's parents have not been checked out by the police? That the child will be abused there and we will get the blame? Surely, if we have vetted foster carers, we must pay some respect to the judgement of these carers who are the people best placed to respond to these sorts of every-day requests. This is an aspect of the healthy risk-taking I referred to earlier. We must foster in foster carers the knowledge and insight to make these judgements and the confidence to exercise this discretion. Judgements will sometimes be faulty and some mistakes will occur. Foster carers must not be made to feel that the world will turn on them if, as is bound to happen in some cases, they weigh the matter up, make a considered judgement and things go wrong. The alternative is the curtailment of the normal freedoms of the many for the sake of the aberrations of a few.

At the other end of the scale from overnight stays, we have holidays abroad. I had one enquiry from a foster carer keen to take the child abroad on the family holiday. The birth parents were objecting. The child was under a supervision requirement, and there were plans to assume parental rights, but this had not yet happened. I advised the enquirer to contact the reporter to the child's panel, but expressed doubt that even the hearing could authorise a holiday abroad in the face of parental refusal.

With holidays abroad becoming increasingly common, we need to look at this matter. It seems unfair that a parent who does not have care of the child should be able to say no if the child wants to go and the foster family want him or her to go.

I have already touched on access arrangements, suggesting that the child be party to the Regulation 23 agreement made between the local authority and the foster carers.

Access can be a thorny issue: there may be suspicion and even hostility in some cases between the foster carers and the birth family. And indeed, it *is* a lot to ask of foster carers to deal with and accommodate some of the parents involved. And it *is* a lot to ask of parents, to be "at home" and natural with their children in someone else's house.

I believe we are coming around more to the view that access is primarily a right of the child, rather than of the parents; that access is for the benefit of the child. Although we cannot, in practice, force reluctant parents to have contact with their children, we can facilitate it by explicit agreements and appropriate practical arrangements.

Viewing access as the right of the child also means extending the network of contacts. There may be people other than parents who are important to the child – relatives, friends, people who have cared for the child. The child should be asked about significant people in his or her life, and all effort made to facilitate continued communication.

Redressing an imbalance

No one would suggest that everything and everyone must centre their lives on the needs and wishes of the foster child. The big bad world outside is not going to centre its movements on the life of any individual, and a foster child would be ill-prepared for that life were she or he to expect such attention.

Part of growing up involves learning to live with others, to respect their wishes, to compromise your own. Foster children need to learn this too. Once again, we are asking for a delicate balance. Our efforts today are set at redressing an obvious imbalance, at trying to ensure that the law and practice on foster care recognise the right of the child to be party to the process.

I started by describing children as the "pawns" of adult concern, with a metaphor centred on the game of chess. But pawn also has another meaning, slightly downmarket. It means a pledge – something we hand over as security in times of trouble to redeem when circumstances have improved. Now I would not like to imply that foster carers are the pawn-brokers of the child care world. I would not like our foster children to be seen merely as items – albeit items of value – stashed away for safe keeping for the convenience of adults, although I think there are elements of that in our system. There are some respects in which children could be seen as pawns in this sense too.

Children are persons not items and their true redemption will only be achieved if they are empowered to be party to the processes which most intimately affect them.

Note

Since this article was first published, the Children (Scotland) Act 1995 has given chidren greater rights to be consulted about coming into the care system, about decisions made while they are in it, and about adoption. The Arrangements to Look After Children (Scotland) Regulations 1996 require local authorities to consult children (so far as practicable) when devising care plans, which must include the extent of contact with members of the child's family and any other significant person.

The Fostering of Children (Scotland) Regulations 1996 are not in themselves specific about involvement of the child, although the general provisions of the 1995 Act under which they are made will require this, as the supporting Scottish Office guidance points out.

While these are welcome developments, the question today is whether the principles are being internalised and applied in a way that is meaningful to the child. As well as the more weighty decisions which are contemplated by legislation and regulation, some of the information requirements highlighted in the article above might seem mundane to adults, but might well be important for the child's quality of life. We need to engage with foster children to ensure that their real needs are taken account of. We need an agenda that is set by them.

Postscript

Malcolm Hill

The chapters in this book have illustrated some of the key developments that took place in fostering practice and our understanding of fostering in the 1990s. In one sense there has been relative stability in that the numbers of foster carers and placements were fairly constant throughout the decade. However, the range of tasks undertaken has diversified. Foster carers are now expected to deal with more demanding and complicated situations than formerly, often with a more family-oriented and not simply child-centred approach. In different ways, foster carers, birth parents and children are now all seen as having greater rights to express their views and influence decisions than formerly. Most people see this as a positive change, but managing the often different and sometimes competing wishes and interests is not an easy process.

One of the key concepts of the 1990s has been partnership. While this is a laudable ideal, it is not easy to achieve. Certainly there are signs that short-term placements can be used flexibly in a way that genuinely shares care with birth parents. Also the majority of foster carers report that they get on well with social workers, especially link workers. Increasing use of contracts and fees or salaries signifies better remuneration for foster carers and acknowledgement of their role. On the other hand, a significant proportion of foster carers appears to be at heart fairly "exclusive" in their role or else "conditionally inclusive". They like caring for or working with the child. They may also be sympathetic and friendly towards certain parents, but find it hard to work with those birth family members who they see as disruptive in relation to the foster family or a bad influence on the fostered child. It seems that more concerted attention to contact issues is required in preparation and training. Birth parent involvement in these processes may well assist.

Carers may also find it hard to deal with children who do not want to become closely attached, whether on account of existing loyalties or the opposite – repeated failures in parenting which have left them detached or disenchanted. Some children and young people do want to live in a family but often with a looser commitment than foster carers expect (Downes, 1992; Triseliotis *et al*, 1995a; Butler and Charles, 1998).

Reports from many different directions show dissatisfaction with social workers. Chapters in this book have included complaints about neglecting foster carers' views in decision-making, carers' role in the use of the Looking After Children (LAC) materials, foster siblings and placement endings. This should not be exaggerated since most carers do see social workers positively. However, there is scope for workers in fieldwork teams to be more available and more knowledgeable about fostering.

Much remains to be done to improve understanding and practice with respect to foster care. At its heart is a complex interaction between children, their birth family members and foster carers (and usually also their children and other family members). All the parties have their own history, needs, wishes, rights, feelings and relationships. Fostering is also a service, provided by a combination of social work agencies and volunteers or semi-professionals, within a legal and social policy framework. Many valuable concepts have been applied to fostering but not yet developed into a fully coherent theory. With regard to the core individuals concerned, ideas about attachment, separation and loss have been central to practice for many years, mostly applied to children but also to parents and even foster carers (Falhlberg, 1994; Jewett, 1996; Farnfield, 1998). The biographical significance of fostering has been embraced theoretically in the concepts of care career and resilience, practically in life story work. The inter-relationships among the key parties have been viewed in terms of triangles, prisms and networks and by means of roles and expectations. More specifically, terms like inclusiveness, partnership and contracting have been used at various times to capture or promote particular ways of conducting these relationships. Networks and protective (or supportive) environments help to encompass the wider influences of extended kin, local communities and society at large. The impact of agency policies and structures have been frequently described, but much less often analysed. Demographic, technological, economic and employment changes are known to affect both the need for foster care and the availability of potential carers. One of the challenges of the new millennium is to understand better and provide a more integrated account of all these complicated elements and factors which make up fostering.

There are many gaps in the literature about fostering. Structures for delivering foster care to children are diverse and change frequently, yet the empirical or theoretical rationale for these developments is thin. Some matters have been explored in the past but not recently (e.g. private fostering), while others have received much attention abroad but not in the UK (e.g. fostering by relatives – see Colton and Williams, 1997; McFadden, 1998). The placement experiences of children from minority ethnic backgrounds or with disabilities merit much deeper exploration. The challenges of abuse-related trauma and behaviour are now a major issue.

This book has provided some signposts for the future, but the map is far from complete. For the sake of the children, it is vital to keep developing and reviewing our understanding of foster care in all its complexity.

References

Aldgate J, Tunstill J, Ozolins R and McBeath G, *Family Support and the Children Act*, University of Leicester, 1994.

Aldgate J, Bradley M and Hawley D, 'Respite accommodation', in Hill M and Aldgate J (eds) *Child Welfare Services: Developments in law, policy, practice and research*, Jessica Kingsley, 1996.

Atkinson C and Horner A, 'Private fostering – legislation and practice', *Adoption & Fostering*, 14:3, 1990.

Barn R, *Black Children in the Public Care System*, BAAF/Batsford, 1993.

Barn, R, Sinclair R and Ferdinand D, *Acting on Principle: An examination of race and ethnicity in social services provision for children and their families*, BAAF, 1997.

Bebbington A and Miles J, 'The background of children who enter local authority care', *British Journal of Social Work*, 19:5, 1989.

Bebbington A and Miles J, 'The supply of foster families for children in care', *British Journal of Social Work*, 20:4, 1990.

Bell M, 'The Looking After Children materials: a critical analysis of their use in practice', *Adoption & Fostering*, 22:4, 1999.

Berridge D, *Foster Care: A research review*, HMSO, 1997.

Berridge D and Brodie I, *Children's Homes Revisited*, Jessica Kingsley, 1998.

Biehal N, Clayden J, Wade J and Stein M, *Moving On*, Wiley, 1995.

Borland M, 'The child: changing perception of children and childhood', in Wheal A (ed), *The Companion to Foster Care*, Russell House, 1998.

Black S (ed), *The Impact of Re-organisation on Particular Services*, Edinburgh University Unit for the Study of Government, 1995.

Borland M, Pearson C, Hill M, Tisdall K and Bloomfield I, *Education and Care Away from Home*, Scottish Council for Research in Education, 1998.

Brown H C, 'Competent child-focused practice: working with lesbian and gay foster carers', *Adoption & Fostering*, 15:2, 1991.

Brown H C, 'Gender, sex and sexuality in the assessment of prospective carers', *Adoption & Fostering*, 16:2, 1992.

Bullock R, 'The implications of recent child care research findings for foster care', *Adoption & Fostering*, 14:3, 1990.

Bullock R, Little M and Millham S, *Going Home*, Dartmouth, 1993.

Butler S and Charles M, 'Improving the quality of fostering provision', in BAAF, *Exchanging Visions*, BAAF, 1998.

Butler S and Charles M, 'Thematic representations of fostering disruption', *Child & Family Social Work*, 4:1, 1999.

Cleaver H, *Focus on Teenagers*, HMSO, 1996.

Colton M and Williams M, *The World of Foster Care*, Arena, 1997.

Craig G and Manthorpe J, 'Small is beautiful?', *Policy & Politics*, 26: 2, 1998.

Department of Health, *Patterns & Outcomes in Child Placement*, HMS0, 1991.

Department of Health, *Child Protection: Messages from research*, HMS0, 1995.

Department of Health, *Children Looked After by Local Authorities*, Department of Health, 1999.

Downes C, *Separation Revisited*, Ashgate, 1992.

Fahlberg V, *A Child's Journey Through Placement*, BAAF, 1994.

Farmer E and Parker R, *Trials and Tribulations*, HMSO, 1991.

Farnfield S, 'Attachment and the care of children "looked after" in their middle years', in *Exchanging Visions*, BAAF, 1998.

Fox Harding L F, *Perspectives in Child Care Policy*, Longman, 1991.

Field S, 'Young Offender Community Support Scheme – Hampshire, England', *Community Alternatives*, 4:2, 1992.

Fletcher B, *Not Just a Name: The views of young people in foster and residential care*, National Consumer Council/Who Cares? Trust, 1993.

Fletcher-Campbell F, 'In care? In school?', *Children & Society*, 12:1, 1990.

Fletcher-Campbell F, 'Progress or procrastination?, *Children & Society*, 4:4, 1998.

Fonagy P, Steele P, Steele H, Higgitt A and Target M, 'The theory and practice of resilience', *Journal of Child Psychology & Psychiatry*, 35:2, 1994.

Garrett P M, 'Mapping child-care social work in the final years of the Twentieth Century: a critical response to the "Looking After Children" system', *British Journal of Social Work*, 29:1, 1999.

Gilligan R, 'Beyond permanence: the importance of resilience in child practice and planning', *Adoption & Fostering*, 20:2, 1997.

Graham J, Hazel N, Richards A and Wadell T, 'Foster family care for homeless young people – the RAFT programme', *Community Alternatives*, 4:2, 1992.

Hazel N, *A Bridge to Independence*, Blackwell, 1981.

Herts B, 'Local government reorganisation and children's services in England', *Adoption & Fostering*, 21:2, 1997.

Hill M, 'What children and young people say they want from social services', *Research, Policy & Planning*, 15:3, 1998.

Hill M, and Aldgate J (eds), *Child Welfare Services*, Jessica Kingsley, 1996.

Hill M and Shaw M, *Signposts in Adoption*, BAAF, 1998.

Hill M, Triseliotis J, Borland M and Lambert L, 'Fostering adolescents in Britain: outcomes and processes', *Community Alternatives*, 8:1, 1996.

Ince L, *Making it Alone: A study of the care experiences of young black people*, BAAF, 1998.

Jackson S, 'The education of children in care', in Kahan B (ed), *Child Care: Research, policy and practice*, Hodder & Stoughton, 1989.

Jackson S, 'Looking After Children: a new approach or just an exercise in form filling? A response to Knight and Caveney', *British Journal of Social Work*, 22: 1, 1998.

Jewett C, *Helping Children Cope with Separation and Loss*, Batsford, 1996.

Jones H, Clark R, Kufeldt K, and Norman M, 'Looking after children: assessing outcomes in child care: the experience of implementation', *Children & Society*, 12: 3, 1998.

Katz L, 'Permanency action through concurrent planning', *Adoption & Fostering*, 20:2, 1996.

Kelly G and Coulter J, 'The Children (Northern Ireland) Order 1995', *Adoption & Fostering*, 21:3, 1997.

Kelly G and Pinkerton G, 'The Children (Northern Ireland) Order 1995: prospects for progress', in Hill M and Aldgate J (eds), *Child Welfare Services*, Jessica Kingsley, 1996.

Knight T and Caveney S, 'Assessment and Action Records: Will they promote good parenting?', *British Journal of Social Work*, 22:1, 1998.

Kosonen M, 'Sibling relationships for children in the care system', *Adoption & Fostering*, 18:3, 1994.

Kosonen M, 'Foster children's sibling relationships: compensation and/or reflection of adversity', in BAAF, *Exchanging Visions*, BAAF, 1998.

Kufeldt K, 'Inclusive foster care: Implementation of the model', in B McKenzie (ed.) *Current Perspectives on Foster Care*, Wall and Emerson, 1994.

Kufeldt K, Armstrong J and Dorosh M, 'Connection and continuity in foster care', *Adoption & Fostering*, 20:2, 1996.

Lowe K, *Teenagers in Foster Care*, NFCA, 1990.

Marsh P, 'Leaving care and extended families', *Adoption & Fostering*, 22:4, 1998/9.

McAuley C, *Children in Long-term Foster Care*, Avebury, 1996.

McColgan M, 'Recruitment, selection and preparation of foster parents in Northern Ireland', *Community Alternatives*, 3:1, 1991.

McFadden E J and Downs S W, 'Family continuity: the new paradigm in permanence planning', *Community Alternatives*, 7:1, 1995.

Millham S, Bullock R, Hosie K and Haak M, *Lost in Care*, Gower, 1986.

Moyers S, *Report on an audit of the Looking After Children forms in 1996*, University of Leicester, 1997.

Mullender A (ed.), *We are Family: Sibling relationships in placement and beyond*, BAAF, 1999 forthcoming.

Natural Children's Support Group, *Children Who Foster*, (video) Vera Publications, 1990.

National Foster Care Association, *Focus on Teenage Fostering*, NFCA, 1998.

Oppenheim L, 'The importance of networks to partnership in child-centred foster care', *Adoption & Fostering*, 16:1, 1992.

Packman J, *Child Care Needs and Numbers*, Allen & Unwin, 1968.

Packman J and Jordan B, 'The Children Act: looking forward, looking back', *British Journal of Social Work*, 21, 1991.

Parker R, Ward H, Jackson S, Aldgate J and Wedge, *Looking After Children: Assessing outcomes in child care*, HMSO, 1991.

Richards S, 'LAC placement patterns', *Adoption & Fostering*, 22:4, 1998/9.

Rhodes P, *"Racial Matching" in Fostering*, Avebury, 1992.

Rhodes P, 'Charitable vocation or 'proper job'? The role of payment in foster care', *Adoption & Fostering*, 17:1, 1993.

Rowe J, Cain H, Hundleby M and Keane A, *Long-term Foster Care*, BAAF/ Batsford, 1984.

Rowe J, Hundleby M and Garnett L, *Child Care Now: A survey of placement patterns*, BAAF, 1989.

Rutter M and Rutter M, *Developing Minds*, Penguin, 1993.

Schaffer H R, *Making Decisions about Children*, Blackwell, 1990.

Scottish Office, *Statistical Bulletin: Children in care or under supervision*, The Scottish Office, 1998.

Sellick C, *Supporting Short-term Foster Carers*, Avebury, 1992.

Sellick C and Thoburn J, *What Works in Family Placement*, Barnardo's, 1996.

Singh S and Patel V, *Regarding Scotland's Black Children*, Barnardo's, 1998.

Shaw M and Hipgrave T, *Specialist Fostering*, Batsford, 1983.

Smith S, 'Permanence revisited – some practice dilemmas', *Adoption & Fostering*, 19:3, 1995.

Stein M, *What Works in Leaving Care?*, Barnardo's, 1997.

Stein M and Carey K, *Leaving Care*, Blackwell, 1986.

Thoburn J, Lewis A and Shemmings D, *Paternalism or Partnership*, HMSO, 1995.

Thomas N, 'The reality of participation in decisions for "looked after" children', in BAAF, *Exchanging Visions*, BAAF, 1998.

Trasler G, *In Place of Parents*, Routledge & Kegan Paul, 1960.

Triseliotis J, 'Foster care outcomes', *Adoption & Fostering*, 13:3, 1989.

Triseliotis J, Borland M, Hill M and Lambert L, *Teenagers and the Social Work Services*, HMSO, 1995.

Triseliotis J, Sellick C and Short R, *Foster Care: Theory and practice*, BAAF/Batsford, 1995b.

Triseliotis J, Borland M and Hill M, *Fostering Good Relations: A study of foster care and foster carers in Scotland,* The Scottish Office Central Research Unit, 1998.

Triseliotis J, Borland M and Hill M, *The Structures, Organisation and Functions of Fostering Services in Scotland*, The Scottish Office Central Research Unit, 1999.

Ward H, *Looking After Children: Research into Practice*, HMSO, 1995.

Waterhouse S, *The Organisation of Fostering Services*, NFCA, 1997.

Webb S, 'Preventing reception into care: a literature review of respite care', *Adoption & Fostering*, 14:2, 1990.

Wheelaghan S, Hill M, Borland M, Lambert L and Triseliotis J, *Looking After Children in Scotland*, Scottish Office Central Research Unit, 1999.

Wedge P and Mantle G, *Sibling Groups and Social Work*, Avebury, 1991.

Yelloly M, *Independent Evaluation of 25 Placements*, Kent Social Services, 1979.